Vivienne Marquis & Patricia Haskell

THE

CHEESE

BOOK

*A definitive guide to the cheeses of the world—
from fresh country cheeses to Cheddars and blues,
Parmesan, Camembert and Brie, pungent goat cheeses
and the richest crèmes. How they taste, how they are made,
how to select and use them, their history and lore—
and a collection of great cheese recipes.*

A FIRESIDE BOOK PUBLISHED BY
SIMON AND SCHUSTER • NEW YORK

WITH AFFECTION AND GRATITUDE
TO EVELYN GENDEL

Contents

ACKNOWLEDGMENTS

We wish to express our thanks to the many people who gave us information and help in writing this book. Foremost among them: Benjamin O. Villa, President of Otto Roth & Co., Inc., whose exceptional knowledge of cheeses is equaled only by his generosity in sharing it; Roberto Ugge, S.p.A. Egidio Galbani, Milan; Heinz P. Hofer, Switzerland Cheese Association, New York; Jacqueline Flêche and Germaine Castets of the Société Auxiliaire de l'Agriculture et de l'Industrie du Sud-Ouest de la France, Paris; J. Lapadou-Hargues, Propagande Agricole Centre National du Commerce Extérieur, Paris; Henrik Tholstrup, Copenhagen, and Gudren Winkel, Danish Agricultural Marketing Board, Copenhagen; Dirk Uges, Bel Paese Sales Company, New York.

Valuable help was also given by Rachael Reed, The Borden Company; Dr. Carlo Grassi, Unione Casearia Italiana, Milan; J. F. Ch. Kleijn, Nederlandse Zuivelbeurs, The Hague; Ove Holst-Knudsen, Copenhagen; Dr. Ernesto Bellinzona, S.p.A. Egidio Galbani, Milan; Martine Segalen and Jacques Canton, Foods from France, New York; Fred Heyward, Bloomingdale's, New York; Hedy Guisti-Lanham, America-Italy Society, New York; Walter V. Price, Emeritus Professor of Dairy Food Industries, University of Wisconsin; James Toomey, Agricultural Marketing Service, U.S. Department of Agriculture, Washington, D.C.; Jean Richard, Confrérie Nationale Brillat-Savarin du Taste-Fromage, Paris; J. P. Denisot, Union de Producteurs en Produits Laitiers et Avicoles, Paris; B. V. Aanhetrot and J. Arnoldi, Het Kaasboertje, Amsterdam; H. R. Cornwell, The English County Cheese Council, London; Murray Greenberg, New York; Consorzio del Parmigiano-Reggiano, Reggio Emilia, Italy; and James Holloway of the Milk Marketing Board, Surrey, England.

And, finally, our thanks to Margaret L. Reynolds, Frances M. Gingerich, Ingrid Mann, Daniel W. Jones, Laurel Rollins, Ann Goodwin, Lydia Strong and Robert M. Hertzberg, all of the United States; and to Freya Noah, St. Croix, V.I.; William and Geneviève Novik, Paris; Flora and Sandro Carraresi, Florence; and Joan and John Lambert, Addlestone, Surrey.

About This Book

What does it taste like? This is what most people want to know about a cheese they have never tried. And yet almost everything that is written about cheeses classifies them by texture: hard, firm, semifirm, semisoft and soft. But how useful is it to know merely whether a cheese is firm or soft? It may only confuse because cheeses with the same consistency may be worlds apart in taste. For this reason we have taken a different approach and have grouped cheeses by their flavor.

There are many different types of Cheddars, for example, and whether those Cheddars are mild or sharp, moist or crumbly, fresh as buttermilk or mellow as Armagnac, they all have a certain taste, a certain recognizable common character. Among the fifty-odd veined cheeses there are decided differences, but they too have a certain flavor in common. Similarly, cheeses with the taste of Swiss belong to a close-knit and easily recognizable group. There are bland and buttery cheeses, cheeses of the Camembert-Brie family, the great grana cheeses of which Parmesan is the archetype; the fresh country cheeses; the sheep and goat cheeses that are entirely different from cow's-milk cheeses, and the ultra-strong cheeses like Limburger and Liederkranz that are in a class by themselves.

Each cheese we discuss is placed in a flavor group with other cheeses that are something like it. Here and there we had to make some arbitrary decisions, and differences of taste being what they are, you may feel that a particular cheese should have been placed elsewhere. Nevertheless, as we worked, we found that these classifications generally held up—the borderline cases were few and far between.

Most important, grouping by flavors makes it easy to enlarge one's experience of cheeses. Someone who likes Cheddar will be encouraged to try other cheeses in the same flavor range whose names may be unfamiliar—cheeses like Leicester, Dunlop, Caerphilly and domestic Kasseri. And going into stores with large assortments of cheeses will no longer be the frustrating and discouraging experience described by one man who recalls the first time he walked into a big cheese store in a big city. He walked in, took one look and almost walked out again. There were hundreds of cheeses—on counters, in open refrigerator cases, inside giant iceboxes; cheeses rising one upon another from the floor, huge wheels and millstones piled as high as the ceiling, each pierced with a marker bearing its name. He saw a round Pipo Crem', its veins of pale blue etched sharply against its white body; an orange Leicester, brilliant as an illumined paper moon; a Welsh Caerphilly, white and fluffy as angel cake. He looked at the gold, amber, alabaster cheeses; cheeses with exotic names like Wensleydale, Warsawski, Nazareth Blue; cheeses studded with cloves, streaked with sage leaves, wrapped in laurel; coarse-grained, crumbly, honey-soft cheeses. Then the clerk asked him what he wanted. Desperately he took in the panorama—and fixed upon one safe and familiar object. With all the authority he could summon, he said, "Half a pound of Swiss, please."

This book deals with hundreds of cheeses. It does not deal with every cheese, for there are thousands, many of them lesser imitations of others, many of them obscure cheeses that few of us will ever encounter. We have tried to include every important cheese, imported or domestic, that you are likely to find in the United States and in major cities abroad—and also some cheeses that can be found only off the beaten track but that have something about them that is interesting or worth knowing. Undoubtedly you will now and then come across cheeses that are not discussed or even mentioned here because new imports are constantly being introduced—and so, for that matter, are new cheeses.

After you read this book you should have no difficulty in placing any new cheese you encounter—whether it is mentioned here or not—because you will be able to see its relationship to cheeses you already know. And this is far more important than the specific information about specific cheeses. For no reader is likely to remember all those details, or to "learn" every cheese we discuss. But he is likely to feel more at home with any cheese, with all cheeses, after reading this book. At least that is our hope.

I

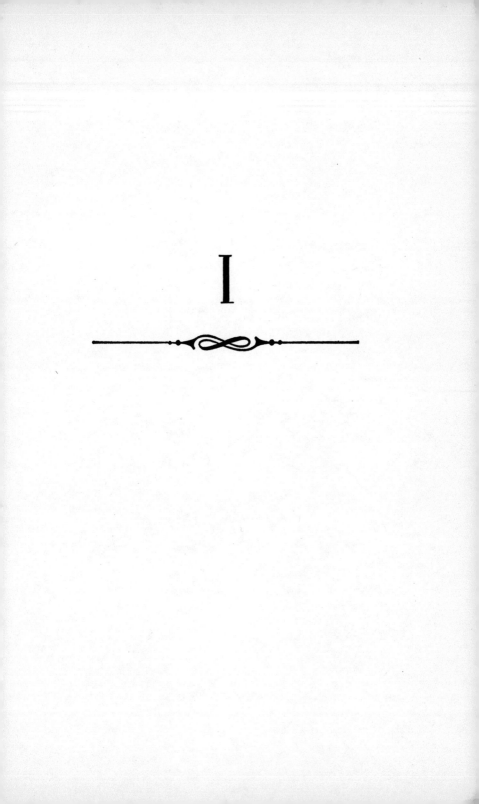

1

Cheese:
The Wine of Foods

As between mice and men, man is easily the more devoted to cheese, and always has been. The mouse, scientists have found, will content himself with cheese for want of something better, but his real passion is for gumdrops.

But men have loved cheese for thousands of years: every kind of cheese, from the simple, fresh country cheeses that have graced the poor man's table since Biblical times to the exquisite worldly cheeses that are the essence of luxury—of cream within cream within cream.

Cheese has been described as "milk's leap to immortality"—and as the food that most resembles wine. For cheese, like wine, is a preserve, and it bears the same relation to milk as wine bears to grapes. Like wine, it has countless varieties, and because of dissimilarities in grasses and herbs, waters and climate,* no two cheeses, however similar, can be identical if they are made in different places. A master cheesemaker with all his secrets and skills can be moved to another locality, and he will be unable to make the same cheese. This has not kept people from trying. They have tried to make Camembert in Britain and Stilton in the United States, with dismal results. But sometimes a so-called imitation turns out better than the original, and sometimes an entirely new and great cheese is produced—as in the case of Liederkranz. In fact, the story of cheesemaking is a long history of imitation, ever since the first cheeses were made.

Many different lands claim the discovery of cheese as their own, and they all have legends, told with countless local variations, which have these elements in common: a rider sets out on a journey, taking with him some milk in a leathern pouch made from a young cow's stomach. Hours later he discovers that the milk has turned into a sour, curdy substance that is not unpalatable. (Today we know that rennet, which is made from rennin, an enzyme found in the lining of a calf's stomach, is the agent that quickly converts milk into curds and whey, and is almost universally used in cheese-making.) But the legend grew up long after the fact; for cheese actually dates back to the earliest domestication of animals, at about 9000 B.C., and it has been made wherever animals produce more milk than people use in fluid form.

Archaeologists have established that cheese was well known to the Sumerians (4000 B.C.), whose cuneiform tablets contain references to cheese, as do the Egyptian and Chaldean artifacts. It is as much a staple of the Old Testament as honey and almonds and wine, and is associated with stories of great daring: David was delivering ten cheeses to Saul's camp when he encountered Goliath; and with great despairing: "Thou has poured me out as milk," says Job, "and curdled me as cheese."

The ancient Greeks had a deity—Aristaeus, son of Apollo—who was considered the giver of cheese, and Homer sang of cheese in the Odyssey. Thus we read how Ulysses discovered the Cyclops' "cheese-racks loaded with cheeses," and how he and his men devoured them. And when Polyphemus returned, "he sat down and milked his ewes and goats all in due course, and then he curdled half the milk and set it aside in wicker baskets."

Those wicker baskets for the draining of cheeses were known to the Greeks as *formos*—the word which became *forma* in Latin, and from which come the Italian word for cheese, *formaggio*, and early

French *formage* which later became *fromage*. From the Latin *caseus* for cheese comes the German word *käse*, the Dutch *kaas*, the Irish *cais*, Welsh *caws*, Portuguese *queijo* and Spanish *queso*. In Anglo-Saxon it was *cese* or *cyse*, which later became *chese*.

The Greeks were so fond of cheese that they rewarded their children with it as we give ours candy—and "little cheese" was a special term of endearment. Their Olympic athletes also trained on a diet consisting mostly of cheese. The island of Delos engraved a cheese on its coins, and the island of Samos was noted for cheesecakes, for which Athenaeus even gives us a recipe: "Take some cheese and pound it, put in a brazen sieve and strain it, then add honey and flour made from spring wheat and heat the whole together into one mass." Wedding cakes of that early era were almost invariably cheesecakes, and at Argos it was customary for the bride to bring little cakes that were roasted, covered with honey, and served to the bridegroom's friends. A delicious-sounding variation was *tuniai*—small cheesecakes that were deep-fried and then covered with honey—of which the playwright Mayris wrote, about 500 B.C.: "Have you ne'er seen fresh tuniai hissing when you pour honey over them?"

Ancient Romans, too, knew a great variety of cheeses, which played such an important part in the Roman diet that the rich had special kitchens for cheesemaking, while the rest of the populace brought their cheese to public smokehouses for curing. Like the Greeks, they also used "little cheese" as an affectionate diminutive. They ate it with fruit, about which Virgil wrote so invitingly: "Yet this night you might have rested here with me on this green leafage. We have ripe apples, mealy chestnuts, and a wealth of pressed chesses." And in the second century Lucius Apuleius wrote that Hypata, the principal city of Thessaly, was so renowned as a place for "fresh cheeses of exceeding good taste and relish," that traders used to journey there to buy cheese and honey for resale.

Cheeses traveled far from their native lands in the knapsacks of soldiers, from Caesar's legions to the armies of Genghis Khan, who carried it with them as a mainstay, as have armies ever since.

Another traveler, Marco Polo, brought back from the East this report of what well may have been the earliest method of preserving cheese: "They make provision also of milk thickened and dried to the state of a paste, which is prepared in the following manner: they boil the milk, and skimming off the rich or creamy part as it rises to the top, put it into a separate vessel as butter; for as long as that remains in the milk, it will not become hard. The latter is then exposed to the sun until it dries. Upon going in service, they carry with them about ten pounds for each man, and of this, half a pound is put, every morning, into a leathern bottle, with as much water as is thought necessary. By their motion in riding, the contents are violently shaken, and a thin porridge is produced, upon which they make their dinner."

So far we have been speaking of the simpler cheeses—fresh cheeses like our cottage cheeses of today, which were followed by the hard-pressed cheeses like Parmesan and Emmenthal, and also the veined cheeses like Gorgonzola and Roquefort that were known almost a thousand years ago.

Far more complicated were the host of elaborate cheeses that came out of the monasteries in the Middle Ages—the soft-ripening cheeses for which France is so noted. They are among the most urbane cheeses in existence, and their development marked an important turning point in the art of cheesemaking.

For all that it has been prized through the ages, cheese has not had a history of universal acceptance. Renaissance and Elizabethan physicians wrote polemics against it, and Shakespeare's references to cheese almost always reflect distaste. Among other things, cheese was thought to have almost occult powers: "Cheese, it is a peevish elf," wrote John Ray in 1670, "it digests all things but itself." People often became so suspicious of it that, wholesome or not, cheese had the power to make them ill. And the superstitions that clung to it, particularly during the sixteenth and seventeenth centuries, are best summed up by the legend, recounted by Horace Annesley Vachell, about a boy . . .

[whose birth] took place in a rocky cave near the Peak of Derbyshire. As a child he could make a hearty breakfast of pebbles. When other boys ate cherry pie, he was content to be apportioned the stones. Later on he served oysters to his guests and ate the shells. Marbles were a *bonne bouche.* Bigger boys used to pick him up and shake him to hear the marbles rattling in his stomach. But, to his dying day, he swore solemnly that he could not digest cheese.

Nevertheless, by the nineteenth century, cheese regained its respectability almost as spontaneously as it had lost it. The change in attitude was not marked by any particular event. Pasteurization, for example, was unheard of until the late nineteenth century, and even then it was applied to milk used for drinking but hardly at all to the making of cheese.

All we know is that the cheeses revered in the Old Testament, whose praises the Greeks sang, the cheeses that were prized for centuries after, suddenly fell into disfavor and just as unaccountably, a few hundred years later, were received back, their good reputation restored.

2

How Cheese Is Made

All cheese is made from milk—usually cow's milk, but also from the milk of sheep, goats and other animals including buffalo (whose milk is still used in making mozzarella in Italy), camels, asses, reindeer and even yaks.

To make cheese, something must be done to the milk to cause it to separate and form into curds (white, milky lumps of the consistency of soft custard) and whey (the thin, cloudy liquid that remains after the curds have formed). This separation is brought about by adding rennet to the milk, or by means of a "starter," which is a culture made of bacteria.

The addition of either of these to the milk creates a small storm within it—the sort of thing you may have noticed if you've ever poured whiskey or brandy into milk and seen it look as if it were about to curdle—a reaction that in a moment subsides as the milk absorbs the spirits. In cheesemaking the milk cannot absorb the rennet or starter, and so after a moment it literally goes to pieces.

The milk may or may not be heated before or during the time the starter is added. It may or may not be skimmed first, and it may or may not have extra cream added. It may be the milk of one milking only, or it may be the morning's milk combined with the milking of the previous evening. A few degrees more or less in the temperature to which the milk is heated will produce distinct differences in the cheeses, as will the way in which the curds are cut. They may be cut into pieces as small as sugar lumps or as large as sandwich loaves, or "combed" into long thin strips with a cheese harp, as in the case of Swiss. Not only the size and shape of the cutting instrument but the motion that is used in cutting the curd will help decide the kind of cheese that will result.

After the curds are cut or broken up by one means or another, they may be drained thoroughly or hardly at all, they may be salted or not, they may be pressed or not. They may or may not be inoculated or their surfaces sprayed with some kind of mold. They may be put to ripen in a warm moist place or in a cool, dry one; they may rest on mats, or in baskets, or be left in hoops or under weights for further pressing. Even small variations in temperature and other atmospheric conditions in the ripening place will change the cheese, and so of course will the length of time that it ripens—it may be days or months, but each day will make a difference. Whether the cheese is rubbed with salt or washed in brine or something else (Maroilles, for example, is bathed in beer) will also make a difference. And so will the number of times the cheese is turned from one side to another while it ripens. Even one small difference in a single step can produce a cheese quite different from the one the cheesemaker may have started out to make. And this is one reason we have so many different cheeses.

To the cheesemaker the capriciousness of the whole process may suggest a prevalence of witches. Consider what can happen when the "friendly bacteria" used in certain kinds of cheesemaking refuse to cooperate. When the Borden's Liederkranz plant was moved from upper New York State to Van Wert, Ohio, all the original equipment was taken to the new plant, as was the "mother culture" used in starting it, and the secret formula used in making it. With all this went a small contingent of cheesemakers who had been making Liederkranz for years—everything, in fact, was moved to Ohio except the shell of the old plant itself.

Operations were resumed in the new plant and everything was done the same way—but the cheese was different. They tried again and again, but they simply could not duplicate the Liederkranz they had been making before. Finally, they took some Liederkranz cheeses made in the old plant and smeared them all over the new tile walls. That done, the cheeses came out right. No one had realized till then that the curds had been affected just as much by bacteria floating free in the air as by the cultures that were mixed directly into them.

This kind of problem is by no means unusual, and though a great deal of scientific research is being focused upon cheesemaking, the most sophisticated dairy technologists will be quick to admit that they do not understand *why* certain things happen in cheesemaking; their primary concern is to find ways to make happen again and again the desirable things that do happen.

All this suggests that cheesemaking is complicated—and it is. It can also be as simple as heating some sour milk (the starter is not even needed if it is sour enough), and scooping out the resulting curds, to be drained in cheesecloth. This is the simplest way of making cheese, and the result is of course the simplest kind of cheese—the fresh pot cheese that goes back to Biblical times. To arrive at a more complicated cheese you may require a Salers cow, a bundle of scented Alpine grasses for her breakfast, an ancient press, a drafty cave, and the guidance of a Benedictine monk.

3

Keeping the Names Straight

Hundreds of cheeses are named for the places in which they were first made—Cheddar, Edam, Camembert, Gorgonzola, for example, and almost all the French blues: Bleu d'Auvergne, Bleu de Causses, de Limousin, de Bresse. Many other cheeses are named for the city or town in which they were first marketed—like Limburger, Stilton and Parmesan.

The sound of the name and the presence of certain prefixes or suffixes will also give a clue to the origin. Names of cheeses from Spanish-speaking countries are commonly prefaced by the word *queso* (meaning cheese)—as in Queso Serra or Queso Cabrales—just as many cheeses from Yugoslavia, Montenegro and thereabouts are prefixed by *sir* or *cyr*. In Norway and Sweden, cheese names commonly end with *ost*, which also means cheese—as for example Noekkelost, Gammelost, Gjetost, Primost, Kuminost. Denmark in 1956 decided to rename all major cheeses to make them sound more authentically Danish—as a result, most of the better known Danish cheeses end with the suffix "bo," starting with Danbo (which means one who lives in Denmark) and Fynbo (for the island of Funen), and on through Elbo, Tybo, Molbo and Maribo. Thus cheeses whose names end with "ost" or "bo" are immediately recognizable as Scandinavian.

Or else, the name of a cheese may refer to some ingredient

mixed with it—as Pepato, an Italian cheese that is studded with pieces of black peppercorn. Others are Nagel ("nail" in German), named for the spikes of clove and caraway that are mixed throughout the cheese; Kümmelkäse (for caraway); Sage (for the herb), and Grappe, the French dessert cheese that is covered with dried grape seeds.

Or a cheese's shape may give it its name: thus from Greece we have Kefalotyrie, which is shaped like a Greek hat or *kefalo;* Hand Cheese, which is pressed into its final shape by hand; the Italian Cacciocavallo, which some maintain got its name because two cheeses are often tied together and hung over a pole, as if astride a horse; Provo, which means oval in Italian, and which becomes Provolone if it is large—or in the smaller size, Provoletti or Provolatine. There is Brick Cheese, which was originally shaped and pressed with bricks; Pineapple Cheese, whose rind is scored to resemble the fruit in texture as well as shape; and Ovoli, the small, egg-shaped Mozzarella.

Or a cheese may be named for the milk it is made of: Pecorino is a generic first name for all Italian cheeses made with sheep's milk, just as Chèvre is the name for French goat cheeses. Double Gloucester refers both to the Gloucester breed of black cattle whose milk was originally used and to the extra-large size of this cheese.

Or a cheese may be named for its maker—like Gervais, originally a brand name and now commonly used as a generic name for this type of French cream cheese, or Bleu de Laqueuille, first made by Antoine Roussel-Laqueuille in 1854. Petit-Suisse, another French cream cheese, was named for the young Swiss cowherd who first suggested adding a little fresh cream to the curds of the local cheese. His advice was followed, and the result was a cream cheese that is one of the softest and fluffiest of them all.

Cheeses are also named for the things they go with or are used for—for instance, Bierkäse, a cheese strong enough to hold its own with any brew, and Raclette, a Swiss cheese named for a melted-cheese dish called Raclette.

And then there is that great group of cheeses made originally by monks, whose names have a decidedly ecclesiastical ring: Pont-l'Évêque, Port-Salut, Munster, Trappist—and a roll call of saints (St. Paulin, St. Florentin, St. Claude, St. Benoit, among others) as might befit the Last Judgment.

II

4

---◦◦◦◦◦---

The Fresh Country Cheeses

Little Miss Muffet
Sat on a tuffet
Eating her curds and whey . . .

Those curds and whey Miss Muffet was addressing herself to
before the arrival of her uninvited guest were, of course, the sixteenth-century forerunner of our cottage cheese. It was wetter and
sourer, and doubtless to an American palate would have tasted like
clabbered milk—which it was—but among Miss Muffet's con-
temporaries it was considered a choice and tasty dish.

Even at that time, however, it had a venerable history, for
although its origins are obscure, there is little doubt that this sour
and separated milk—curds and whey—was the beginning of
what we now call cheese. In this chapter we shall consider the
simple cheeses made directly from curds and whey—simple in the
sense that they are not pressed or aged into hardness or seasoned or
subjected to the various other processes that most other cheeses go
through—but which nevertheless include some of the most elegant
cheeses available here or in Europe.

In piecing together the story of how the fresh cheeses were first
made, it seems likely that early nomadic tribesmen, wandering with

31

their flocks, must at times have had a good deal of sour milk to dispose of. After using what they could, they were faced inevitably with the choice of throwing the rest away or carrying it with them—a hard decision for poor people who had to keep moving to keep alive.

At some point or other—some say about 9,000 years ago—these wanderers appear to have realized that milk, like meat, could be more easily preserved and transported if it could somehow be dried. Eventually they hit upon two ways of doing this. One, probably the first, involved the process of evaporation: they put fresh milk into shallow earthenware utensils and exposed it to the heat of the sun. The milk first turned sour and then began to evaporate. The result was a semidry acid curd characteristic of the fermented milk preparation we know today as yoghurt. This was also probably the primitive beginnings of cream cheese, for the first cream cheeses were—and some are today—simply dried cream. This, indeed, was Mrs. Beeton's impression when she wrote, "Cream cheese, although so called, is not properly cheese, but is nothing more than cream dried sufficiently to be cut with a knife."

It is also "nothing more than" the famous Devonshire clot which is so highly regarded that at the time of the present English queen's coronation an advertisement appeared in a London paper offering a choice window seat along the Queen's route in exchange for a full pint of this delectable cream.

In any event, the simplest way to make a cream cheese, still, is to pour heavy cream into a perforated box lined with two loose layers of cheesecloth. In about four days, the cream's superfluous moisture will have evaporated or drained away, leaving a firm but spreadable cheese.

The other method of "drying" milk that eventually evolved among primitive peoples consisted of spooning the curd of soured and separated milk into a wicker mold, then pressing and draining off the remaining whey. This is what Polyphemus the Cyclops was doing in Chapman's translation of the *Odyssey*, when he

> . . . *quick did dress*
> *his half-milk up for cheese,*

and in a press of wicker pressed it—put
in bowls the rest.

Today, some 3,000 years later, the steps for making a simple pot cheese (which is the same as cottage cheese, only drier) do not differ greatly, as witness this recipe:

Take a quart of milk. [Polyphemus used skim milk, as do many pot-cheese manufacturers.] Add 1 teaspoonful of rennet. Put the milk in a warm place overnight where it will set into a junket. Pour the junket into a piece of cheese cloth. Tie the ends of the cheese cloth together and hang it—full of curds and whey—on a hook over a basin, and let the whey drain and drip away until the curds are nearly solid. Thereafter, add salt and pepper for pot cheese or stir in some heavy cream for creamed cottage cheese.

Most of the cheeses we shall be talking about in this chapter are variations of these—cream or pot cheeses. They have only one life to live, and live it as fresh cheese. But occasionally a cheese will have a particularly distinguished "fresh" stage before it goes on to be another cheese. Mozzarella is one of these, for a mozzarella, if the cheesemaker wishes, can eventually become a provolone. And sometimes it is not the cheesemaker but the consumer who decides whether a cheese is to be left to mature or to be eaten "green." For example, many of the people who live in Van Wert, Ohio, where Liederkranz is made, regularly eat uncured Liederkranz and think the rest of us peculiar for liking it when it is "smelly"; and it is not unusual for the inhabitants of one Wisconsin cheesemaking town to pile raw Cheddar curds into a paper bag and eat them in the movies like popcorn.

Many variations of pot cheese and cream cheese can be found in every country that makes any cheese at all: Germany has its Glumse which resembles cottage cheese; Latin America has an assortment of *queso blanco* (white cheese), fresh skim-milk cottage-type cheeses; Holland has a one-day cheese, fresh, sweet and full of whey, which is called May cheese although it is made all year round by local farmers; Austria has a fresh Rahmkäse, or cream cheese, as well as a fresh butter cheese. Even India, which makes practically no cheese, has a kind of cottage cheese called Surti and a cream cheese called Surtal. The list is endless, ranging from the sweet and mild to the sour, salty, and briny. Only a few of these ever reach the major cities, for they are indeed "country" cheeses, consumed for the most part where they were made.

Because of their similarities, we shall not attempt to deal with this multitude of fresh country cheeses. Instead we shall focus on a few of the more outstanding and typical cheeses found in the principal cities of two primarily rural countries—Italy and France—and after that we'll take a look at some of the fresh cheeses available in our own country.

ITALIAN FRESH CHEESES

MOZZARELLA

Mozzarella at its best is very tender and dripping with its fresh whey as one bites into it. At one time it was made only from buffalo's milk, and in southern Italy it still is. Elsewhere in Italy, as in the United States, mozzarella is now made mostly from cow's milk. It isn't difficult, however, to find the *autentico mozzarella da bufala* almost anywhere in Italy, for refrigerated transport and a less intricate distribution system than ours make it possible to ship buffalo mozzarella as far north as Milan and still have it reach the customer in good condition. One we tasted in Florence had been shipped from Battipaglia, the principal southern Italian center for buffalo mozzarella. About the size of a medium tomato, it was tender, sweet and full of juice. Some people will disagree, but to us the difference between buffalo's- and cow's-milk mozzarella is not great. They are both mild; the buffalo has perhaps a more definite character, which emerges as one eats it.

In Italy you can also find tiny mozzarellas no larger than sea scallops, which come six in a pack (but not a vacuum pack) and are white, wet with whey, and have the same tender texture as the larger mozzarella. Like the larger ones, some are lightly smoked and some are not.

The pliable texture of fresh mozzarella has modeling possibilities which the Italians have not overlooked. A friend of the British gastronome Osbert Burdett wrote from Italy describing mozzarellas "fashioned into the shapes of animals and rude images of Saints" which she had found in the shop of an ancient lady called La Mozzarellara, "the one who sells mozzarella." (And La Mozzarellara herself looked "like a Chelsea jug: very squat and square, with ten chins under a black straw hat, an impassive face, and earrings which seem to drag the lobes of her ears to where might have once been her waist.")

Even the word mozzarella has been pressed into different meanings. As Roberto Ugge of Milan's Galbani cheese company wrote to us:

"In Italy 'mozzarella' is also used as a deprecatory term for young men who aren't very manly. 'He's a mozzarella,' people say. Also football and basketball teams that don't play well in the championships are called 'mozzarelle.' This is because mozzarella is soft, delicate and mild, which explains why it is used for weak young men and weak teams."

SCAMORZA

The oval-shaped, yellow-tinted Scamorza made in Central Italy is a little more solid, but very like mozzarella in texture. There are small Scamorze weighing between four and eight ounces, and large ones weighing as much as two and a half pounds. It has the mild flavor of the mozzarella, and like mozzarella it is often smoked. Italians toast it on bread or fry it in a pan with an egg.

RICOTTA

Ricotta is white and creamy, with a bland, verging on sweet, flavor, and it has much in common with cottage cheese. Despite the resemblance, when a large Italian cheese company once tried to introduce cottage cheese into Italy, it was for some reason unacceptable to Italians and was quickly withdrawn from the market. Perhaps it was because of the texture: ricotta is much smoother than cottage cheese and has no solid curds because it is not made from milk—not even skim milk. It is made from the coagulable substance in whey—whey that comes from the manufacture of still other cheeses such as provolone, mozzarella, and in this country, Swiss and Cheddar. It is no accident that this cheese, which is a by-product of other cheeses, proliferates in all the poorer countries of central and southern Europe where whey is considered too nutritious to be wasted. These whey cheeses are known variously as Ricuit, Serac, Ceracee, Mejette, Ziger, or Schotenzger. It is also no accident that in the affluent United States ricotta is now made from a combination of whey and whole milk, when it isn't made entirely from whole milk.

The traditional whey ricotta with its satiny texture is also most accommodating to the textures and flavorings of other foods, which is what makes it such an important ingredient in lasagna, manicotti and cannelloni. Indeed ricotta is so adaptable as to be a chameleon among cheeses, for it is also used as a creamy filling for pastries and puddings.

Crescenza Stracchino

For those who love the texture of a melted, collapsed Liederkranz but who recoil from its strong flavor, the Crescenza Stracchino is the answer, although unfortunately you have to go to Italy to find it. Ten minutes out of the icebox and the Crescenza is literally beside itself. Glistening, supercreamy, mildly tart, it is often used instead of butter—and is a way of having butter, cream and cheese all in one. If you come away from Italy having tried just one new cheese, this should be it.

The "Stracchino" part of its name is a generic term applied to cheeses which since around A.D. 1100 have been made in the plains of Lombardy from the milk of cows passing through on their way south for winter grazing. The word *stracca* corresponds to the now more frequently used *stanca,* meaning tired, which is what the cows were. Stracchino cheeses were made from their milk, which was greatly affected by their fatigue. Today, however, the cows no longer go south for the winter and all stracchino cheeses are made from well-rested milk.

CREMINO

Cremino is very much like our familiar silverfoil-wrapped cream cheeses. It too is foil-wrapped and it is sold all over central and northern Italy.

MASCARPONE

"The Mascarpone," wrote Osbert Burdett's friend, "is a large ball-shaped kind of Petit-Suisse tied up in muslin—a little kerchief for each. At home in town, these can be spread on chocolate cake or be eaten with strawberries. In the country you eat them with bread and salt. They are a sort of Devonshire clot without the clot." This exquisite butter-colored cheese that tastes like whipped cream is indeed made from fresh cream. It is eaten with sugar and fruit, and is sometimes served beaten up with brandy or liqueurs and sugar. It is made all over Italy but, alas, hardly ever here.

THE FRESH CHEESES OF FRANCE

Not surprisingly, the country that gives us our most cosmopolitan cheeses also produces an infinite number of fresh country cheeses—reminding us again that it is invariably the sophisticated palate that values simplicity.

Few of these cheeses reach here, however. Most French cheese manufacturers see little reason for pitting their fragile and perishable fresh cheeses, so costly to ship, against the scores of inexpensive—and often excellent—American cream and cottage cheeses. And so almost the only French fresh cheeses we get here are the little two-ounce foil-wrapped double-crème, Gervais, which has been well known for over a hundred years, and the equally famous

Petit-Suisse, also a double-crème, and so perishable it must first be frozen before it can be flown here. For the other fresh cheeses one must go to France; and even there, to sample all of them, one would have to make an extensive tour of the country. For only a few of France's fresh country cheeses—like the farmer cheeses, Fromage à la Pie, Maigre, and Ferme—ever get even as far as Paris.

But wherever you find them, French fresh cheeses do not have quite the fresh cheese flavor that we are accustomed to. Our cottage and pot cheeses and cream cheeses are, by and large, milder and sweeter, with only a trace of sourness. An American abroad often has to cultivate a taste for the more intense sourness of the French fresh cheeses, and he quickly learns to eat many of them in the French manner—that is, with sugar and cream. The sour flavor of these fresh cheeses is also found in the French favorite, *crème fraîche,* which in turn is not unlike our sour cream. *Crème fraîche,* too, is usually eaten with sugar.

Fromage Blanc

The simplest of all French fresh cheeses is the Fromage Blanc, which is our old friend sour milk poured into a cheesecloth bag and drained of its whey. This cheese travels under three names: when the sour milk curds are eaten with salt and pepper, its name is simply Fromage Blanc. When heavily sugared and eaten with sweet cream, it is called Fromage à la Crème. And when the sour and separated milk is set to drain in small heart-shaped wicker baskets lined with cheesecloth, and the heart-shaped curds are then turned out onto a plate and covered with cream and sugar, it becomes the classic dessert Coeur à la Crème.

Demi-Sel

Next in simplicity is the Demi-Sel, a small, moist cream cheese weighing about four ounces. As its name indicates, it is salted (although not salty), and in this respect is more like American cream cheeses than most French cream cheeses—which, unless they have to travel any distance, are largely unsalted. Demi-Sel is made all over France, but the best usually comes from Normandy.

Fresh Double- and Triple-Crèmes

The fresh double- and triple-crèmes are the richest of all the fresh cheeses, in and out of France. They bear the same relationship to each other as do the *cured* double- and triple-crèmes of Chapter 10—which is to say that rich as the double-crèmes are, the triple-crèmes are far richer. A fresh double-crème is more like our cream cheese than any other French fresh cheese, except that it is a little sourer and also more buoyant in texture—perhaps in part because it contains no preservatives.

The delicate double-crème Petit-Suisse is rather like a coagulated *crème fraîche,* and although not so sour as the double-crème Gervais, most Americans will doubtless feel that it is quite sour enough and that Petit-Suisse is at its best—and, indeed, it is exquisite—with sugar and strawberries. Most frozen Petit-Suisse—which is the only Petit-Suisse we receive here—has an odd texture when it defrosts, a kind of curdy wateriness, but the flavor is still excellent, and there is nothing to do but to pour off the curdy water and get on with eating it. The Petit-Suisse we import (called Demi-Suisse) comes in a box of six little rollmops, about an inch in diameter, each wrapped in its own paper. One of these tiny cheeses makes a pretty dollop for a dish of strawberries.

The most sumptuous of the fresh country cheeses—the triple-crèmes—can be had only in France. These snowy-white, thick, soft cheeses have the taste of a sour, moist cheesecake, without the sugar and vanilla.

No trip to France should fail to include a generous sampling of as many of these triple-crèmes as you can find. Those that should not be missed are the incomparable Fontainebleau, whipped into a white cloud (with or without *crème fraîche,* raspberries, or strawberries), the fresh St. Florentin, which requires nothing but a spoon and the privacy of a hotel room, and the fresh Boursin and Boursault, which are different brands of the same superb cheese.

These two companies, Boursin and Boursault, are passionate rivals—when one comes up with something the other is sure to follow suit. As each claims to be first in everything, we have no idea which was responsible for that little tour de force of a cheese, the fresh Triple-Crème aux Fines Herbes, a cheese infused with French garlic but so delicately that "Fines Herbes" is indeed the more appropriate name. Very little of this cheese comes here because neither company seems to have solved the problem of keeping it fresh until it gets to the American consumer's table. The Fines Herbes that one does occasionally find here is often disappointing because it tends to be bitter. It is best to wait until you are in France to try it—and try it you must, for this cheese is nothing short of spectacular.

THE UNITED STATES

Cottage Cheese

The American taste for mild cheese and the American preoccupation with weight-watching are both clearly reflected in our remarkable consumption of cottage cheese. Of the twelve pounds of cheese per person we eat each year, four and a half pounds are cottage cheese. The names we eat it under are various and confusing (in some regions, for example, "country style" means small curd, in others it means large curd), but in general we eat two kinds: plain and creamed. And there are about five different varieties: large curd, small curd, flaked curd, home style (soft and creamy with rather large curds), and pot or "whipped" style, as it is known in some parts of the country.

Ideally, the flavor of cottage cheese is much like that of fresh milk with a slightly acid but delicate taste and aroma. The texture is firm enough for the curd to hold its shape, and the curd is smooth and tender with a bright creamy-white color. If it is creamed, the curd has a smooth, glistening coat of cream that does not flow off when the cheese is spooned onto the plate. Of the hundreds of tons of cottage cheese made on a small and large scale throughout the country, some do live up to this ideal. But not all, unfortunately, according to a disheartening study made by Consumers' Union recently. In sampling the cottage cheeses in one typical metropolitan area, Consumers' Union found that the poor samples slightly outnumbered the mediocre ones, "and in no case could all samples of any brand be classed as at least good."

One of the principal conclusions was that cottage cheese is often stored too long before it is sold. Regrettably, no manufacturer dates his cartons to give the purchaser a guide to freshness, although some manufacturers have code dates for their own edification. (For example 0423 means April 23, as does 2232, except that to crack the second code, you have to add the first two digits and reverse the last two.)

About the only guide one has to quality is the U.S. Department of Agriculture's "Quality Approved" shield. Whenever you see it imprinted on the carton, it means that the cheese has been voluntarily submitted to a Department of Agriculture inspection (there is no compulsory inspection) and that it fulfills the Department's minimum requirements for quality. As for freshness, one can confine the buying of cottage cheese to stores that have a lot of turnover, buying only as much as will be used in a few days' time. As with any fresh cheese, even with good refrigeration, each day counts against its quality.

Like most cheese, cottage cheese is at its best when it is at room temperature, so for the fullest flavor it is best to take it out of the refrigerator a few hours before serving it. And the cottage cheese you would take to the office for lunch, if only you had an icebox there, will taste better and richer, we can promise you, if it is *not* refrigerated for those few morning hours.

FARMER CHEESE

Farmer cheese, which is closely related to cottage cheese—or, more exactly, to the drier pot cheese—once used to be sold only in bulk, in the shape of a sleeve board, but now it also comes in small, prepacked rectangles. There is no one kind, for it is made differently in different localities and even within the same locality. It is also called "pressed cheese" in some parts of the country. But if it is good, its flavor is clean, mild, and slightly sour, and its texture is firm enough to slice without crumbling. For a light summer lunch, nothing beats a thick slice of farmer cheese sprinkled with salt and pepper, and topped with two or three tablespoons of sour cream—for the dry farmer cheese and rich sour cream have a natural affinity.

Cream Cheese and Fresh Neufchâtel

American cream cheese is one of the greatest values around. Where else for so little money can you get the sense of luxury you feel when you spread a good cream cheese on a slice of fresh, heavily seeded rye bread, or a chewy bagel?

In addition to the familiar national brands, almost every major community has its own local brand of cream cheese—although the local brand will often be owned by one of the giant cheese corporations, because so many small cheese companies are being absorbed by larger ones. Consequently, a large company will often have two brands of cream cheese competing in the same locality. A chief difference from brand to brand is that many contain gum arabic while a few holdouts still do not. Cream cheeses without gum arabic (the label will tell you) have a lighter, more natural texture, even though they are not quite so long-keeping.

American Neufchâtel is like cream cheese except that it is smoother, spreads more easily, and contains less butterfat than cream cheese, but more protein and moisture. It is richer than the French fresh Neufchâtel from which it is copied and, as made here in the United States, it may or may not contain a stabilizer such as gum arabic.

On the whole, American cream cheeses and Neufchâtels are very good, although we're inclined to agree with one cream-cheese lover who said wistfully, "None of them has as much tang as they did when I was a kid—but then, something seems to have happened to the rye bread, too."

MOZZARELLA

If you're lucky enough to live near an Italian neighborhood, you'll most likely be able to go, some early morning, to an Italian grocery with its provolones suspended overhead, its large, ornate tins of olive oil and boxes of exotically shaped pastas lining the shelves, and buy a freshly made mozzarella dripping in its own sweet whey. Even earlier that morning, the proprietor will have received his daily shipment of mozzarella curd from a local distributor and will himself have completed the final steps of manufacture, heating the white, pliant curd, kneading it until it is soft, and molding it into irregular spherical shapes.

He will doubtless ask if you want a large mozzarella (about eight ounces) or a small one (about four ounces). Take either or both, and don't wait until lunch—eat it without delay, sprinkling it with salt and a few grains of pepper. Never mind those, unalterably committed to strongly flavored cheeses, who insist that mozzarella has no flavor. The body of the newly made tender mozzarella, which pulls apart in clean strips, is permeated with refreshing whey juices and has a sweet, milky freshness that only the coarsest palate could disdain.

FACTORY-MADE MOZZARELLAS

The factory-made mozzarella that is sold largely in supermarkets is another—and a most uninteresting—cheese. It is older, firmer, and without juice, because unlike the mozzarellas one finds in Italy or in Italian-American neighborhoods, these are manufactured and packaged for a longer shelf life, and toward that end its juices—one of its most beguiling characteristics—have been wrung from it. Nevertheless, some of these mozzarellas are better than others, as the process of trial and error will confirm.

The recently developed "pizza cheese" made in the Middle West and shipped to Eastern states is even drier than the factory-made mozzarella. And so it must be, we are told; otherwise it would never reach the customer's pie in good condition. From the customer's viewpoint this may seem unreasonable—there are, after all, such things as fast trains and refrigerated cars. From the manufacturer's standpoint it makes sense. Even after they reach their destination, these cheeses must pass through the hands of many middlemen and endure long waits before they finally reach the pizza joint or the retailer's refrigerated case. The result is a "pizza cheese" with even more of its juices removed than the factory-made mozzarella, and so much drier that it is really a different cheese—not a very good one perhaps, but acceptable when it is melted, doused with tomato paste and covered with anchovies.

RICOTTA

Ricotta made in this country, as we have said, is made of whole milk and whey, or entirely of whole milk. This of course makes for a thicker, creamier cheese—more like creamed cottage cheese, but sweeter and smoother. Italian-Americans are very fond of it, and with reason. You can make a wide variety of dishes with it, depending on your ingenuity. For example, you can make a delicious pasta—with something of the textural contrasts of cannelloni—by spooning some ricotta into hot, well-buttered noodles. Or you can combine instant coffee and confectioners' sugar with ricotta to make delicious coffee pudding. But it is most commonly used in making Italian cheesecake and *lasagne al forno*.

5

The Bland
and Buttery Cheeses

"I would have hated Sevruga caviar and Château Margaux 1899 if I'd had them five days a week," wrote Joseph Wechsberg. And so with cheeses. A daily regimen of Roquefort or Brie—or any cheese whose brilliance of flavor shocks the palate—would quickly pall. No, what is wanted for every day, to serve hunger rather than appetite, is a cheese that is as simple and sustaining as fresh bread and butter.

We have many of them. Lovely cheeses. Not great, but dependable in their goodness and amiability. Bel Paese is an example, and others—there are a couple of dozen in all—include Italy's Taleggio and Fontina, France's Bonbel, Holland's Edam and Gouda, Denmark's Samsoe, Tybo, Danbo, and other "bo's," and America's Munster and young brick. People who are not venturesome in their tastes usually like these mild cheeses to the exclusion of any others, and so of course do children, but an appreciation of them is by no means confined to the unsophisticated palate. For the connoisseur usually goes full circle before he is done, and as he becomes less infatuated with rich and exotic foods, he develops a regard for the taste of things that are delicate and pure. And at half-circle he needs them, too—for respite. Thus the mild cheeses are appreciated universally—they are eaten at all times of the day or night, in some countries even at breakfast—and people the world over consume more of them than any other kind. Today, in fact, the dominant trend in all countries is toward milder and milder cheeses. In Italy, for example, during the past few years the sharp flavors of the provolone and Gorgonzola sold domestically have been deliberately muted to meet the change in tastes. English cheeses, never very strong, are much milder now than they used to be, and harder to tell apart. And even in France, home of the world's most sophisticated cheeses, one group of cheeses that has recently become extremely popular is almost as bland as butter.

ITALY

BEL PAESE

One of the best-known Italian cheeses in the United States and all over the world is the delicately flavored Bel Paese—an ivory-colored cheese that is soft and yielding, not only to the touch but somehow to the taste, too. Its popularity has grown so in the past ten or fifteen years that the familiar round chipboard box showing a map in beige and pale green and a picture of an elderly priest can be seen in the display cases of most supermarkets and even in smaller shops that do not carry an extensive variety of cheeses. In restaurants, too, Bel Paese is often among the four or five cheeses at the bottom of the menu. It is a cheese you can order with confidence, because it has exceptional uniformity of quality and keeps well. Provided that you do not get an outside cut that has been exposed too long to the air, it is difficult to find a poor piece of Bel Paese, even in a second-rate restaurant.

Bel Paese is the brand name of one of a group, generically classified as "Italico" cheeses, which have been made in Italy, with minor variations, for about seventy years. It is the best known of the Italicos, and its three chief competitors in Italy (they are not imported here), Pastorella, Bick, and Fior D'Alpe, are excellent cheeses but not quite on a par with Bel Paese.

The name, of course, means "beautiful country," and it was used to refer to Italy in Dante's *Inferno* and in a sonnet by Petrarch. Much later, *Bel Paese* was the title of a popular book about Italy written for young people by an Italian priest, Antonio Stoppani—the same one whose picture appears on the Bel Paese package. Stoppani was a friend of the Italian cheesemaker Egidio Galbani, whose chief avocation was mountain climbing and who went every Sunday to Lecco, near Lake Como, to climb. He was impressed by the local cheeses there and he studied the methods used in making them. At that time—this was around the turn of the twentieth century—native Italian cheeses were eaten principally by the poor; with the exception of Parmesan, local cheeses were spurned by Italians of means, who bought only French luxury cheeses. Galbani wanted to make a luxury cheese in Italy at a popular price. The particular formula he developed was one of the foundation stones for what was to become the Galbani empire—a corporation that today occupies the place in Italy that Kraft holds in the United States, with an export business that reaches to every corner of the world.

Bel Paese is made in Melzo, not far from Milan, and it has literally put that town on the map. For on the Italian map that appears on every Italian Bel Paese cheese, there is little Melzo, larger than life—larger, in fact, than Rome.

Imported and domestic (Wisconsin) versions of Bel Paese are both available in the United States, and their wrappings, showing the picture of the priest against the background of a map, at first glance look identical. However, the map on the imported Bel Paese is that of Italy; the map on the domestic Bel Paese is of North and South America. If you always assumed, as we did, that all Bel Paese was Italian, you probably never noticed the difference in the maps, but once you know you can't miss it. Both cheeses are good, but because of the differences in the water and vegetation from one part of the world to another, cheeses made in different locations are always bound to be slightly different, and these are no exception. To the credit of Wisconsin it must be said that the American version of Bel Paese, which is delightfully creamy and has a most agreeable tartness, is one of the closest copies of any cheese we have encountered. But the Italian Bel Paese is even better; it is less likely to have the ever so faintly bitter aftertaste sometimes found in the domestic Bel Paese, and it has the more rounded and pleasing flavor.

Though Bel Paese is primarily a table cheese—a most versatile one, for it is companionable to many other foods—its fatness makes it a good melting cheese too, and it can be and often is used instead of fresh mozzarella for cooking. This makes it a good all-purpose cheese to keep on hand, particularly since few Americans buy mozzarella unless they intend to use it for cooking—and sometimes it's not possible to get mozzarella. Such was the case of a Japanese lady who wrote the makers of Bel Paese in Milan a few years ago that she had started a school of domestic economy in Tokyo. The Japanese at that time were importing very few cheeses, but she reported that her girl students were getting highly satisfactory results by using Bel Paese instead of mozzarella to make a dish that was fast becoming a Japanese favorite—pizza.

And at the Parisian restaurant that specializes in cheeses, Androuet on the Rue Amsterdam, a dish was invented by M. Androuet himself thirty-three years ago which is still featured on the menu, called

CROQUE MADAME BEL PAESE
(assembled in layers as follows:)
slices of toast
Béchamel sauce topped with grated Parmesan
slices of prosciutto
and little slices of Bel Paese on top—all melted

This dish was presented by Androuet at the 1932 World's Fair Exposition in Paris.

TALEGGIO

Taleggio (also sold here under the brand name of Tal Fino) is the only representative we in the United States ever see of the stracchino cheeses. Most of these (as described in Chapter 4) are so little aged, so delicate and fresh, that they cannot travel out of their own country. Only Taleggio, which is older and not exactly typical, ever comes here. Named for the small town in Lombardy in which it is believed to have originated, Taleggio is ripened in natural caves for at least forty days. By the time we see it, it has achieved a great age compared with most stracchinos. It is soft and creamy under its rough, rosy crust, and if the piece you get is a recent arrival it will be bland and mellow, with however just the slightest edge to it—a faintly aromatic quality that is entirely pleasing. This edge sharpens as the cheese gets older, and many people prefer it that way—up to a point. The only way to judge it before you buy (assuming that the wrappings are fresh and loose on the cheese, and the cheese plump and springy) is to sniff it if you can. If you are reminded of a ripe Camembert or Brie, you are too late; put it back. But if it's mild and inviting, you have a cheese that you are almost certain to enjoy.

FONTINA

Most of the cheeses in the bland and buttery group are, as we have said, good though not great. The one exception that merits the word "great" is Italy's Fontina—the best and the original of which is designated by its full name, Fontina d'Aosta. Just as the finest Parmesan cheese comes from a particular district in Italy known as the *zona classica,* the true and original Fontina also comes from a rigidly defined zone in the mountains of northern Italy near the Swiss border—the Valley of Aosta (hence the name Val d'Aosta, or the frequently used contraction, Valdostana).

How to describe Fontina d'Aosta? Its physical attributes are easily catalogued. The cheese it most resembles in appearance is Swiss Gruyère—that is, it has a light-brown crust; it comes in wheels twelve to fifteen inches in diameter and three to four inches thick; the cheese itself is a warm ivory in color, the texture fairly firm, and the surface broken here and there by tiny holes. But the flavor and character of this wonderful cheese cannot be so neatly categorized. For Fontina is a cheesemaker's dream come true. Imagine being able to make a cheese that combines the sweet butternut flavor of a select Emmenthal with the special tang of Gruyère—but with a hint of Port-Salut about it, making it more worldly than either Emmenthal or Gruyère; a cheese that at room temperature never liquefies, but neither does it remain quite solid—it is creamy, acquiring in the mouth a certain gloss not unlike that of Brie. This is Fontina d'Aosta, a cheese that belongs with the top dozen cheeses that are being made anywhere today.

It has many imitators, known by names like Fontal, Fontinella, and Fantina, which may be marketed here under the name of Fontina, because that name is not protected by law in the United States as it is in Italy. Some are very good, others not.

One means of identifying the true Fontina d'Aosta is by the rind. It is a light, brightish brown, like the color of cocoa with a good deal of cream in it. This rind is covered by a thin veneer of wax. Whether it is because air gets in between the wax and the rind in certain places, making for patches of lighter and darker brown, or because the rind itself is unevenly colored, the surface of the rind, marked as it is with faint lines and subtle color contrasts, resembles a terrazzo floor.

Beware one Italian "Fontina" that is much in evidence here. It has a bright-red rind, and the cheese itself is yellow rather than ivory. This cheese is sold here (and legally) as Fontina, and it proves how little an unprotected name can come to mean. For this extremely bland so-called Fontina is a nonentity among cheeses; the only bounce it has is in its texture, which is rubbery.

Little is known about the early history of Fontina d'Aosta except that it has been made in Lombardy since the eleventh century. The valley for which it is named is located in the upper Bergamo Mountains, within sight of Mont Blanc, the Matterhorn and Monte Rosa. The city of Aosta, originally founded by the Romans near the place where Hannibal crossed the Alps, is one of the most beautiful in Italy. It is connected to Martigny, Switzerland, by the great St. Bernard Pass—and it is not surprising that the cheese from this vicinity should have something in common with the Swiss Emmenthal and Gruyère, or that it should be the principal ingredient in the Italian version of Swiss fondue, called *fonduta,* which is made with white truffles and white wine (see the recipe in Chapter 22). For in addition to being a table cheese of extraordinary quality, Fontina d'Aosta is a superb melting cheese.

If you do not yet know Fontina d'Aosta, lose no time in finding it. It is a cheese that appeals to people of many different tastes— one that you will want to serve again and again.

FRANCE

France is the last great stronghold of strong cheeses, and one has only to go through a Paris *crémerie* and see there some of the outrageous cheeses, in their outrageous crusts—grown brown, gray, even black, with time, their surfaces hard-winkled and warty—to know that the French will probably always, so far as their cheeses are concerned, put age before beauty. The more affluent the neighborhood the more one is likely to see these ancient cheeses which, as their age increases, are revered the more as "cheeses for the connoisseur." At the other extreme, the French taste goes directly to the exquisite fresh cheeses—as rich and as mild, almost, as newly whipped cream.

And so in France we find only three or four cheeses that fall into the bland and buttery group—cheeses that are midway between the very fresh varieties and the robust cheeses that are typically French. But the fact that *any* bland cheeses should be given house room in France is in itself worthy of note. And that three of them, all marketed under the now ubiquitous trademark of La Vache Qui Rit, should have become household words in France in the past few years is nothing less than phenomenal. This is the Laughing Cow, a Gallic Elsie. Her countenance (not so amiable as Elsie's, and with more than a trace of malice) is to be seen all over the Paris Métro, in the pages of family magazines, on billboards, and in the refrigerator cases of every "supermag." Most Frenchmen will insist that they patronize her only for the sake of their children. But at the very least she will exert some influence upon the tastes of the next generation, and there is reason to think that she may to some extent be having her way with this one.

BONBEL

The first of these three, Bonbel, is small and round, the size of a baby Edam, wrapped in buttercup-yellow paraffin and then in cellophane—a cheese that has become familiar here during the past year or two because it has been imported in considerable quantity. Bonbel is like a very creamy American Munster or Fondutta, very soft and very mild, although it has a nice sour tang to it—a thoroughly pleasant cheese, particularly for breakfast. Nothing could seem more unFrench, but there it is.

BABY BEL

The second is known as Baby Bel, and though it is very big in France, it has not yet made its way here. It's the same size and shape as Bonbel, and also very soft, but the paraffin covering is a bright red. The flavor is indistinguishable from that of a very young, moist Edam.

LA VACHE QUI RIT

The third is a process cheese with the same name as the trade mark, La Vache Qui Rit. Most of the soft, cream-style process cheeses are, like different brands of cream-style corn, difficult to tell apart—except perhaps that one may be yellower or stickier than another. And this one is like all the others, except that it is now being packaged (and sold here) in individually foil-wrapped cocktail squares the size of a bouillon cube. These are better eaten in solitude because they take a certain amount of application to unwrap.

MIMOLETTE

The French have always spurned English Cheddar, when they acknowledge its existence at all, and they have never been much of a market for Holland Edam. But for those stray Frenchmen with a taste for either, there is Mimolette, another most improbable French cheese. Mimolette resembles in texture and shape a Holland Edam ball that has a little age on it and is yellow on the outside instead of red. Broaching it, however, is like cutting into a ripe Cranshaw melon—the interior is brilliant in comparison to the skin. With the exception of English Leicester, Mimolette is the brightest orange cheese there is, and it gets its brilliance in the same way Leicester does—by massive doses of annatto. But for all its color, Mimolette is a drab cheese. It tastes a little like a Cheddar and rather a lot like an Edam—and for all that, not much like anything at all.

HOLLAND

Unlike France, which has hundreds of different cheeses but only a few in the bland group, Holland has only two cheeses of real importance, both of them bland—the well-known Edam, and Gouda. In cataloguing the virtues of these two cheeses (and here we are talking about the very young Edams and Goudas; the aged varieties are something else again) the first word that comes to mind is "dependable," closely followed by "wholesome," "agreeable," and "adaptable." Perhaps not an exciting list of attributes.

But for people who like cheese with a light, clean, pleasant buttery taste and the conventional texture, Edam and Gouda can hardly be improved upon.

Both cheeses date back to the Middle Ages and were being exported from Holland to other countries in Europe as early as the thirteenth century. Holland is the world's largest producer of milk and its biggest exporter of cheeses, and her considerable experience in dealing with world markets, plus the fact that she entered them very early in the game, account for the fact that her two principal cheeses—particularly the Edam—are to be found almost everywhere in the world.

Their excellent keeping qualities have further contributed to their popularity, particularly in warm climates. Throughout South America, for example, Edam, in addition to a few local cheeses, is what people mean when they say cheese (just as cheese here means American or Cheddar), and the same is true of Puerto Rico and other islands in the Caribbean. In fact, Puerto Ricans consider Edam cheese so much their own that dairies around New York that cater especially to the Puerto Rican population are supplying *bodegas* on the upper West Side and in Spanish Harlem with two kinds of "Puerto Rican cheeses"—one a local version of the fresh white, sourish curd cheese that is native to Puerto Rico, and the other a facsimile of Holland Edam.

Young Edam and Gouda

Edam and Gouda are smooth, mellow cheeses, not dissimilar in flavor. The main distinctions between them, both in shape and in taste, arise from the difference in butterfat content—for Edam is made from partly skim milk, Gouda from whole milk. As a general rule, the higher the butterfat content, the softer the cheese. Because Edam turns firmer faster, it can retain the ball shape in which it is made (it is the world's only cheese that is perfectly spherical). Gouda, however, being less firm at a young age, is made in the more conventional wheels. Gouda has a yellow rind; Edam, of course, has the bright-red rind that is as much a part of its identity as its shape. Farmers of northern Holland have taken this way of distinguishing their cheese since the thirteenth century, when they entered into a formal agreement to rub all the cheeses from the vicinity of Edam with vermilion-dyed cloths to impart a characteristic reddish glow to the rinds.

Neither Edam nor Gouda is especially recommended, even by Holland cheesemakers, for grating or cooking. They are intended to be eaten with the fresh, moist white or pumpernickel bread and butter that the Dutch serve with them (particularly at breakfast), or with Dutch rusks—which you can buy here, but which are by no means so tender as the ones you get in Holland. This Dutch bread-and-cheese breakfast is usually supplemented with a thin slice of ham, also a specialty of Holland. And with a pot of fresh coffee—no people in the world make better coffee—these cheeses, by the time one has spent two or three days in Holland, begin to seem as reasonable to eat for breakfast as Wheaties. Edam and Gouda are eaten at all meals, and every bar in Holland features fresh open-faced cheese and ham sandwiches, along with the national drink, Genever, or Holland beer.

Old Gouda

Most of the Edams and Goudas that are exported to the U.S. are perfect examples of good but not great cheeses. They rarely disappoint. But when these cheeses are well aged they become something entirely different. An old Holland Gouda is a liqueur of a cheese, a great cheese—especially if it is farmhouse rather than factory-made. You can tell because a farmhouse cheese has a gray mark on its rind that reads "Boerenkaas, Holland" (boeren means farmer), followed by the number designating the farm on which it was made. Factory cheeses are stamped in red with the word volvet, which simply means "full fat," though in fact they have no more butterfat—and often less—than the farmhouse cheeses. The latter, being more choice to begin with, are usually the ones set aside for long aging. One way to identify a well-aged Gouda (apart from the flavor, which is the unfailing indicator) is by its edges. If the sides form sharp edges with the top and bottom, the cheese is young. If it is well aged, the sides will have become smooth and rounded from the gentle rising of the cheese inside.

We do not import many aged Goudas into the United States, but better shops sometimes have them. They are worth looking out for.

Old Edam

An aged Edam (these, unfortunately, are rarities in the United States) can be an even greater revelation. One two-and-a-half-year-old Edam we sampled in Amsterdam, so hard that it almost had to be opened with a cleaver, was the color of a light vanilla caramel inside. The flavor was like that of a Parmesan anointed with brown butter and a few drops of brandy—pretty stylish for an Edam! But by then it had become another cheese.

There is a story that in 1841 the Uruguayan fleet, under American command, defeated the British-led Argentine Navy after substituting Dutch Edams for cannonballs when they ran out. But if the cheeses were as aged as they would have had to be for shooting out of a cannon, it would be hard to say who was the loser.

DENMARK

The Danes are the world's greatest copiers of cheeses. And with just a few exceptions, such as Danish blue cheese (copied after Roquefort), and Esrom (copied after Port-Salut), and Crema Danica, an original with some of the best features of Camembert and the triple-crèmes, most Danish cheeses fall squarely into the bland and buttery group—and with minor variations they are all copies of one another.

In fact it is almost impossible to keep the bland Danish cheeses straight, because the flavors are so alike that the differences in taste actually vary more with the age of the cheese than with the variety. To make matters even more confusing, in 1956 the Danish government changed all the names of Danish cheeses to new names that make them sound Danish in origin. Thus Danish Port-Salut became Esrom (for the town where it is made); Danish Swiss became Samsoe (for the Danish island of that name); Steppe (originally named for the Hungarian region in which it was first made) became Danbo (which means one who lives in Denmark). Other "bo's" include Fynbo (for the Danish island of Funen), Maribo, Tybo, Elbo, and Molbo. Untie all the "bo's" and you have virtually the same cheese over and over and over again. The sizes and shapes vary from loaf to wheel to sphere; the colors from bone white to buttercup yellow; the holes from pinpoints to peachstones; the flavors from faintly sweet to faintly sour. But they are all minor variations of the Samsoe, which is in turn a buttery variation of an Emmenthal—softer, moister, milder, less distinctive perhaps, but an extremely agreeable cheese nevertheless.

Thus Denmark gives us a lot of different names but really very few different cheeses. One Danish authority feels that a reason for the limited variety is that Denmark has few Catholics and therefore no demand for cheeses interesting enough to take the place of meat on fast days; this also means that Denmark has missed out on all the wonderful cheeses that came out of the monasteries in Catholic countries.

In any event, there is no "best" bland Danish cheese; they are all quite good, and you will have to sample them to see which you prefer. Some of the confusion will automatically be eliminated because few stores carry more than three or four, if that many.

NORWAY AND SWEDEN

The bland cheeses of Norway and Sweden are not markedly different from those of Denmark. One of the best is Norway's Jarlsberg, a wide-eyed, well-textured, buttery cheese. Another is Norwegian Tilsit, which when young is like a very mild brick. Swedish cheeses in this group include Herrgård, or Manor, cheese, one of the most popular in Sweden—a holed cheese with a delicate flavor rather like that of Gouda; and Sveciaost, another mild and agreeable cheese that also resembles Gouda.

THE UNITED STATES

In many supermarkets the best-selling cheese today, other than the process varieties, is American Munster (or Muenster)—a cheese that deserves its popularity. Despite the name, this cheese has no relation to the European Munster, which is very soft and strong and smelly. In fact the chief characteristic of American Munster is its surpassing mildness and almost complete absence of bouquet—two reasons for its success in a country in which bland foods, and particularly bland cheeses, are preferred. But Munster, for all its mildness, is not wishy-washy; at its best it has a light, fresh taste that you will not quickly tire of. The quality varies enormously, but the cheeses sold in bulk are generally better than the prepackaged ones. Munster makes an excellent breakfast cheese and it is one of the best melting cheeses that we have. Try it in scrambled eggs, or broiled on slices of buttered light toast with a topping of thin-sliced onion.

Fondutta, which is made in Wisconsin, is a very close second to Munster—and you may like it even better because it is fatter and softer.

Brick—a cheese very popular in the Western part of the country, and almost a stranger to the East—is sweet and mild when young, cream-colored and firm-textured, and for this short period it belongs with these bland cheeses. As it ages it acquires formidable strength—and old brick is therefore discussed with the strong cheeses in Chapter 15.

Two other American bland cheeses that are very similar to each other are identified by the brand names Gold-N-Rich and Baronet. They are midway in flavor between Bel Paese and Munster, with a dash of young Cheddar thrown in, and like many Cheddars they are colored orange. Of the two (and other cheeses of this type are available under still other brand names) Gold-N-Rich has a little more oomph. But you can't go wrong with Baronet either—unless, of course, what you really wanted was Limburger. These cheeses also melt and cook very well, and though they are themselves tame, they too have a special affinity for onions.

6

---·◦∞◦·---

The Swisses

Swiss cheese is a curiosity. It has always been known not for its special sweetness or its mellow hazelnut flavor, but rather for the cheese that is *not* there—that is, the holes. These holes are found in more than a dozen cheeses made in various countries and commonly called "Swiss," but the original—and easily the best—is the Switzerland Emmenthal. This Emmenthal, the most imitated of all cheeses, is to other Swisses what Baccarat crystal is to simple glass. Unfortunately the difference is not immediately apparent, because all the Swiss cheeses—the good as well as the poor ones— are more or less alike in color, and even in shape after they have been cut; and all, of course, have one attribute in common—the holes. And so it is impossible to say how many buyers of cheeses, the experienced as well as the innocent, have unwittingly accepted second or third best, simply because they looked into, and trusted, those deceiving eyes.

The holes in Swiss cheese—though the term is a misnomer because Switzerland produces many other kinds of cheeses that have no holes, and cheeses with holes are made in almost every country that makes cheese at all—are so much a part of its identity that even a child can tell a Swiss by its holes, and countless jokes have been made about them. In a classic scene in a Charlie Chaplin movie he is a hapless waiter trying to meet an angry patron's de-

THE SWISSES • 61

mand for Swiss cheese by boring holes into a hunk of Cheddar. But this, as we shall see, is only slightly more outrageous than some attempts that have actually been made to fake the holes by mechanical means and thus simulate at least the look of a real Swiss.

The earliest version of Swiss cheese did not have that characteristic look. It was smaller by far, and solid through and through. The holes—which are the consequence of the natural "rising" of the cheese—came much later as the art of cheesemaking developed, just as bread baked with yeast came long after unleavened bread. This precursor did not taste like our Swiss either, for rennet was as yet undiscovered, and salt, a precious commodity, was used sparingly if at all. Methods of making it were entirely different too. We know from early drawings that this ancestral Swiss was made in crude vessels over a wood fire, the curd cut and stirred with pine branches. No one can say with certainty when it was first made by the Celtic mountain dwellers who originally inhabited the Swiss Alps, though the writings of Plinius Secundus place it at least as far back as the ascendancy of Rome, where it was brought by Caesar's legions after the campaigns in Helvetia.

Though a number of cheeses claim the distinction of having been captured by—and, in turn, having captured—the luxury-loving Romans, it is reasonable to think that this cheese could have withstood the long journey to Rome as others could not, and it may well have arrived there in a condition to be admired. This is because Swiss appears to have been the first cheese that was made with a view to durability. Firm even when young, this cheese was made to support age, and its heavy rind, which thickened with aging, was as strong as a leathern skin, making the pale, delicate cheese it encased proof against weather and wet and time itself. For the mountain dwellers who made it in summer it was meat for the following winter, and if needed, for the winter after that. Small wonder, as it came to represent francs as well as food to the Swiss, that so many traditions grew up around it. One that has been handed down for generations is the setting aside, upon the birth of a child, of a great wheel of Swiss—to be partaken of at his christening, at his wedding, and at last at his funeral. Swiss was the first cheese to have been exported on any scale, and with the growth of trade it became known throughout Europe and the Near East. Unofficially, too, it crossed Switzerland's borders thousands of times in the gunnysacks of the ubiquitous Swiss Knights, whose services could be enlisted for almost any cause that could afford their hire. The Swiss economy was, in fact, so geared to the disparate arts of war and dairying for so many hundreds of years that the Swiss had a saying that their country's two biggest exports were Swiss mercenaries and Swiss cheese.

The worldwide success of Emmenthal inspired the making of "domestic Swiss" in virtually every country that made cheese at all. Some of these always were, and still are, indifferent cheeses. Others, such as the wheel Swisses made in quantity in Green County, Wisconsin, until about twenty years ago, and now almost a thing of the past, were superlative cheeses in their own right, even though they did not, and could not, exactly duplicate the Switzerland Emmenthal. But the commercialization of cheesemaking brought a general decline in quality—for one thing, because the cheeses were not properly aged. In the case of some unscrupulous operators the abuses were far worse: holeless cheeses made by entirely different processes or cheeses made by the original process but which emerged "blind"—that is, without holes—were sometimes gouged with a utensil like a melon baller and sold as Swiss. Later, when prepackaged slices came on the market, holeless cheeses were sometimes sliced and then stenciled to resemble Swiss. The honestly made cheeses, for the most part, had virtue but no character. Whereas the flavor should have been sweet and delicate, it was often faintly bitter, as if the cheese, from its surface to its very heart, was all parings. This was particularly true of "winter cheese," made when the cattle, unable to graze outdoors, were fed silage rather than the natural, sun-dried hay used exclusively for winter feed in Switzerland, where the use of silage is forbidden by law. If the cheese that resulted was deficient in flavor, this went largely unnoticed because it was usually (at least in this country) eaten in paper-thin slices and often with ham and plenty of mustard.

Meanwhile, the great Swiss wheels made in this country and in others beside Switzerland all but disappeared. For new technology had ushered in one of the greatest offenses of all: so-called "block" or rindless Swiss that matures not in a great wheel, encased in its natural amber skin, but that comes of age in a shower curtain of a plastic bag, from which it emerges limp and rubbery and in all respects unworthy of the name it bears.

Switzerland Emmenthal

Emmenthal (or Emmenthaler), like so many other cheeses, is named for the district in which it is produced—the Emme Valley, in the canton of Bern. It is one of the most difficult of all cheeses to make. It requires the highest quality of milk (good milk is always a requirement for good cheese, but in some more than others the quality of the milk—its taste—is but little changed through its making and curing, and the excellence of the cheese can be judged by the clarity with which the fresh milk taste comes through, even though the cheese is aged). Equally important, its making requires great skill. Just as in making a soufflé the cook must avoid opening the oven to check its progress, so the cheesemaker must decide, without looking, just when the cheese has developed eyes of the right size and quality for it to be removed from the warm, humid fermentation rooms in which it "rises" to the cool aging places in which it matures. This he does by thumping and tapping the cheese. A good ear and a sure touch tell him—to the day—not only when the eyes are sufficiently opened, but also whether the cheese has the right body to be removed from the warm to the cool curing place.

And well before this stage other skills come into play: the cutting of the curd with a Swiss-cheese harp, for example, is a critical step in its production. After that comes the most spectacular moment, when the massive curd, often weighing more than two hundred pounds, is cradled with heavy cheesecloth and hoisted out of its copper vat like a Gargantuan dripping mozzarella, by a block and tackle. The immense curd hangs draining off its excess whey, and then after being hauled on a rail suspended from the ceiling—much as a side of beef travels inside a wholesale butcher's—it is lowered into the circular wood or stainless-steel hoop into which it is pressed to form the massive wheels in which Switzerland Emmenthal is traditionally made.

In addition to superior milk and special skill, a third requirement for a really fine Emmenthal is patient capital. To come into its own, the cheese must ripen in its own good time, and this of course ties up the maker's investment. Most of the presliced, prepackaged Swiss sold in the United States in vacuum-sealed plastic bags has been aged just sixty days—the minimum our law allows for any cheese made from unpasteurized milk—or it may be aged for even a shorter time if pasteurized milk is used. These cheeses, callow and unseasoned as they are, serve—and perpetuate—the American taste for bland cheeses. In Switzerland, Emmenthal which is to be exported is aged according to the taste of the country to which it goes—varying from the four months' minimum required by Swiss law to ten months or more. Most of the younger cheeses go to the United States, while France, Germany, Belgium and other European customers prefer the riper ones.

As for size, four hundred years ago the weight of a Swiss wheel seldom exceeded ten or twelve pounds. Tradition has it that the wheels became larger and heavier when, at the end of the eighteenth century, street and bridge tolls were instituted in some villages, with levies figured by the piece rather than the weight or size. In any case, by 1800, Swiss expertise had made it possible to have good quality cheese of one hundred pounds or more. Today wheels for export may not weigh less than 145 pounds, and their weight, usually between 155 and 175 pounds, sometimes exceeds 220 pounds. Most of these wheels require at least a ton of milk to make.

Ripening is just one factor—though a critical one—in the development of flavor. Another is the natural rind, which begins to form early as the cheese is taken off the shelf each day, turned over (so it won't be flat on the bottom and curved on top like bread), washed off and rubbed thoroughly with a dry cloth, then with salt. The grains of salt melt in the moist atmosphere of the cellar and the drops of salt water penetrate the rind and gradually season the curd within. The rind, which hardens as the cheese cures, not only nourishes but protects it. It enables the cheese to breathe, while adding to its flavor. The more recently developed rindless Swiss, on the other hand, is a poor thing in comparison, insulated as it is in a plastic skin from the world in which it must later make its way. Thanks to its deprived infancy, it readily relinquishes what little flavor and sweetness it has upon exposure to the air.

The flavor of Switzerland Emmenthal is often likened to that of hazelnuts or walnuts. It is sweeter than any of its imitators, and leaves a far sweeter aftertaste. The Swiss attribute the sweetness not only to the care the cheeses receive at all stages of their making, but also to the good Swiss milk which comes from exceptionally fine cows (Swiss brown, Simmental, Fribourg and Eringer) that graze in the greenest of pastures, rich in aromatic grasses, and Alpine flowers. And this fragrant fare is washed down by the clear glacial waters that have made Swiss spas famous the world over.

The making of Switzerland Swiss cheese today and the maintenance of its quality are regulated almost entirely by the Swiss Cheese Union—one of the tightest and most powerful cartels in the world, exceeded in its strictness perhaps only by the South African diamond syndicate. The sophistication of the top management of the Swiss-cheese industry—which has little to learn from anyone about how to market and promote a product—contrasts interestingly with the Old World traditions that cling, a little cloyingly at times, to the making of the product itself. Little ceremonies, like the bedecking of the cows with flowers and ribbons each spring as they are led up into the mountains to graze until autumn, continue to be observed today as they were decades ago.

Similarly, the cows are still ornamented with bells, the largest bells with the deepest tones being reserved for the "leader" cows. The encouragement of such simplicity is sophistication itself.

EMMENTHAL COPIES—AMERICAN AND OTHERS

In Wisconsin Swiss-cheese making also has its traditions, almost as persistent as those in Switzerland itself—even though the traditional methods are rapidly yielding to new ways. In Green County, in the towns of New Glarus and Monroe, "the Swiss-cheese capital of the United States," there are still many Old World Swiss cheesemakers who are direct descendents of the 121 settlers from Glarus, Switzerland, who came to Wisconsin in 1845 in the wake of a depression that caused them to seek better conditions, if not greener pastures, in the New World. They still carry on the fine old traditions of cheesemaking, and the more fortunate continue to exercise their hard-learned skills in small plants that make fine wheel Swisses according to old Swiss methods—these principally for sale to mail-order customers and to discriminating shops. But a great many of the cheesemakers, and particularly the younger ones, are employed in plants in which the rindless block Swisses come off the assembly line like endless yellow dominoes. Everyone in Green County buys and eats the well-aged wheel Swiss made the old way. We sampled a piece there, almost a year and a half old, and have never tasted a better Swiss cheese from Switzerland or anywhere else. Among the old-timers in Green County, the "other kind" of cheese, the rindless block Swiss, is regarded much as any alien product is regarded whose manufacture keeps a town alive—as something made for immediate removal to little-known and less understood customers.

So-called Swiss cheeses are being made all over the world. The present runner-up to Switzerland Swiss, and Wisconsin and Ohio Swisses, is the Finnish Swiss, which has been widely distributed in the United States in the past few years. This is also a rindless block Swiss, whose overall quality is about on a par with the Wisconsin product, though it may have a little more sharpness (depending upon the piece), accompanied by a slightly more bitter aftertaste. Finnish Swiss is giving serious competition both to Switzerland Swiss and to our domestic Swiss. It is priced so low that it can be sold in reputable shops for the same price as domestic Swiss, or for pennies more. Often, sitting side by side with Wisconsin Swiss marked "Domestic Swiss," the Finnish is marked simply "Imported Swiss." It does not occur to many customers to ask, "Imported from where?" and they buy it assuming that it is the Switzerland Swiss, for which they sometimes pay considerably more.

Other Swiss cheeses available in the United States include Austrian Emmenthal, a mild and undistinguished cheese, and the even milder make-believe Swiss from Ireland called Blarney. It is well named, for its looks are cheerful and its ways deceiving. Butter-yellow, its color is accentuated by its bright-red paraffin rind. The eyes are plentiful, large and glistening. And there the resemblance to Swiss abruptly ends. Even less like Swiss is the Danish Samsoe which, because it has small holes, is sometimes offered as Danish Swiss. The flavor, however, is not that of the Swiss family at all, but is instead very close to Edam. Jarlsberg, from Norway, looks rather like a Swiss but does not taste like one. There is also a Dutch Swiss, made in small quantities to meet the local demand. But Dutch cheesemakers admit it is such a poor imitation that they would be ashamed to export it.

GRUYÈRE

Another great pair of cheeses that fall squarely in the Emmenthal flavor family are the Gruyères, both Swiss and French. A wheel of Gruyère is less than half the size of a Swiss wheel, and though it also has holes throughout, they are smaller than the Emmenthal's—about the size of a cherrystone. The color is the same ivory-to-yellow as Emmenthal, but the rind of the Gruyère is not smooth and ambery but brown and wrinkled like an almond skin. Swiss and French Gruyère have much in common for they are made in similar geographical localities—one on the Swiss side of the Jura Mountains, the other on the French side. Gruyère was originally a Switzerland cheese, and the Swiss claim it all as their own, maintaining that any good French Gruyère was probably made by Swiss emigrés. Whether or not this is so, the French Gruyère (which is also made in the Haute Savoie) can hold its own any day with the Swiss. Both are delicious cheeses. Swiss Gruyère tends to be sweeter than the French; the French has a little more tang. But the ages of the particular cheeses you are choosing between may accentuate this difference, or cancel it out, or even reverse it—so it's best to sample before you buy.

Though Switzerland exports much more Emmenthal, Gruyère is by far the favorite there. It too has a long and distinguished history, having first been made in the Gruyère Valley in the canton of Fribourg in the twelfth century (and later also in the cantons of Vaud and Neuchâtel). It is not so well known as Emmenthal, probably because its appearance is less striking. But Gruyère is no Cinderella. In fact we prefer it.

A variation of Swiss Gruyère which can be found only in Switzerland is the Fribourg Vacherin, which, with Gruyère, is used in making Fribourg Fondue. It is whiter than Gruyère and somewhat milder.

Emmenthal and Gruyère are both cheeses that cook beautifully, and they are therefore well represented in the recipe chapter of this book. Included of course is the classic Swiss Fondue made from a combination of Emmenthal and Gruyère melted in white wine and kirsch. The fondue, which is dipped out of a common bowl with chunks of bread, has come to symbolize amity, the only unpleasant aftermath being the indigestion that surely follows unless the fondue has been prepared correctly. Besides white wine, the other ingredient most commonly associated with them in cooking is the onion, which is also used in making the rich brown Helvetia soup—the local version of onion soup, in which Swiss cheese is melted in slabs. The onion plays a prominent part in Swiss diet the year round but comes fully into its own at the annual Zibeli-Marit—a kind of prewinter Mardi Gras at which "the rose of roots" is displayed, worn in the lapel, and eaten in a variety of ways—particularly in piping hot cheese-and-onion tarts, which are washed down by cold white wine.

The process Swiss Gruyère that comes in triangular foil-wrapped portions is entirely different, and has as little resemblance to true Gruyère as any process cheese has to real cheese. It is discussed with the process cheeses in Chapter 17.

APPENZELL

Appenzell (or Appenzeller) is the name of another—and super-lative—cheese in the Swiss family. It's well worth watching out for, and can be found in many large cheese shops. It is not so well known as either the Switzerland Emmenthal or the Gruyère. But it is a worthy member of this great triumvirate. It looks very much like the Gruyère, with the same wrinkled brown skin and smaller holes than the Emmenthal. The flesh of the cheese near the rind may be of a deeper yellow. Made in the canton of Appenzell, it is also being made increasingly in the cantons of St. Gall, Thurgau and Zurich. It too has a long lineage, dating back to the time of Charlemagne. As eaten in Switzerland this cheese is delicate, but the Appenzell we have tasted here, possibly because it is older, has even more tang than Gruyère and by far more flavor than Emmen-thal. Unlike the other two, Appenzell undergoes a special curing process during its first four or five days, when it is submerged in a vat of cider or white wine and spices; the taste is not recognizable in the cheese, though it undoubtedly contributes greatly to Appen-zell's piquant and rounded flavor.

Another variety of Appenzell, which must be sampled in Switzerland because it is not imported here, is the Appenzell Raess (*raess* means sharp) cheese. This is made of skim milk (regular Appenzell is a full-fat cheese), and is much more pungent.

RACLETTE

Raclette is made in the canton of Valais, and in Switzerland is eaten primarily as a table cheese, though it is better known here as the ingredient for the dish that bears its name. The name Raclette derives from the French verb *racler*, to scrape, and it is made simply (in Switzerland, that is) by placing a cut cheese directly before a wood fire, scraping the cheese off as it melts, and eating it at once. In France the cheese is pan-fried.

SAANEN AND SBRINZ

The two remaining cheeses in the Swiss flavor family, neither of which, unfortunately, is imported into the United States because of the strict import quotas on Swiss cheeses, are Saanen, which is a variety of Gruyère, and Sbrinz, the oldest cheese made in Switzerland and the earliest ancestor of Emmenthal, Gruyère, and all other cheeses in this group. In their youth Saanen and Sbrinz both show a definite family resemblance to the others. But as a rule they are both aged so long that they become hard and granular, and after about four years—a very great age for most cheeses, though a very tender age for Saanen or Sbrinz—the flavor loses its Emmenthal quality and becomes like Parmesan at its majestic best.

Saanen, which is produced in the Saanen Valley of the Bernese Oberland, is usually cured for at least five to six years, and in Switzerland is also called Hobel cheese (which means plane cheese), because it is so hard that a special cheese plane must be used to cut it. There was a time when the social standing of a Swiss family was measured in part by the age and quantity of the cheese it kept in its cellars, and Saanen made a particularly good heirloom, for it is said to be edible after more than one hundred years. Sbrinz too. Probably the Sbrinz we have today comes closest to that earliest cheese which Plinius of Rome praised in his writings; and once you have tasted it you will understand why. No visitor should ever leave Switzerland without trying the well-aged Sbrinz which is to be found there alone. For it is a way of scaling the Matterhorn without taking the climb.

As with all other cheeses, Swiss cheeses probably taste best when eaten on their native ground, where they are understood and well cared for, where there is no incentive or need to offer substitutes for the real thing, and where the wine and other foods are naturally most compatible with the cheese because they have sprung from the same soil. Also, the traveler to Switzerland will find varieties of cheese there that cannot be found anywhere else. Nevertheless, for those who are fond of Swiss and Swiss-type cheese, it is encouraging to know that they (unlike so many others) travel well, and the chances are that they will be good when you get them if they were good to begin with. That last point can be judged only by tasting enough varieties to decide which of the Swisses are for you, and then by tasting before you buy, if possible, to be sure that you are getting what you asked for. For the eyes alone, however appealing, will tell you nothing.

7

Parmesan

In the enchanted land of Bengodi, writes Boccaccio, all the macaroni makers dwelt high upon a mountain—a mountain of grated Parmesan cheese. This Bengodi was a veritable land of Cocaigne, whose streets were paved with pastry, a land where "they tie the vines with sausages, where you may buy a fat goose for a penny and have a gosling into the bargain," a land whose brooks in springtime doubtless brimmed with cool white wine. And atop that mountain of grated Parmesan, the makers of macaroni could be seen at almost any hour lifting the tender hot pasta out of the broth, covering it with sweet butter, and rolling it down the mountain to the people below.

Fortunate people—because we know that any pasta buttered and covered with almost *any* grated cheese is good, even when it is not great. But what must it have been like in Bengodi, a land where there was no second best?

The macaroni would have been superior to begin with, having been mixed and kneaded, rolled out and cut by cooks who doubtless believed they were on Mount Olympus and conducted themselves accordingly. The butter would have been fresh and sweet.

And the cheese. For a moment imagine that pasta—cooked *al dente*, of course, with the steam rising out of it and the golden lumps of butter melting, disappearing among its strands—picture it, while we consider our cheese.

THE TRUE ITALIAN PARMESAN

Without doubt, those macaroni makers would have insisted that only one cheese was fit for their pasta: the true Parmesan, the great Parmesan that must be counted among the half-dozen best cheeses of the world; the Parmesan that can be made only in Italy, and there made only in a certain small section in the north. Delicately grained and subtly flavored, it is the cornerstone of Italian cuisine and the necessity of cooks the world over. For Parmesan is the only true seasoning cheese we have—a cheese that has something in common with the truffle whose essence seems to bring every other ingredient into its own. There is no cooking cheese like it, nor for that matter any table cheese better than Parmesan that is freshly cut and still moist. The true Parmesan is the most distinguished member of a group of Italian cheeses that are very similar to one another and are known by the generic name of grana cheeses. The word *grana*, meaning grain, refers to the peculiarly grainy texture of the cheese when it has been properly aged. The aptness of the name can be appreciated if we look at a piece of choice and well-aged Parmesan. It is not smooth; it is too old and hard to be cut smoothly with an ordinary knife. Usually the big cheese is entered with a small elliptical knife like a dagger, thick on one side and sharp on the other, and the knife is jiggled so a piece breaks off. Its surface is as rough as an unpolished stone. As we look closer, we see that that surface is actually comprised of tiny, pale-golden crystals, millions of them, and each crystal is self-contained and perfect, so solid and separate that, even with a fairly young and moist cheese, and even after the cheese has been grated fine, you can bite on the crystals and feel their delicate snap. These tiny grains, not unlike the grains found in the flesh of a pear, have never been quite duplicated by any cheesemaker outside of Italy, where this remarkable Parmesan has been made for more than nine centuries.

The United States makes a so-called Parmesan, and so does Argentina, but they do not compare. We shall have more to say about these later, but first let us speak of the grana cheeses of Italy, for they are worth dwelling upon.

The Two Major Italian Types

Italy produces two major types of grana cheese, both of which are commonly called Parmesan in the United States and elsewhere in the world. One is the original Parmesan (the *grana tipico,* as it is called in Italy), whose full and correct name is Parmigiano-Reggiano. It comes from a small section comprising Parma (the ancient castled city from which Parmesan gets its name), Reggio Emilia (where most of the cheese is actually produced), Modena, and certain sections of Bologna on the left bank of the Reno, and Mantua on the right bank of the Po. Cheesemakers here were the first to make Parmesan and their skills have been handed down through generations. In no other center of Italian cheesemaking are standards more exacting.

Then there is another Italian grana, whose correct name is Grana Padano. Padano means "of the Po," a river that winds over large stretches of Piedmont and Lombardy so that the Grana Padano name applies to grana cheeses made in many different towns throughout northern Italy.

The differences between these two grana cheeses are these:

Parmigiano-Reggiano is produced in a small, restricted territory where the milk used in making the cheese is absolutely uniform, and each year the cheesemaking time is restricted from mid-April to precisely the 11th of November.

Grana Padano, on the other hand, is produced everywhere in the north from Turin to Verona. The milk differs for better or worse from one place to the other, and Grana Padano may be made all year round. We know, however, that cheeses made during the winter months are not as good as those made during the rest of the year.

Parmigiano-Reggiano must be at least two years old before it may be sold, and only the first-quality cheese may be exported. For Grana Padano the ripening time may range from one to two years, and the standards for export are less exacting.

The difference, in short, is that if you buy Parmigiano-Reggiano you can be almost certain of getting a superlative cheese. If you buy Grana Padano you may also get a superlative cheese—or you may get one that is only good, but not the very best.

The birthplace of Parmesan was Bibbiano, now a rather prosperous rural town in the Reggio Emilia district adjoining Parma and about two hours' train ride from Milan; but it was named for Parma because Bibbiano, and indeed all of Reggio Emilia, was under the rule of the duchy of Parma during the Middle Ages, and because most cheese trading took place there as well. This false attribution was only partly corrected by Italian law in 1951, when the Stresa Convention decreed the present designations of Parmigiano-Reggiano and Grana Padano as well as the regulations governing their production.

If you buy a piece of Italian grana from an uncut cheese, you may see Parmigiano-Reggiano or Grana Padano branded on the rind, because almost all Italian grana imported here is either one or the other. Of course the part of the rind bearing the official brand may not be visible or may have been cut off by the time your piece is cut—in which case how are you to know what you are getting? Recognizing the need for better identification, the Parmigiano-Reggiano cheesemakers' union began in 1964 to stencil the name over the entire vertical surface—much as the "Switzerland" is repeated all over the rind of Swiss cheeses—so that even if you buy the very last wedge you can see exactly what you are getting. But it will probably take at least until the spring of 1966 before cheeses marked in the new way are fully ripened and available in stores here. The Grana Padano union had not at this writing changed to the stencil system, but it makes such good sense that they undoubtedly will.

BUYING PARMESAN

In the absence of an identifying mark, how can you choose a top-quality grana? First, you should seek some assurance that it was made in Italy—not in Wisconsin or Argentina or anywhere else—for the Italian granas have never been successfully imitated. If you ask for it in a good Italian store (one whose salami is not imported exclusively from Chicago), you will in all likelihood get the real thing, because discriminating Italians will not even recognize a Parmesan that is not from Italy. All good specialty cheese stores stock Italian granas, although they may or may not carry domestic Parmesans.

It bears repeating: the first requisite for a top-quality Parmesan is that it be Italian. This is like saying that the first requisite for a good Maine lobster is that it come from New England, but since the Parmesan name is not protected in this country—as, for example, the name Roquefort is—the buyer cannot be too explicit in asking for *Italian* Parmesan.

In selecting Parmesan, remember that a well-aged cheese will be a pale yellow; a younger cheese is whitish. Sometimes even a well-aged cheese will have whitish marks here and there because all Parmesans bruise white when the surface grains are crushed by the cutting action of the knife; even so, it should look appetizing. If the surface shows a lot of chalky white in sporelike formations, the piece is probably dried out and will not taste good.

An aged cheese will have more flavor and character than a younger one and is therefore the best choice for cooking or seasoning. As with other cheeses sold in bulk, the best thing is to sample any grana before buying. This will show whether the cheese has the mild yet piquant flavor and fragrance—not too salty, and with a sweet rather than a bitter aftertaste—that you can expect of a top-quality Parmesan. Sampling will also quickly show whether you are being offered a cheese that resembles, but is not, Parmesan—for example, the black-rinded and equally grainy-looking Romano, a sheep's-milk cheese that is much stronger than Parmesan; or Sardo, another sheep's-milk cheese, as hard as Parmesan but with an entirely different flavor.

If you want the Parmesan for table use rather than for grating, a younger and less yellowed piece may be a good choice. It will not have quite as much flavor, but it will be more moist and crumbly. If you prefer the sharper taste, stick to the well-aged cheeses, using the part farthest from the rind for the table, the rest for grating.

We have been speaking of Parmesan as a table cheese because it *is* a superb eating cheese, though most Americans associate it with grating and cooking only. Cheese experts such as P. Morton Shand and Hilaire Belloc have praised Parmesan's exceptional eating qualities, which are fully appreciated in Italy, where Parmesan is often served with fruit for dessert. Mr. Belloc, in fact, suggests that Parmesan turns hard in self-defense: "It is the world," says Mr. Belloc, "that hardens Parmesan. In its youth, the Parmesan is very soft and easy—and is voraciously devoured."

That thick rind of Parmesan has been thought to serve other purposes than mere self-protection, as witness a verse entitled "The Mouse That Turned Hermit," by the eighteenth-century Italian poet Pignotti:

> *"Once upon a time there was a mouse," quoth she,*
> *"Who, sick of worldly tears and laughter, grew*
> *Enamoured of a sainted privacy.*
> *To all terrestrial things he bade adieu*
> *And entered, far from mouse or cat or man,*
> *A thick-walled cheese, the best of Parmesan."*

But the rind's true purpose is to give privacy to the cheese itself. To this end it thickens as it ages, and both the rind and the cheese become so hard that the cheesemaker cannot use an ordinary cheese plug to sample it. Instead, he inserts a long needle threaded like a screw, whose grooves pick up particles of the cheese as it is drawn out again. And he also takes soundings with a small metal hammer especially made for that purpose. The rind is also rubbed during the final months of ripening with a mixture of oil and *terra umbra*—a superfine dark earth, rich in mineral salts, that gives it an almost ebony look. This effectively shuts out any light that might cause the cheese to become rancid.

DOMESTIC AND OTHER PARMESANS

"Beware of American Parmesan, which is cheaper and tastes like tallow," P. Morton Shand wrote. By and large, he is right. Run-of-the-mill domestic Parmesan has only the most superficial resemblance to Italian grana—its taste quickly turns flat and then becomes so shockingly salty that it all but pulls the tongue out of your head. There is no grain at all, and the range of textures goes from rubber tire to Bakelite.

There is one exception—a Parmesan cheese produced by a company by the name of Stella, whose products are marketed from coast to coast. This cheese, which has good grain and flavor, is made in an Italian colony near Fond du Lac, Wisconsin. The company was set up in business by an Italian diplomat connected with the World Food Commission who was concerned with the plight of Italians who had to be relocated after World War I. The firm is now thriving, and the quality of its products, though not entirely uniform, is such that it deserves to prosper. They can be found in specialty cheese stores, but unfortunately most of Stella's Parmesan is sold under the house names of better supermarkets and grocery chains so that it may be hard to track down.

Argentine Parmesan, which is the cheapest of all, has an acceptable flavor, but it is very salty.

GRATED PARMESAN

Unless you have no alternative, do not buy the grated cheeses in shaker boxes or jars that are marketed by various cheese companies, large and small, all over the United States. These pre-grated, prepackaged "Parmesan" or "Parmesan-Romano" or "Italian Style" grated cheeses compare in flavor with a select Italian Parmesan, bought by the piece and freshly grated, in almost the same way that canned hamburgers compare with prime steak. One reason is that the cheeses used are domestic, unless the package is explicitly marked otherwise—and often they are inferior domestic cheeses at that. Another is that the flavor of freshly grated Parmesan, like that of fresh-ground coffee or pepper, is at its peak immediately after it has been grated, and from there on the flavor fades with every passing hour. And often other cheeses, especially Romano, are blended with the grated Parmesan. This Romano, strong and salty, is probably added to compensate for the deficiencies of flavor in the Parmesan—which is usually no great shakes to begin with. Also present in some of the inferior brands of grated cheeses may be rejects of other, non-grana cheeses, known as "grinders" by the trade. Finally, cheese does not continue to age after it is ground—it simply gets old, and there is a difference.

The label should be read carefully for it describes the cheese or blend of cheeses within the package. The makers are not required to state whether the Parmesan is domestic—and this is ascertained only by the absence of the word "Italian" on the wrapper. The word "imported" is no guide to quality, because the cheese could have been imported from anywhere.

Some grocers, notably in Italian neighborhoods, also carry a grana cheese that they grate themselves for sale by the scoopful, and this, though it is unlabeled, is usually better than most pre-packaged grated cheese, though not as good as imported Italian Parmesan that you buy and grate for yourself. In a pinch, almost any grated cheese is better than having no cheese at all for your onion soup; but the difference between pre-grated and freshly ground Italian Parmesan is so great that it can hardly be over-stressed.

Parmesan in Cooking

Parmesan cheese has played an important role in Italian cuisine for at least eight hundred years. The first historical document in which it is mentioned is the *Chronicle* of Adamo Salimbene, a monk who lived in Parma in the twelfth century. Boccaccio's references to it in the *Decameron* show that by the fourteenth century it was well known not only in his native Florence but probably throughout northern Italy. And perhaps the inspiration for his mountain of Parmesan in Bengodiland came from his observations on the flourishing cheese trade he saw in Parma, and on the enviable position of the cooks—who were rewarded for their labor with as much Parmesan cheese as they wanted for their own use.

In another old document we find one Bernardo Navagero, a sixteenth-century Venetian envoy to the Vatican, gossiping to the doge that "the Holy Father is getting fat, being very partial to Parmesan cheese, of which he eats plenty." And in 1568 Bartolomeo Scappi, a Dominican in charge of Pope Pius V's household, published his *Cookery Book* in which he proclaimed Parmesan the best cheese on earth. Two other popes, Leo X and Benedict XIV, are reported to have shared this view. According to the Parma historian Botti, Parmesan was a favorite of Leonardo; and other experts on local lore suggest that it is no coincidence that a city capable of producing such a great cheese should also be closely identified with some of Italy's greatest artists and musicians.

It would be difficult to overstress the role of Parmesan cheese in Italian cookery or the influence of Italian cookery on world cuisine. Though France is regarded as the gastronomic capital of the world today, it had no cuisine until the mid-sixteenth century when Catherine de' Medici took leave of her native Florence to become the bride of Henry II, bringing with her an entourage of chefs the like of which France had never known. She also brought a number of forks. The cuisine of Catherine's Tuscany was unparalleled in Europe, and many of the specialties for which Florence and Bologna are now famous were well known then, too. As early as the tenth century the renowned house of Ricasoli was producing Chianti in the vineyards surrounding its castles of Brolio and Meleto. And pasta had already assumed many sizes and shapes besides the thin ribbons that Florentines baked between layers of beaten eggs and cheese and spinach. And while the pasta that Catherine brought with her did not leave an indelible mark on French cuisine, the cheese that accompanied it did. The French were not slow to recognize the greatness of Parmesan, or the variety of ways it could be used, and its introduction into France marked the beginning of all the *gratinée* dishes that are topped not only with breadcrumbs but with cheese as well—and the French onion soup that requires this cheese as surely as it requires onions. These and many other French dishes owe their supremacy to Parmesan.

If Parmesan is an ornament to French food, it is an absolute essential of Italian cooking, transforming a simple vegetable into a superlative dish, and working the same magic upon soups, risotto and polenta, but chiefly, of course, on pasta. Macaroni—and cheese. Spaghetti—and cheese. Fettuccine, ravioli, cannelloni—and cheese. There is nothing quite like that combination. What a sense of the harmony of things was shown by Sir John Squire, the British gastronome, when he described a perfect holiday: "I have just come back from a holiday in the mountains above Lake Como —staying with Italian friends, spaghetti, cheese, and wine."

So important a role does Parmesan play in Italian cookery that it may make its appearance in any course from soup to dessert. Minestrone demands Parmesan as surely as onion soup does, and without it either one is like an unresolved chord. In Tuscany in summer, minestrone is also served chilled. This is a great dish because the soup (which has been skimmed of fat) is very green and summery and the vegetables are crisp. The flavor is, if anything, better than that of a good hot minestrone, except that the Parmesan sprinkled on it does not melt but rests on the surface, every grain dry and separate. In Italy, Parmesan is used not only in minestrone but in soups of all kinds, including clear chicken broth. And the test of a good, well-aged Parmesan is that it must instantly dissolve in the soup, and not become, as the Italians say, *gumosa*, clinging to the bottom of the dish like soft taffy.

Stracciatella, a soup that is a specialty around Rome, is a kind of Italian chicken egg-drop soup with Parmesan as a basic ingredient. The eggs are beaten with a few tablespoons of grated Parmesan (or Romano, which is stronger) and some minced parsley, and the mixture whipped into consommé that has been brought to a boil. The result is a chicken soup delicately flavored by Parmesan, in which are suspended the sheerest yellow shreds, similar to egg noodles but thinner and lighter by far.

As for pastas, they merit a book by themselves. The colors range from pale ivory to the deepest yellow, except for *lasagne verde* and *pappardelle,* which are green. The shapes go from tiny stars, hats, springs and crescents to great ribbed tubes of rigatoni. The sauces may run the gamut from simple melted butter (with a good cheese, this is the desert-island choice) through much more complex blendings of meats and herbs, tomatoes, onions, mushrooms, truffles—but they all demand Parmesan, and each is a different vehicle for the cheese. No Italian pasta is eaten without Parmesan, with the single exception of spaghetti with clam sauce, which for some curious reason is denied that privilege by all but the most unorthodox diners.

One of the most popular dishes of northern Italy is its *risotto,* for which Parmesan, again, is absolutely essential. Indeed Parmesan plays such an important role in the cooking of the north—which is where the finest Italian cuisine is to be found—that the per capita consumption of Parmesan in such cities as Milan and Bologna is twice that of Italy as a whole. Risottos are made with as many different sauces as pasta, but the risotto Milanese is the classic (the recipe is in Chapter 22).

One of the delights of Parmesan is the contrasting textures it adds to other foods. Small wonder that the Japanese, whose cuisine reflects a special regard for contrasts of texture, have been so taken with Parmesan that since the war they have imported more of it than any other cheese. But the biggest customer for the grana cheeses is the United States, followed by the United Kingdom, Switzerland, France and Germany. Because of their great hardness and durability (which prompted Mrs. Beeton to describe them as "made for sea voyages principally") there is no spot on the globe too distant or too intemperate in climate to import the granas. And how fortunate for all of us. For as one Milanese put it, "No Italian export, with the possible exception of our Sophia Loren, has brought so much pleasure to the world."

8

The Great Cheddars

To most Anglo-Saxons, cheese means Cheddar—for in almost every country where Englishmen and their tastes and notions have prevailed, you'll find their descendents and almost everyone else making and eating a variety of what Horace Vachell called "the cut-and-come-again cheese, the best cheese for every day." Whole generations of English-speaking people have never tasted any other cheese; many, principally in the United States, have never even tasted real Cheddar—only its illegitimate offspring, process American cheese.

Though Cheddar originated in England, we do not eat English Cheddars here. It is one of the milder ironies of Anglo-American relations that England, which sent the original Cheddaring process, a few cows, and some colonists to these shores in the 1600s, is not allowed to export Cheddar to the United States. For this we are doubtless indebted to our congressmen from the dairy states who act as minutemen for their constituents, defending the lucrative American Cheddar market against the redcoats.

This is our loss—as British connoisseurs would be the first to tell us. They disdain non-English Cheddars, insisting that the only true Cheddar is made in England, in Somerset County. But the "true" Cheddar is in short supply even in England, which has itself become an importer of Cheddar cheeses—from Canada, the United States, New Zealand, and elsewhere—to the dismay of British cheese lovers. Even forty years ago, P. Morton Shand excoriated "base colonial imitations, fraudulently sold under names that for centuries have been the pride of two of our foremost agricultural counties [Somerset and Cheshire]." Canadian Cheddar, he added, would not even wash clothes, and New Zealand Cheddar was utterly useless as furniture polish.

Although he was equally despondent over the scarcity of true Cheddar, Osbert Burdett nevertheless had some words of consolation for the lover of Cheddar cheese who is confused by the many different varieties available today. "If there ever was, there has long since ceased to be a uniform flavor for Cheddar," Burdett wrote. "By this time Cheddar has become a word no more precisely descriptive than sherry. As diverse flavours are now required of Cheddar cheese . . . as of Jerez wines. Unfortunately, the differences are unreflected in nomenclature. Even the grocer's loose division of sherry into pale, golden, and brown, not to mention the individual names of the sherries included under each division, have no counterpart at a cheese-counter."

The "Best" Cheddars

Nobody really knows what the original Cheddar tasted like; we have only the assurance of the Elizabethan historian Camden that Cheddars "were excellent prodigious cheeses . . . and of delicate taste." But over the years, among epicures, a fine Cheddar has come to mean one that, whatever part of the world it comes from, is made of the whole, unpasteurized, summer milk of cows which have drunk fresh, clear water and fed upon green grasses, free from any flora that might taint the milk; a cheese that is never forced into maturity before its time but is aged slowly and lovingly until it is eighteen months to two years old; one that is close yet porous in texture, full in flavor, and sharp without being bitter; a crumbly cheese that sometimes seems moist with its own richness; one whose savor has the sensuous, penetrating quality of a fine old brandy; a cheese to be eaten at the end of a meal without bread or biscuit.

This is one kind of Cheddar—a great Cheddar—and its flavor

and texture are unforgettable. But there is another Cheddar, much younger and in its way also the "best." It is about six to nine months old and has the close, firm texture of cold butter. Its flavor, neither sweet nor acid, faintly suggests newly churned buttermilk. It is far less rich than the connoisseur's aged Cheddar, but it is unsurpassed when eaten with fresh whole-wheat bread and butter, or unsalted soda crackers and sweet gherkins, or with buttered homemade white bread and crisp lettuce accompanied by a glass of hard cider. You will note that we include butter as a suitable companion to the younger Cheddar despite those who echo the old Somerset saying that "bad cheese asks butter to eat with it; good cheese asks none." We feel that the flavor and texture of the firm and sometimes rather dry cow's-milk cheeses are often enhanced by sweet butter and that it is no reflection upon a cheese to be eaten with butter. Butter seems to impart a welcome unctuousness to the younger Cheddar in particular, and to accentuate all that is sweet and fresh about it.

Both the older and the younger Cheddars are excellent for melting; the only difference is that you need to use less of the older Cheddar because its flavor is more intense. But whether young or old, a pan of golden, bubbling, melted Cheddar and a stack of hot toast or baking-powder biscuits right out of the oven are wonderfully good. One taste makes anyone understand Ben Gunn's heart-rending cry, "I dream of cheese—toasted mostly!"

ENGLISH CHEDDAR

In England there are two kinds: farmhouse Cheddar and factory Cheddar; whereas in the United States and Canada there is only factory Cheddar (although here and there a gentleman cheese-maker may turn out an occasional farmhouse Cheddar). English farmhouse Cheddar, like most farmhouse cheeses, is better than the factory-made, and it is more expensive simply because there is less of it. It is made only from May to October, from the milk of a single herd of cows—usually Shorthorns—which means that only as many Cheddars can be made as there is milk from that herd.

The cheese is always made by an expert. Factory Cheddar, on the other hand, is made from mixed milk—that is, from milk of many different herds owned by many different dairy farmers; it is made in large quantities, all year round, and as economically as possible by cheesemakers who may be supervised by an expert but who are not experts themselves.

More farmhouse Cheddar makers are still to be found in Somerset County than anywhere else in England, but their numbers are dwindling because they have found that they can make more money by selling their milk to the Milk Marketing Board, either to be resold in fluid form or used for factory Cheddar. But then, good farmhouse Cheddars have never been plentiful. Over three hundred years ago one Lord Poulet wrote to a friend telling him that Cheddar cheeses "are grown of late to be of such great esteem at the court that they are bespoken before they are made." And so it is today. London clubs, private persons, and a few select shops place their orders well in advance. In short, farmhouse Cheddar is hard to find and getting harder. A motor trip through Somerset County and its diverse byways might yield a farmhouse Cheddar, but this is by no means certain. However, if you start your journey reconciled to failure, you are certain to have a splendid trip. The countryside is charming, the town of Cheddar, though largely Cheddarless for a century, has its nearby Cheddar Gorge with its caves and their stalactites and stalagmites, while farther east the city of Wells can be depended upon for some excellent factory Cheddar—and, of course, a handsome cathedral. The area surrounding Wells and Shepton Mallet, a few miles away, takes in the establishments of the best farmhouse Cheddar makers. But, again, there's no guarantee that they will have an unbespoken cheese.

It is a pity, of course, that no English farmhouse Cheddar comes to the United States. Occasionally some large cheese retailer may prevail upon an importer to bring in a Cheddar under a pseudonym, but most importers decline to do so because, ethics aside, the penalties are severe. A whole shipment can be refused entry and turned back if a U.S. inspector decides that even one cheese is really good old English Cheddar in disguise. Inevitably, of course, the absence of English Cheddar from their shelves encourages some American retailers to sell a Cheddar as "English," or at least to imply that it is English when it isn't.

CANADIAN CHEDDAR

In the United States, Canada's factory Cheddar is very often the closest we can get to English farmhouse Cheddar. Not the small bars of packaged Canadian which one is beginning to find in supermarkets (though this is, generally, a reliable medium-to-sharp cheese), but the aged five-pound wheels which you can buy only in cheese specialty shops. This Cheddar is usually excellent, sometimes great.

AN ITALIAN CHEDDAR

An excellent Cheddar is made in, of all places, Italy. This is Friulana, named for the district in the north, around Venice, where it originated. Exceptionally piquant in flavor, and very much like English Cheddar, Friulana is almost equally hard to come by in the United States. You can, however, get it at the New York restaurant Giambelli, whose owner is the only importer of Friulana we know of.

SOME AMERICAN CHEDDARS

New York, once the center of the Cheddar industry until a growing population pushed the cheese industry west, prides itself—and properly—on dry, crumbly Herkimer County Cheddar with its sharp, full flavor. Other New York cheeses are labeled simply "New York State—6 months," or one year, or two years.

Wisconsin now produces more Cheddar than any other state and you can find Wisconsin Cheddars in supermarkets everywhere. From the very mild to the very sharp, they appeal to a wide range of tastes, and their quality also varies, from mediocre to excellent.

Vermont Cheddar, sharp, almost white, and well cured, has a faithful following among New Englanders and others who have spent their holidays in New England, while up and down the Pacific Coast Oregon Tillamook is the preferred Cheddar. Tillamook, like Wisconsin, ranges in flavor from the excessively mild to the very sharp, but unlike most Wisconsin Cheddar, Tillamook is made exclusively from raw milk, as are Vermont, Herkimer and Canadian Cheddars.

Coon Cheddar has a short, crumbly body with a dark surface color and is cured by a patented method which involves a higher temperature and humidity than is customary in curing fine Cheddars, and which, incidentally, requires that the cheese be of exceptionally high quality to begin with. A good one-year-old Coon in a ten-ounce stick is now marketed by a prominent manufacturer. It can be found in many supermarkets, wrapped in a smart, shiny black wrapper. The cheese within is the color of sweet butter. This is a Cheddar you might pick up when you need a full-bodied, well-cured Cheddar and have no prospect of getting to a specialty shop.

The same cheese company, one of the largest producers of Cheddar and Cheddar-flavored products in the world, also has three other Cheddars that merit attention. But it must be added that the wedge of Cheddar wrapped in silver foil and labeled mild is actually bland; the Cheddar in gold foil, labeled sharp, is medium; and the Cheddar in red foil, labeled very sharp, is sharp—and often slightly bitter. The middle cheese in gold foil, however, is a dependable young Cheddar. You can find it in supermarkets and grocery stores everywhere; it is a good cheese to buy when you're in a hurry and in no mood to take a chance on unknown brands.

Inexplicably, a great favorite in California is a cheese that is often called a Cheddar but which, in our view, qualifies as a very distant relative, and then only when it has been cured for a few months. This is the Monterey. For the most part, the Monterey is cured from three to six weeks and is semisoft and bland with a high moisture content. It seems more appropriate to classify this cheese as a variety of American Munster along with the high-moisture Jack, which is the same as the young Monterey except that it contains even more moisture. A grating cheese sometimes called "dry Monterey," sometimes "dry Jack," is made from partly skimmed milk or skim milk and is cured for at least six months.

Colby, which is made mostly in the Middle West, is softer than standard Cheddar, more open in texture—sometimes almost lacy— and has a higher moisture content; as a result (as is the case of all high-moisture cheeses) it does not keep as well. Corn Husker, first made by the Nebraska Agricultural Experiment Station around 1940, falls roughly into the same category; it has a softer body than Cheddar, more moisture, and it perishes quickly. Both Colby and Corn Husker (of which very little is made) are very mild.

BITTER CHEDDAR

Ideally it is better to taste a Cheddar before buying even a quarter of a pound, but obviously this is practical only where cheese is sold in bulk. As more and more cheeses are sold pre-packaged, it becomes necessary to trust to previous experience with a brand, and count oneself lucky if the Cheddar comes near to tasting as one wants it to taste. Nevertheless, whenever Cheddar is sold from a wheel, remember to sample it first.

You will doubtless refuse a Cheddar with a soapy flavor and a putty texture, an improperly cured Cheddar. But be sure also to reject a Cheddar that has even the slightest taste of bitterness—or one that leaves a bitter aftertaste. Many people live out their lives believing that all sharp Cheddars are slightly bitter—that that is what "sharp" means. But there is a profound difference between sharpness and bitterness, despite what some enterprising cheese dealers may say.

A bitter Cheddar is a bad Cheddar and its bitterness can have several origins. Among the causes are bitter milk, forced curing, and pasteurized milk.

Bitter milk can come from cows that, during the winter months, are forced to feed upon sour, fermented silage grasses instead of sun-dried grasses; or from grazing in pastures choked with noxious weeds; or from cows that are denied respite and milked too long. Bitter milk makes bitter cheese—this is the unalterable rule, no matter how great the cheesemaker's skill.

Forced curing occurs when cheesemakers rush their Cheddars into early maturity rather than go to the expense of letting them develop at their own pace. Overhead is high, and to cure them faster they step up the temperature in the curing room, a process not unlike the forcing of blooms in a hothouse or forcing green tomatoes into premature ripening. Inevitably something is sacrificed—the fragrance of the flower, or the flavor and texture of the tomato. In the case of a Cheddar something else happens: it develops a bitterness that assails the palate immediately and lingers on. Some dairy chemists maintain that all Cheddars go through a period of bitterness while curing and that a properly made Cheddar will pull out of it. The problem again is overhead. Some manufacturers feel that they can afford to let the cheese take its own time; others do not.

As for using pasteurized milk, this has always been a matter of controversy. All connoisseurs, and some people in the cheese industry, insist that any cheese—with the possible exception of fresh cheese—suffers irreparably if it is made of pasteurized milk. In Cheddar, they say, the unhappy consequence is often a bitterness that may only show in the aftertaste. And why, they ask, should anyone want to make Cheddar from pasteurized milk when it has been established with certainty—even embodied in law—that harmful bacteria in raw milk cannot survive in cheese that is cured for sixty days? Further, who wants a Cheddar less than sixty days old? Nonetheless, some 75 per cent of the Cheddar made in this country is made from pasteurized milk because, among other advantages, it permits cheese manufacturers to use milk that is not of uniform quality. We have compared enough raw-milk Cheddar with pasteurized Cheddar to suspect that bitterness all too often follows in the wake of pasteurizing.

RINDLESS CHEDDAR

Tastelessness or "greenness" in a Cheddar is another common failing—probably the consequence of the cheesemaker's desire for a quick turnover, combined with the new taste for bland cheese. In any event, as Osbert Burdett said, such cheese is made to be sold, not eaten. Which brings us directly to the rindless Cheddar, that "breakthrough" of recent years that delights cheese manufacturers and packaging experts almost as much as it depresses cheese lovers. Rindless cheese is a triumph of packaging because often it is "cured" in the same plastic wrapper in which it is sold, thereby uniting a manufacturing step with a merchandising step and saving everybody a great deal of bother and money. The only loss is in flavor. This rindless cheese, clothed in transparent plastic and lying in wait in supermarkets everywhere, is labeled "natural" Cheddar. This is technically correct because it is not a process cheese, but the truth is that this cheese is to natural Cheddar what a Madame Tussaud dummy is to a human being. The offense of the "natural" rindless Cheddar is not just the absence of flavor—it is the illusion it gives when you taste it that the full Cheddar flavor is just a step ahead, just a bite away. The truth is that it has no flavor worth pursuing.

These reflections upon a Cheddar's possible shortcomings may seem harsh, but over the years, Cheddar's good name has been most shamefully traded upon. Excellent Cheddars are made in many different parts of the world—but so are bad and indifferent Cheddars, and whenever you buy a piece of any Cheddar without tasting it, you are buying a pig in a poke.

COLORS, SHAPES, AND SIZES

Although Cheddars range in color from pale butter to pumpkin to a Halloween orange, a Cheddar's color has nothing to do with its quality. People in different regions have become accustomed to particular shades, and cheesemakers very sensibly see no reason to complicate their marketing task by quarreling with regional preferences, since all that is required is a little more or a little less annatto (a tasteless vegetable dye), or none at all, to give the Southerner his deep orange, the Midwesterner and Westerner their medium orange, and the New Englander his "white" Cheddar.

American Cheddars come in an assortment of shapes and sizes, while English Cheddars, by and large, tend to retain the traditional Cheddar shape, which is cylindric, about 14½ inches in diameter, 12 inches high, and weighing between 70 and 78 pounds. Other sizes—and these are American primarily—are the daisy, which is about 13½ inches in diameter but only slightly more than 4 inches high, and which weighs 21 to 23 pounds; the larger flat or twin, which is 14½ inches in diameter, slightly more than 5 inches thick, and weighing 32 to 37 pounds; and the longhorn, which is 13 inches long, 6 inches wide, and weighs 12 to 13½ pounds. There are also 11-pound "midgets" and 5-pound "peewees."

The Mammoth Cheddars

In general, Cheddars do not exceed the traditional Cheddar size of approximately seventy-six pounds. But from time to time, Cheddar makers seem to be seized with an unconquerable urge to make mammoth cheeses. English cheesemongers appear to have confined this craving to the nineteenth century and to cheeses that weighed around a half ton—such was the heft of the Cheddar presented to Queen Victoria and her consort as a bridal gift—but New World cheesemakers are altogether out of hand. Even now, a seventeen-ton Cheddar, the handiwork of Wisconsin cheesemakers, sits under a specially designed refrigerated glass at the New York's World's Fair, having journeyed there in a specially constructed truck and, for part of the way, over specially built, heavy-duty roads. This monstrosity dwarfs by eleven tons the Cheddar that appeared at the 1937 New York State Fair and by thirteen tons the Cheddar exhibited at a Toronto Fair in 1883.

Not content merely to perpetrate these freaks, cheesemaking communities also tend to celebrate their efforts in verse. The

Toronto cheese, for example, prompted mortician James McIntyre to write:

> *We have thee, mammoth cheese,*
> *Lying quietly at your ease;*
> *Gently fanned by evening breeze,*
> *Thy fair form no flies dare seize.*
>
> *All gaily dressed soon you'll go*
> *To the greatest provincial show*
> *To be admired by many a beau*
> *In the city of Toronto.*
>
> *May you not receive a scar as*
> *We have heard that Mr. Harris*
> *Intends to send you off as far as*
> *The great world's show at Paris.*
>
> *Of the youth beware of these,*
> *For some of them might rudely squeeze*
> *And bite your cheek; then song of glees*
> *We could not sing, oh, Queen of Cheese.*

Upon an earlier occasion, after the entire community of Cheshire, Massachusetts, had thrown itself into making a cheese for President Jefferson, eleven stanzas entitled "The Mammoth Cheese—an Epico-Lyrico Ballad" appeared in *The Mercury and New England Palladium*. It begins:

> *From meadows rich, with clover red,*
> *A thousand heifers come;*
> *The tinkling bells the tidings spread,*
> *The milkmaid muffles up her head,*
> *And wakes the village hum.*

Understandably, the beneficiaries of these preposterous cheeses are often confronted with a storage and disposal problem. Even a modest 76-pounder can prove troublesome: it needs its own cool room and must be turned over and wiped with a cloth every day;

also its peak of goodness comes in its own time, not at its owner's convenience. Queen Victoria managed to sidestep both of these difficulties, however, when the cheesemongers who bestowed the 1000-pound Cheddar upon her became so enamored of it themselves that they asked to be allowed to exhibit in a round of country fairs. The queen quickly consented, and when, sometime later, they attempted to return the Cheddar—grubby, nicked, and showworn—she declined to take it back again. Thereupon the would-be donors fell to quarreling over its disposition. In due course, seeking proper adjudication, they turned the cheese over to the British Chancery, where it disappeared forever.

When a 1400-pound Cheddar was thrust upon Andrew Jackson by a New York cheesemaker, Old Hickory characteristically stood his ground and met the crisis head on. For almost twenty months he kept the Cheddar in the middle of the White House vestibule until it was ready to eat. He then gave a party the like of which Washington has not seen since. Everyone in the city was invited. It was, according to one contemporary account, a blowout of some proportions:

> This is Washington's Birthday. The president, all departments, the senate and we, the people, have celebrated by eating a big cheese. The president's house was thrown open. The multitude swarmed in. The senate of the United States adjourned. The representatives of the various departments turned out. Representatives in squadrons left the capitol, and all for the purpose of eating cheese: Mr. Webster was there to eat cheese, Mr. Woodbury, Colonel Berton, Mr. Dickerson, and the gallant Colonel Trowbridge were eating cheese. The court, the fashion, the beauty of Washington, foreign representatives in stars and garters; gay, joyous, dashing and gorgeous women all in the pride and panoply and pomp of wealth, were there eating cheese. Cheese, cheese, cheese, was on everybody's mouth. All you heard was cheese; all you smelled was cheese. It was cheese, cheese, cheese, streams of cheese were going up the

avenue in everybody's fists; balls of cheese were in a hundred pockets; every handkerchief smelled of cheese. The whole atmosphere for half a mile around was infected with cheese.

The mammoth Cheddar was devoured in two hours, leaving the White House carpet slippery with cheese. Only a small piece was saved for the President's table.

9

The Cheddar Relatives

What was that wonderful orange cheese, bright as a lantern and sharp as a pick, that so delighted Dr. Johnson? The cheese that graced Elizabeth's table—the great cheese of old England? Not the Cheddar that we immediately associate with tankards of ale, bubbling rabbits, and English cheese. It was Cheshire, the cheese that preceded Cheddar by some five hundred years and was a part of the English daily fare for at least two centuries before Cheddar was even thought of, and which remains, to this day, the cheese that Englishmen eat more of than any other.

Cheshire is possibly Cheddar's most distinguished relative, but by no means the only one; in this prolific family there are about a dozen cheeses that are closely related to Cheddar. Most are available in the United States, and at least four or five have become staples in specialty cheese stores.

Most of these Cheddar relatives are British (and these are the ones that are easiest to find) although a few are not, such as Cantal, which is French, and Warsawski, which is Polish-American. Each of these has its own distinctive character yet all share a common flavor, a flavor which—whether sweeter in one cheese or saltier in another, subtle, or more direct—is essentially the flavor of Cheddar.

The American taste for Cheddar is, of course, the reason for the growing popularity and availability of these cheeses. Since the

British cannot send Cheddar to the United States, they are doing the next best thing: they are capitalizing on our preference for the Cheddar flavor to sell us their Cheddarlike cheeses—in ever-increasing numbers. Even the French, who generally deplore the Cheddar hegemony in the United States, are sending us more and more of their Cantal, the only Cheddarlike cheese that they make in any quantity. (They have begun to make a real Cheddar, on a small scale, in south-central France. A little gets to London; none comes here.)

CHESHIRE

Cheshire is probably Great Britain's oldest cheese. Some Cheshire-philes maintain that Britons were making Cheshire long before Caesar raised his Roman wall around Chester, now the capital of Cheshire county, and at that time the headquarters for the Roman 20th Legion. Others are content to point out that a cheese by the name of Cheshire was first recorded in the Domesday Book.

But even if Cheshire is not Great Britain's first cheese histori-cally, there is little doubt of its place in English affections—it is and always has been first. During the Elizabethan period, when Englishmen were becoming acutely conscious of their own Eng-lishness and making everybody else aware of it too, Cheshire was declared by one historian to be the best cheese in all Europe. Cheshire was the favorite cheese of Dr. Johnson and other lumi-naries who frequented Ye Olde Cheshire Cheese. They appear to have eaten it ceaselessly and in quantity—sometimes plain with chunks of bread, sometimes toasted, and sometimes "stewed"— their name for Welsh rabbit. But always with gallons of ale. Eight-eenth-century recipes for Welsh rabbit never called for ale—doubt-less because the cooks knew they could rely upon the guests to supply it in ample measure.

In the seventeenth century, Sir Kenelm Digby's *Closet Open'd* described Cheshire's two chief virtues as truly as they ever could be. Sir Kenelm called Cheshire a "quick, fat, well-tasted cheese to serve upon a piece of toast." "Quick, fat" are precisely the words for Cheshire's excellent melting properties, and "well-tasted" can not be improved upon to describe the satisfying Cheshire flavor which intensifies in the melting. These two characteristics have made Cheshire one of the great toasting cheeses.

Although the British are fond of saying that Cheshires, like the Union Jack, come in red, white, and blue, a foreigner soon learns that their red isn't red, their white isn't white, and their blue is really blue veining. The white or uncolored Cheshire is a pale, pale yellow. The red, as Edward Bunyard once pointed out, is more of a warm apricot, the consequence of adding annatto, the vegetable dye that is also added to Cheddars.

The blue is another story. It starts out as a perfectly ordinary red or white "long-keeping" Cheshire—that is, a Cheshire that has been cured for eight or ten months. This Cheshire changes color, we are told, only if a spore of *Penicillium glaucum* chances to get at it. In other words, a blue Cheshire isn't made, it just happens. Although this may be true of most blue Cheshires, there is reason to believe that sometimes a Cheshire is helped into its blue period by a shot of penicillium. Blue Cheshires are very good, though terribly expensive, and their goodnesses will be dwelt upon at greater length in Chapter 13.

Regrettably, long-keeping Cheshires are not made in large quantities, and most Cheshire today is of the medium-ripened variety, which means it is cured for only six to eight weeks. Obviously there is less overhead and quicker turnover in medium-ripened than in the longer-ripened Cheshire, and this is why well-aged Cheshire has almost become a delicacy of the past. Certainly in the United States it is all but impossible to find. A few remaining farmhouse Cheshire makers still turn out an occasional well-cured Cheshire for special customers, usually on order, but cheese factories concentrate on medium Cheshire. The medium Cheshire is good and highly reliable in quality, more so than some of the other Cheddar relatives, but the long-keeping Cheshire has a richer, more penetrating flavor. It is made during July and August when grazing is at its best and the Shorthorn milk is at its richest. The medium-ripened cheese is made during the next best grazing months, May, June, and September. Some early-ripening cheese is made until the first of May, but it is young and callow and sold for immediate consumption.

No other country has ever seriously tried to imitate Cheshire—at least not for long—because, unlike Cheddar, it really cannot be counterfeited successfully outside the Cheshire area. Even the enterprising cheesemakers of the United States have forborne to make a Cheshire, as have the Australians—although the Canadians, according to P. Morton Shand, once tried and made a mess of it.

Cheshire cannot be imitated because of the peculiar character of the Cheshire county soil. Its grazing lands are impregnated with rich deposits of salt, and substantial quantities of salt inevitably are passed along to the Cheshire milk which is famous for its saltiness. The result is that Cheshire is intensely salty—although, curiously, it does not seem so at first taste. The initial flavor of a medium-ripened Cheshire is that of buttermilk—and its moist, crumbly texture also seems to deepen the buttermilk flavor. It is only after perhaps the third or fourth bite, when one has settled down to eating it, that one can detect Cheshire's saltiness. Even then it is not intrusive, possibly because it is intrinsic to the milk and therefore permeates the cheese so evenly that the palate is not suddenly and harshly assailed by a massive concentration. Nevertheless this pervasive saltiness makes it a perfect cheese to eat with celery, radishes, cucumbers—or indeed with any vegetable that needs salt and can be eaten raw. And of course Cheshire can be eaten with fresh bread or toast, buttered or unbuttered, or just by itself in chunks, with perhaps a sweet gherkin.

All British cheeses are scrutinized by the English Country Cheese Council and the Milk Marketing Board of England and Wales, the first awarding a green trade mark to fine-quality factory cheeses, the second giving a red trade mark to superior farmhouse cheeses. This does not mean that cheeses not complying with their standards cannot be sold; they can be and they are, but they are not allowed to carry either trade-mark, and as a consequence usually bring a lower price.

Cheshire is probably the most consistently reliable of British cheeses. It is less necessary to taste it before buying. This trustworthiness goes back forty years to the founding of the Cheshire Cheese Federation, an organization which no longer exists but whose excellent work has been continued by the Milk Marketing Board and the English Country Cheese Council. The Federation, alarmed at the uneven quality of Cheshire emerging from farmhouse dairies and factories, decided to reverse the ominous trend and began judging Cheshires on the basis of flavor, texture, color, and keeping quality. If a Cheshire received ninety-two out of a possible one hundred points, it received a trade mark which denoted excellence. Cheshire makers coveted the mark for its market value, and their need to hold onto it once they had acquired it got them into the habit of making consistently good Cheshires. Thus are traditions of excellence born.

Justifiably or not, Cheshiremen have always been inordinately proud of their cheese. When, for example, Elizabethan England was wresting control of the seas from Spain, Cheshiremen had no less than three versions of a tiresome doggerel whose general point was that Cheshire county cheeses were far better than anything the Spanish had, or were ever likely to have.

And at one time vanity prodded Cheshire makers into making outsize cheeses which they, like Cheddar makers, could present to monarchs. This petered out by 1910, perhaps because Cheshire makers began to realize that in the matter of size they could never compete. Cheshire is not so firm as Cheddar, and the largest cheese they were ever able to put together was only three hundred pounds—hardly a match for the outsize Cheddars.

From time to time, the French have made a number of observations about Cheshire. Victor Meusy, for example, writes:

> *Dans le chester sec et rose*
> *A longues dents, l'Anglais mord*

> (*Into Chester dry and pink*
> *The long teeth of the English sink*)

He calls Cheshire "Chester," as do the rest of his countrymen. Englishmen rarely complain about this, doubtless because they realize how extraordinary it is for the French to recognize the existence of any British cheese. And the French do recognize Cheshire. They have gone so far as to admit it into their *cuisine classique*. Cheshire is used in one or two sauces and, crowningly, one is allowed to use Cheshire instead of either Gruyère or Parmesan in making *paillettes de fromage,* those cheese sticks that are so delicious for luncheon with salad greens.

But by and large, the French are on such unfamiliar ground when they discuss British cheeses that they are not to be taken seriously even when they praise them. One suspects that when they profess a liking for a British cheese it may be for all the wrong reasons. Maurice des Ombiaux, for example, who was a gastronome of some distinction during the early part of this century, and who was brimming with good will for Cheshire, was equally full of misinformation. Coming as he did from a country not given to coloring its cheeses, he thought red Cheshire was naturally red and that its color was the proof of its virility. "There is nothing anemic about it as in other cheeses," he wrote; "it is, on the contrary, high in color as a Scotsman fresh from his mountains for whom whiskey has no terrors."

Double and Single Gloucester

"One can pass from Cheshire to Double Gloucester as from a fine bourgeois to a fine vintage wine. . . . [It is] perhaps the single hard English cheese that can be compared for richness and delicacy of flavor with the great blue cheeses." So wrote Osbert Burdett before World War II, and there is every evidence to suggest that at that time Double Gloucester could and did challenge Cheshire in excellence.

Nevertheless, even as Burdett wrote, the dairy farmers of Gloucester County were replacing their Gloucester cows—those strikingly handsome black beasts with the broad white stripe running the full length of their backs—with more profitable if less splendid animals. In richness of milk, not even Guernsey could surpass the Gloucester cow, but her daily yield was small. Inevitably other breeds that gave thinner milk, but more of it, began to appear in Gloucester pastures, and today the Gloucester strain has all but vanished. So, too, has the cheese of which Burdett wrote; now all Double Gloucester is factory-made from thinner milk. Still, there are some good Double Gloucesters to be had, and occasionally they can be found in the United States—in specialty cheese stores of course, not supermarkets. But by all means ask for a sliver to taste before you buy it. If a Double Gloucester is mature—that is, if it is about one year old—its flavor will be pungent but not sharp. "Put a crumb no bigger than a pinhead on your tongue," said one Gloucester lover, "and it will fill your whole mouth with its savor." If the sample seems to be indifferent, pass on to some other cheese, and return to Double Gloucester another day in another season. Sooner or later you'll hit Double Gloucester at its best. When you do, it will be one that was made in August when the milk is richest; its texture will be hard, close and satiny, and its flavor will have been worth waiting for. Cut off a chunk and wrap it in two or three of the greener leaves from a head of iceberg lettuce; the textures go well together and the lettuce will not distract your palate from the mellow ripeness of the Gloucester flavor.

The name Double Gloucester implies that there is a Single Gloucester, and so there is. Both cheeses have the same diameter (sixteen inches) but they differ in girth and age. Side by side they look like millstones of different thicknesses. Single Gloucester is only about half as thick (two to three inches) and only two-thirds as heavy (sixteen pounds) as the Double Gloucester. It is a young cheese and is eaten when it is about six weeks old, whereas Double Gloucester—"the thick sort"—as S. Rudder called it in his *New History of Gloucester County* published in 1779, "requires to be kept to an age proportionate to its size and thickness, to make it ready for the table." This age is anywhere from six months to a year.

Single Gloucester never strays too far from its native Gloucester or Berkeley (another name by which both cheeses are called) because it is too young to travel far and not at all appreciated when it gets there. At home its mild fresh flavor is highly regarded—which Osbert Burdett would have taken as proof that "local taste is less discriminating than that of London clubs."

Single Gloucester is always uncolored and the shade of Guernsey milk. So, in its own vales, is Double Gloucester, which is given its carrot color only for Londoners and other foreigners. At one time the exteriors of all Double Gloucesters were painted red, a practice which developed in the mid-eighteenth century when many dairywomen were already coloring the curd with carrot juice, in the hope of deceiving customers into thinking that their cheeses were made from richer milk than the uncolored cheeses of their competitors. By the time Double Gloucesters came into favor all hard cheeses were colored, and so the distinctions were lost. Then, at the urging of cheese merchants bent on finding a "characteristic" that would set the Gloucester apart from other cheeses, dairywomen took to painting it—they stained the Gloucester's surface with a mixture of Spanish brown and Indian red, and then rubbed its perimeters until the carroty yellow of the cheese showed through. The results were impressive. But they were probably never more splendid than when they were piled high on a great barge, their dark-red burnish gleaming in the sun, as they moved slowly and regally down the Thames from Lechlade to London.

Much earlier, Double Gloucester wore a hard, practical, everyday coat of bluish-black, designed to protect it from mites, or so it was hoped. Putting this exterior on the cheeses must have been a most disagreeable chore—for every fortnight the dairywomen had to rub the curing-room floor with bean tips and potato haulm "and other green and succulent herbage" until the floor was wet and brackish black. The Gloucesters were then placed on the floor and turned twice a week. When they were completely cured, their coats were hard and blue-black. Painting the Gloucesters red put an end to this, and although the dairywomen are reported to have hated painting the cheese—which they apparently thought more deceitful than coloring the curd—they probably preferred it to the fortnightly rubbing.

One final word about Double Gloucester. A glance at the latest calendar of events for visitors to Great Britain reveals that it is still the custom in Gloucester to celebrate the arrival of spring by honoring Gloucester's cheese. They no longer festoon three large Gloucesters with flowers and carry them on litters through the streets "accompanied by a joyous throng, shouting and huzzaaing . . ." to the churchyard, where they roll the Gloucesters around the church three times before eating them. But they do still eat a good deal of cheese on that day, just as their forebears did.

LEICESTER

What strikes you first is its flamboyant color—it is an orange to end all orange. Although the added coloring has no effect on its flavor, nevertheless Leicester's orange succeeds in its original purpose: it easily persuades the buyer that the color of the cheese is synonymous with a rich flavor. Fortunately the color is not misleading, for when you put a morsel in your mouth, Leicester's flaky shortness dissolves into a rich creaminess that also has a singular tang—one that can be only imperfectly described as the flavor we associate with lemon.

Some have said that Leicester was once the second greatest English cheese (the first being its better known Leicestershire neighbor, Stilton). But despite its undeniable virtues, it is doubtful that Leicester ever was or ever will be a really great cheese, because it has some intrinsic shortcomings. Compared with Cheddar, Leicester has a higher moisture content and consequently a shorter life span. It is at its best when it is between three and nine months old, and is likely to be overripe when it is a year old—just when a good Cheddar is entering its prime. And it is subject to a truly serious fault. Some Leicesters develop patches of flavor that are unpleasantly stronger than the rest of the cheese. Not even the cheesemakers know exactly why this happens, but it does. However, this is where Leicester's high color becomes useful to the buyer in a way not intended by the cheesemaker. These patches of strong flavor show themselves as bleach marks on the cut surface—

so that whenever a buyer sees these white marks on the orange cheese, he can correctly conclude that this is a Leicester to avoid.

Although Leicester is shaped like a millstone, its body and texture are anything but hard, as one soon discovers when cutting it. It is impossible to cut a good Leicester briskly and cleanly. This loosest of the hard-pressed cheeses must be gentled along; it must be cut softly, and the knife bearing its creamy smudges must be withdrawn slowly and easily, otherwise the cheese will crumble. Yet this also has its advantages: it makes Leicester a highly desirable melting cheese for rabbits and sauces. And as it melts quickly, it is ideal for quick things like simply melting some cheese on bread.

In the United States, Leicester is available wherever you can find other British cheeses. Don't buy too much at a time because it doesn't keep well, but do buy it. Leicester is really an excellent cooking cheese and very good to eat, too, particularly with spring onions and watercress.

Note: After all we said about Leicester's traditional bright-orange color, we find, just as this book is going to press, that current shipments of Leicester have become unaccountably paler and are all but undistinguishable from Cheshire or Double Gloucester in appearance. The texture, too, is different; it is less flaky and short. Perhaps, instead of Leicester, we are getting the new all-purpose cheese mentioned on page 110, but nobody at this writing seems to know.

CAERPHILLY

As Ernest Oldmeadow once said, those who like buttermilk will like Caerphilly very much and those who hate buttermilk had better leave it alone. Depending upon one's tastes, this will serve either as a warning or an inducement, but it is, at any rate, a fair statement. Snow-white Caerphilly—which looks rather like a single-layer cake newly turned out from a nine-inch baking tin and freshly sprinkled with confectioners' sugar—does indeed have the distinct flavor of country buttermilk. Its flavor is not unlike that of medium-ripened Cheshire, but its texture is vastly different: it is firmer and leaner, and has a slightly granular shortness which—if one can imagine it—is not dissimilar to the texture of a farmer cheese that has been so compressed that the individual curds are as solid as chocolate. And like farmer cheese it is very good eaten with cracked pepper.

Welsh miners and their families, for whom Caerphilly has been a mainstay for five generations, eat this cheese in brown-bread-and-butter sandwiches and with salad greens, but more often than not just by itself in neat slices. In fact, Caerphilly's two-and-a-half-inch height is said to have been chosen originally for a very practical purpose: to enable a pitman to hold a slice between his thumb and fingers and eat it while working, without getting any more coal dust on it than he has to.

For other reasons too, Caerphilly has often been spoken of as an ideal cheese for miners. For one thing, it does not dry up, as other cheeses do, when it is taken underground in the miners' wallets. And it is mildly but distinctly salty because it has been steeped in brine to toughen its coat—which has a special appeal for men whose work makes them sweat profusely. And finally, Caerphilly is easy to digest, an important consideration for men who work all day in cramped positions.

Although Caerphilly was first made in and around Caerphilly, Wales, one would be hard put to find any Welsh Caerphilly there today. Now it is all made by Englishmen, and most of it is made just across the Bristol Channel in Somerset County. This shift came about during the last century when Welsh dairy farmers, unable to meet a growing urban demand for cheese, sought assistance from their Somerset neighbors—and never recovered from it.

Traditionally, Somerset farmers made Cheddars, but Cheddars take time and money. For example, it takes one hundred pounds of milk to make a ten-pound Cheddar, which then must be cured for at least six months. To make a seven-and-a-half-pound Caerphilly, on the other hand, you need only seven gallons of milk—and the

Caerphilly can then be sold within five to ten days. Such factors were not lost upon the enterprising Somerset cheesemakers, who felt that they more than offset the risks involved in selling to a market composed exclusively of miners whose jobs and incomes were so precarious. They felt that a nice penny could be turned, and they were right. It is only conjecture of course, but it is possible that the highly prized Somerset County Cheddars have maintained their superior quality over the years just because the Somerset farmer has had a source of ready money in Caerphilly. As the economic pressures intensified, Somerset farmers were perhaps not so tempted to compromise the quality of their Cheddars as were dairymen elsewhere. They had the luxury of an alternative; they could either make Caerphilly and get out of the Cheddar business altogether, or they could make both.

The Caerphillys that we get here are cured for a little longer time—for at least two or three weeks. Nevertheless it is well to remember that Caerphilly is a young and short-lived cheese, although you can prolong its life by keeping it wrapped in a damp cloth.

Summer is a particularly good season to buy Caerphilly because it has been made from the year's richest milk—and also because it is a good refreshing cheese to eat when it is hot. It is particularly inviting if, as Mr. Oldmeadow once put it, you "associate it" with your salad. And it makes an excellent fondue for those who like fondue but who have perhaps wished that it were not so rich.

SCOTCH DUNLOP

Scotsmen may prefer not to think of Dunlop as a kind of English Cheddar, but there is really no other proper way of describing its flavor. A mature Scotch Dunlop has the same sweet flavor as a buttery young English Cheddar. It has some bite to it, but not much—and no bitterness. In the United States it can be found where other British cheeses are sold, and in our view it is perhaps the nearest thing to a young English Cheddar that can be found in this country. Scotsmen very often eat it while it is young—that is, about two months old—but at this age Dunlop is so mild that the comparison with Cheddar ceases to be useful. Here we are speaking of Scotch Dunlop that is at least four months old.

We are told that Dunlop cheese originated in Ireland at the time of Charles II and the religious troubles, when one Barbara Gilmour learned to make such cheeses before crossing the North Channel to Scotland, and more than likely, to the county of Ayer—which is today the major producer of Dunlop.

Dunlop is never dyed; its true color is somewhere between butter and cream, which is a faithful representation of its flavor—because in biting into a Dunlop one somehow has the sensation of going straight through the cheese into the fresh, rich milk. The Dunlop surface, when it is cut, is smooth and unbroken, its texture moister than Cheddar, and in the opinion of one admirer, "it does not dry the mouth so forcibly." It is a pleasant eating cheese, good with coarse-textured whole-wheat bread spread lightly with butter, and—although you'll probably have to make them because they are not easily come by—with Scotch oatcakes.

It is excellent as a melting cheese, and it can be used in any recipe calling for Cheddar, although you will need more of it for flavor than if you used an aged cheddar.

LANCASHIRE

Should you ever find yourself in Lancashire, by no means miss tasting Lancashire cheese. The chances are against finding it anywhere else, more's the pity, for it is a poor traveler with a short life span. Since Lancashire must be eaten at two or three months, but no later, not much gets even as far as London. Practically the entire production of Lancashire, therefore, is consumed locally.

This is the softest of the hard-pressed cheeses, and even at three months of age it spreads like butter. But softer does not mean milder, for Lancashire is stronger in flavor than either Cheddar or Cheshire. Indeed, its strength and soft texture make it eminently suitable for Welsh rabbits and toasting—it turns custardy when melted—and it is ideal for sauce Mornay. All of which seems to suggest that if you do stop in Lancashire some day, you should also arrange to have kitchen privileges.

ENGLISH DERBY

Though by no means a spectacular cheese, English Derby is mild and good-tasting. It is at its best when it is aged for six months, even though in England it is frequently sold when it is only six to eight weeks old—probably because Derby manufacturers are eager to "move" a cheese which has certain inherent faults that tend to manifest themselves as the cheese matures. For one thing, as it ages its moistness encourages the development of undesirable and un-Derby-like flavors. It can be found in the United States, perhaps not as readily as the other British cheeses, but that is really no great loss.

WHITE WENSLEYDALE

The white Wensleydale we import is stronger than the cheese eaten in Yorkshire, where it is made. Ours has more age, and whereas young Wensleydales are much like Caerphilly in flavor, fresh and buttermilky, the older ones taste more like aged creamy Cheddar with overtones of Reblochon. These older white Wensleydales come in one-pound cylinders about three inches in diameter, three and three-quarter inches high, and are wrapped in plastic wrap. Not too long ago they were disappointing indeed, because for some reason a kind of gaseous odor developed within the package, and the cheese was malodorous and bitter. This has since been corrected, and though you may have tried and rejected Wensleydale during this unfortunate period, it's worth trying again. It is a good, nippy, spreadable cocktail cheese.

THE ALL-PURPOSE CHEESE

These days, the American buyer of English cheeses is more likely to get what he asks for than the Englishman who buys cheese in his local supermarket. The growing taste for mild cheeses in England has encouraged one manufacturer to turn out a cheese with the texture and flavor of a young Cheshire and sell it variously as Cheshire, Cheddar, Double Gloucester, Leicester or Derby. No one apparently takes this misrepresentation very seriously. The buyer who is particular about his cheeses usually goes to a specialty shop anyway, while the supermarket shopper seems content with this all-purpose cheese regardless of its name. "After all," one official of the English Country Cheese Council said, "It *is* a good cheese."

Domestic Warsawski

The original Warsawski, which comes from Poland, is a strong cheese made of sheep's milk. But there is another Warsawski which is made here from cow's milk—and this is an entirely different cheese. Whereas the Polish cheese is grayish in color and has a decidedly barnyardy flavor, the American one is almost pure white and has a faint Cheddary flavor infused with another taste not unlike an Asti Spumante or some other sweet but light sparkling wine. It is all a matter of taste, of course, but here is one instance in which we think the copy is far more pleasing than the original. Domestic Warsawski is a cheese worth looking for.

Domestic Kasseri

The original Kasseri comes from Greece—and here again we think the American reproduction is vastly superior to the original. Greek Kasseri is a sheep's-milk cheese, and if anything it is even stronger than Polish Warsawski. The domestic Kasseri has a flavor somewhere between Cheddar and Parmesan, with the same light winy taste that domestic Warsawski has. Neither of them is around in any great quantity, though some specialty cheese stores do stock them and they can sometimes be found in Greek and Polish neighborhood stores. It is a pity that they are not as well known as they deserve to be.

Cantal

"There beside the pound pats of butter, wrapped in pear leaves, arose a giant Cantal which looked as if it had been split open with an ax." It is only proper that in his classic description of the Paris cheese market Zola should mention Cantal first, because in all probability it was one of France's first cheeses. Cantal almost certainly preceded France's dozen or so other hard-pressed cow's-milk cheeses, and it is far, far older than the infinitely more sophisticated soft-ripening cheeses with which France is more usually associated.

Cantal comes from the somewhat insular region of Cantal and Auvergne, an area well known for its mutton and pigs, its wonderful pastureland with whose aroma the cheese itself seems to be imbued. And Waverly Root has described its cows as having bright-colored curly hides with a luminosity that vanishes, according to local legend, if the animals are removed from these volcanic pastures and taken to different soils.

Cantal is a big cheese—around a hundred and ten pounds, and fifteen inches tall. It is cylindrical in form—in fact, it is sometimes called Fourme de Cantal, Fourme referring to the mold in which the cheese is pressed and shaped; its cut surface is smooth and pale yellow, and its rind is tough and callused.

You can find Cantal only in well-stocked specialty stores, and it is at its best between November and May. It has a Cheddary taste but be warned—it can either have a strong barnyard flavor or it can be sweet and mellow. Again, it is a good idea to see whether it is really to your taste before you buy it.

10

---···❦···---

The Double-
and Triple-Crèmes

For seventy or eighty years, France's double-crèmes were regarded as the world's richest cheeses. Then, in the 1950s, the unbelievable triple-crèmes began to appear, sweeping aside all previous standards of richness, until now it is safe to say that anyone who has not tasted a triple-crème doesn't know what rich is. One distinction should be made at once: we are not speaking now of the fresh cheeses made of cream, those innocent country cheeses discussed in Chapter 4. Here we are dealing with their sophisticated elders, the cured double- and triple-crèmes—cured meaning that they have been brushed with special molds and allowed to ripen.

The typical double-crème has the rich curdy flavor and texture of a heavy cheesecake, and a pronounced sourness which gives way to piquancy when the cheese has been at room temperature for several hours and the thick creaminess has taken over. As for the triple-crème, it is calculated to appeal shamelessly to the sybarite in all of us. Its taste is not unlike that of a Brie, but milder. And perhaps more than any other cheese, its texture is incorporated into its flavor—a flavor that one can summon by imagining the satiny paste of a perfect Brie mixed with equal parts of thick sour cream and whipped sweet cream.

It is unlikely that these voluptuous crèmes could have appeared at any other time (and certainly they could have come from no other country), for these are the cheeses of affluence. They owe their existence to France's new prosperity—which is to say that there is enough cream to make these cheeses and, in and out of France, enough people with money to buy them.

Double- and triple-crèmes are rich and expensive because they contain more cream than other cheeses—cream that cheesemakers deliberately and willfully add to curds of cheese already rich in butterfat.

What exactly do "double" and "triple" crème mean? Under French law the definitions are explicit. A double-crème must contain, and be labeled, "60% *matière grasse*"—which means that 60 per cent of every 100 grams of cheese is butterfat. A triple-crème contains 75 per cent *matière grasse*. Now an average cheese—a Camembert, for instance—has 45 to 50 per cent. So a double-crème is 10 to 15 per cent richer, and a triple-crème is 25 per cent richer than other cheeses—roughly the equivalent of having two eggs in your beer.

But to experience an astonishing sense of geometric progression, one must taste a double- and a triple-crème in quick succession: whatever a double-crème is, a triple-crème is many times more so—many many more than its mere 10 or 15 per cent difference in butterfat would seem to account for.

How Crèmes Are Made

The surface of the fresh crème is treated with a mold that gradually ripens the cheese from its exterior to its interior. This mold, which varies from one kind of cured crème to another, more closely resembles those used in making the milder soft-ripening cheeses like Crema Danica or Caprice des Dieux than those used for Liederkranz, French Camembert, or Brie. The crème is then placed in a curing room to ripen for ten days to two weeks. It continues to ripen as it moves from the factory to the distributor and to the consumer, who ideally receives it a few weeks later when it is at its prime.

DOUBLE-CRÈMES YOU CAN BUY HERE

Only a few double-crèmes come to this country in any quantity. One is Fromage de Monsieur Fromage, a cheese from Normandy that was first made about seventy-five years ago. This is a small round unctuous cheese whose only shortcoming is that it is occasionally too salty, which suggests that it may have been oversalted to preserve it for its long journey to the United States. Another double-crème is Une Gourmadise!!! (the exclamation marks are the manufacturer's), which is relatively new here, and not unlike Monsieur Fromage in flavor and texture. A third, which is now well known, is the ivory-colored triangular Hablé Crème Chantilly (Swedish, despite its French name), which has a smoother texture than Monsieur Fromage but essentially the same flavor. This cheese created a mild sensation when it first came to this country—this was before the advent of the triple-crèmes—and Sheila Hibben's remarks about it in the *New Yorker,* in 1950, reflected the feelings of many people at that time:

> Endeavoring to be as restrained as I can, I shall merely suggest that the arrival of Crème Chantilly is a historic event and that in reporting it I feel something of the responsibility that the contemporaries of Madame Harel, the famous cheesemaking lady of Normandy, must have felt when they were passing judgment on the first Camembert.

TRIPLE-CRÈMES

As we have said, triple-crèmes are astonishingly richer than double-crèmes, and the difference is as much in texture as in taste. When a triple-crème has been at room temperature for seven or eight hours, its interior has the consistency of the custard in an éclair, and you have only to press its crust gently to feel the cheese move within. But when it has been at room temperature for only two or three hours, it has *two* textures and *two* flavors—the very center of the cheese is still solid (although not unyielding), and should you eat it at this point you will find that it is really like two cheeses in one—a delicately sour double-crème suspended in a fondue of triple-crème.

TRIPLE-CRÈMES YOU CAN BUY HERE

Of the half-dozen triple-crèmes that come to the United States, the deservedly popular Triple Crème Parfait is perhaps the best known because it was the first to be imported in any quantity, and it is an excellent cheese of its kind. The Parfait has a burnt-orange crust streaked with white mold, indicating that it has lain on straw mats during its curing period, and is about three and a quarter inches in diameter and two and a quarter inches high. Like most crèmes, it is packed in a round, light chipboard box.

The pretty, rosy-crusted Brillat-Savarin is a more recent arrival, and the only real difference between it and other triple-crèmes is that its texture, when it is cold, becomes a little grainy, almost like a hard sauce. However, this graininess (which is not unpleasant and does not detract from the flavor) tends to disappear the longer the cheese sits at room temperature.

Le Roi, another of the newer imports, has a wrinkled, light-beige crust etched with fine lines of white mold, and a brilliant yellow paste which, at room temperature, is threaded through with what looks like tiny rivulets of melted butter.

Excelsior, although not officially a full triple-crème, since it has only 72 per cent *matière grasse*, is nevertheless rich enough to hold its own with the others.

Boursault and Boursin are two relatively recent, and widely distributed, triple-crèmes produced by the two companies which are rivals on both sides of the Atlantic. They are superior triple-crèmes, and unlike all others, they are packaged in layers of paper, not in boxes. One minor point about Boursault: although some packages are labeled "Special" while others are not, the cheeses within are the same. The reason for the difference is that one of the distributors here is apparently eager to distinguish his cheese from his competitor's.

WHEN YOU BUY A CRÈME

The crèmes, like all perishable cheeses, are at the mercy of slow turnover—and if they are not bought soon after they arrive at the cheese store, they are likely to deteriorate. Even refrigerated, the crèmes run a fast course from youth to age, and some cheese dealers, anxious to avoid loss, tend to push those that have gone beyond their prime. One wishes that they would order fewer of them in the first place, or not handle them at all. Keeping their high mortality rate in mind, the only thing to do is to go to a reputable shop and cast an alert and wary eye over the stock. One should always examine a crème carefully, for even on the refrigerated shelves of the most honorable cheese store these perishable crèmes have been known to run away with themselves.

Whether the crème is wrapped in a layer of paper and then packaged in a box, or simply wrapped in two or three layers of paper, the paper around the cheese itself should be clean and fresh, never brown and sticky. If any part of the paper looks dark and disagreeable, the cheese will also probably have a strong smell, another indication that it is over the hill, or at least well on its way. Obviously this is a cheese to avoid.

Although triple-crèmes are usually refrigerated until they are sold, some stores let a few stand on the counter at room temperature throughout the day. Assuming that a cheese is in good condition to begin with, and that you intend to serve it that day, you can buy it in the certain knowledge that by cocktail or dinnertime it will be at its sublime best.

By all means serve triple-crème to your guests at the end of a good dinner—with wine and good French or Italian bread, or unsalted biscuits. They'll love it. But for solitary or family occasions you may yield to the temptation that is somehow always present with a triple-crème—and that is to plunge your spoon right into its center and eat it without anything else at all.

11

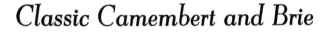

Classic Camembert and Brie

*Both are "vintage" cheeses at their ripe moment;
and everyone is free to maintain his preference.
Neither could be spared. I can only repeat that
none would have thought Camembert could be
surpassed were it not for Brie. For Brie to be
surpassable seems impossible.*
—*Osbert Burdett in* A Little Book of Cheese

CAMEMBERT

In England the heroine of cheesemaking is a Mrs. Paulet of
Wymondham, who is credited with having invented Stilton. In
Denmark it is Hanne Nielsen, a farm woman who traveled all over
Europe about a hundred years ago, studying methods of cheesemaking; it was she who started Denmark on imitating the cheeses of
other lands. Italy has no such heroine but has instead a patron
saint—Santa Lucia, whose features adorn the pure gold medal
awarded each year to the cheesemaker in Lombardy who has produced the most of the best Parmesan. But in all the world only one
person associated with cheesemaking has rated a statue—and not
just one statue, but three. This is Marie Harel, who is credited with
having invented France's favorite cheese, the Camembert. Camembert is to France what "American" cheese is to the United States

and Cheddar is to England, and there is hardly a French man, woman or child who does not know Camembert and eat it often. It is their most plentiful cheese and one of the cheapest. Yet it is also prized by connoisseurs, and people who think nothing of serving a score of luxury cheeses at a reception will give the same attention to the selection of their Camembert that they give to their wines.

It is one of the best known of the foreign cheeses in the United States, where a good deal of Camembert is imported from France, and considerably more of it is made, principally in Ohio. Not surprisingly, there are decided differences between the imported and domestic Camembert, though a comparison does not give the imported French Camembert as many points over the domestic as we might expect—even though it is the superior cheese to begin with—simply because, by the time it reaches us, it is often past its prime and may also give evidence of the rude and capricious treatment it has received along the way.

The Camembert you can get in France is something else again, not merely because it has not had to travel, but because the milk used in making it is unpasteurized, which makes a difference in the flavor. French Camembert in France (unlike ours and unlike the French Camembert packaged in portions for export) comes in small uncut rounds, and the rough crust, scored by the straw mats on which it has lain, is gold flecked with white, like a lightly browned butter pastry sprinkled with confectioners' sugar. The flavor when it is at its prime—that is, neither hard at the center nor runny to the point of collapsing when it is cut into—the flavor of Camembert is such that one can believe the story that Napoleon kissed the waitress in Normandy who first served it to him.

The cheese was nameless at that time, and Napoleon is also reputed to have named it, uninspiredly enough, for its place of origin, Camembert, a tiny commune three miles outside of Vimoutiers in the department of Orne. There the cheese is supposed to have been invented around 1790 by a Mme. Marie Harel, a farmer's wife, in whose honor an eight-foot-high stone obelisk was placed many years ago, not far from the farm where she lived. Its inscription:

EN

L'HONNEUR

DE

MME. HAREL

NÉE

MARIE FONTAINE

QUI

INVENTA

LE

CAMEMBERT

In the nearby town of Vimoutiers, a more personal memorial was erected—a granite statue of Mme. Harel, shown with a massive milk jug balanced on her hip. Writing of this statue, T. A. Layton reports, "She has flowing robes and on her head she wears what, with respect, can best be described as a large, elongated, inverted, tapering flower pot." The statue lost its head in the bombing of World War II, however, and was hauled away.

Some ten years later it was replaced by a second statue—this one a gift from the employees of the large American company that produces most of our domestic Camembert. A small replica (the third statue) stands in Ohio, in front of the cheese factory that was the donor. But there is good reason to believe that the Camembert "invented" by Marie Harel was in existence before she was born, just as the Stilton credited to Mrs. Paulet is supposed to have preceded her by perhaps thirty years. Very few cheeses of this world, in fact, are sure of their ancestry or even their early associations. And invariably when we come upon new information, it is to place it earlier, not later, than generally supposed. Of Camembert, André Simon notes: "As a matter of historical fact, the fame of the cheeses of Normandy can be traced back to the twelfth century, and Camembert is named as one of the best Normandy cheeses in two old French dictionaries, that of Thomas Corneille, published in

1708, and that of M. de Lamartinière, published in 1741: 'Vimoutiers . . . every Monday is Market Day when they sell the excellent cheeses of Livarot and Camembert.' "

Waverly Root reports that the question of whether Marie Harel
invented or reinvented Camembert cheese was a matter of hot
debate in the French press at the time the second statue was in the
news. Root says, with some resignation, that the only thing that is
certain is that she was born in Vimoutiers. He, with many others, is
inclined to think that Marie Harel probably made not the first but
the best Camembert of her day, and thus brought the cheese into
its own. He also points out that the "original" Camembert—the one
mentioned in these early accounts—was probably a blue cheese
anyway, and would therefore have been quite different from the
Camembert we know today. The mold used for the present-day
cheese, he reports, "was taken from the Bondon cheese of the Pays
de Bray, in northeast Normandy, which has perhaps since regretted
the gift to a competitor."

This mold, called *Penicillium candidum*, is related to penicillin,
and is sprayed on the surface of the cheese shortly after it has been
drained of its whey and before the aging process begins. It is different from the mold used in making American Camembert and is the
chief reason that the French Camembert crust is golden, whereas
the American Camembert is crusted in shades of white and off-
white.

André Simon also salutes a Monsieur Ridel, also of Vimoutiers,
who had the wit to invent a light, round wooden box in which to
store and transport this fragile cheese. "It was he who deserved a
statue," says Simon, "for it was he who made the fortune of the
Orne farmers, and others. Until he introduced his box, Camemberts were sold in six, wrapped up in straw, well enough protected
to arrive in Paris in good shape, but not fit to stand much longer
journeys. Monsieur Ridel's packaging made it possible to export
Camembert all over the world."

But whoever invented Camembert would sternly disapprove the
practice of cutting the cheese into individual triangular portions

instead of leaving it intact. For Camembert, like Brie, is never the same once its rind has been cut into; cutting into it, connoisseurs insist, puts an end to its normal ripening processes. A cut Camembert or Brie that has been prematurely broached may go on to ripen as best it can and achieve a certain goodness, but it has been denied the wherewithal for perfection. Anything that affects the ripening processes must be accorded importance because even under ideal conditions a Camembert moves very rapidly from underripeness to perfection to overripeness, and the period when it is at its prime is short indeed—two or three days, sometimes less. As P. Morton Shand says: "Camembert must be eaten à *point*, for a day or two before it is ripe it will still be rather hard, dry, and even chalky, while a day or two after it has reached its brief prime, it is overpowering and positively unwholesome. A curiously 'jealous' cheese is Camembert," he adds, "for one box will differ from its neighbours on the stall in the most astonishing way."

If a Camembert shows a hard, caky white center even when it is at room temperature, there is nothing to do except cover it with a damp cloth, put it in a cool place, and hope for the best. With great luck it may ripen fairly uniformly and become the cheese you hoped it would be. But many Camemberts whose normal ripening processes were disrupted in one way or another will pass from youth to old age, as some people do, without any discernible interval. If the Camembert you have bought is already past its prime and beyond help, you will quickly know it by the gusts of ammonia that waft from its wrappings, the ominously rusted look of the rind, and the bitter, disagreeable taste.

FINDING A GOOD CAMEMBERT

There are many ways of identifying a good Camembert, but unfortunately most of them await opening and cutting into the cheese, which you can do only after you have bought it and got it home. Here are some general rules to help you choose it. First, don't buy imported Camembert in the summer. It is good only from October to June, its best months being January to April. Domestic

Camemberts (which are made to be sold all year round and which, as they are made differently, are a different kind of cheese from the French Camembert) are more dependable in the warmer months. Whether imported or domestic, a cheese should be passed up if it is not plump and somewhat yielding to the touch. If its box seems too big for it, beware—it probably fitted perfectly when it was packed, but it has lost needed moisture; a raised rim means the same thing. It will be refrigerated when it is offered to you, and if the aroma is anything but mild while it is cold, you can be reasonably sure that when it comes to room temperature the smell will protest its age.

It is always desirable to compare the cheeses in the refrigerator case, if you can. The differences from one cheese to the next are often due not so much to temperament—even though Camemberts *are* highly individualistic—as to the fact that old cheeses are not always removed when new ones are delivered. And it is not always by accident when the old cheeses are found on top or out in front of the case, as they often are. Recently, we were looking over the Camemberts in an open refrigerator case. The clerk said, "I'll get you a *good* one." And he reached back and drew the prize from the very bottom of the stack.

As with almost any cheese, the integrity of the seller is the best guarantee of the quality and condition of a Camembert. Domestic Camemberts can be bought with reasonable confidence in almost any store with a brisk turnover. But French Camemberts should be bought only at the best shops. Once in a great while you can find a good French Camembert at a supermarket, but more often, in comparison to the other cheeses there, the French Camemberts are a sorry sight indeed.

Differences Between French and American Camembert

Domestic Camembert is a safer bet than the French, and it is a different cheese, patterned more closely after the French Carré de l'Est than French Camembert. At all stages the French Camembert tends to be stronger in flavor than ours and moves to ripeness more rapidly; and it is much the better cheese when you can get it at its best—which is seldom possible here.

A recent development in France is the production of Camembert that has been "stabilized"—that is, made from pasteurized milk and treated to produce a more uniform cheese with a longer life span— a cheese that is not at any point so good as Camembert made in the old way. This is not a process cheese, but it might as well be, because of the almost plastic perfection of its even texture and color. Years ago the United States took some lessons from the French in developing a method for making Camembert. Now, much later, one suspects they may have taken a leaf or two from our book in developing these new stabilizing processes. It also means that the great Camembert of the past is becoming harder and harder to find, even in France.

Near-Camemberts

There are many French cheeses that resemble Camembert but are not Camembert. One of the most important is Carré de l'Est, a square-shaped cheese that is milder than Camembert and a little softer, with a white crust. It is imported into the United States, and so is the delicious Four Seasons, another cheese very similar to Carré de l'Est. Others are Chaourcée, a much larger copy of Camembert, which is made in the Champagne district; and Rollot, a Camembert type made in Flanders. These, like half a dozen other near-Camemberts, are rarely seen except where they are made.

Camembert is produced in many countries besides France and the United States—including Germany, Denmark, Holland, Belgium and Austria. Of these the only two that you are likely to find here are the German and the Danish, and then most likely in cans. We do import a German Camembert from Bavaria that is fresh, and a singularly attractive-looking cheese it is. Handsomely packaged, it promises much: the rind is golden, the flesh plump, white and glistening throughout. At room temperature it shows a marked willingness to run and overrun onto the plate. Fair and handsome it is—but it leaves a bitter, bitter taste.

CANNED CAMEMBERT

As for the canned Camemberts from Germany and Denmark and elsewhere—the idea of having a luscious, soft-ripened cheese on the shelf for use at any time is a fine one. But so far no one has succeeded in canning them. Some canned cheeses are better than others: they look good and they don't taste bad—just peculiar. Others are dark and evil-looking, with a taste to match. On the whole, they are not good cheeses. The skin on all of them, when cut or bitten into, pulls off eerily in one piece like a thick wet leather glove. If it is one of the poorer specimens it may taste like a piece of greasy lamb fell that has been soaked in evaporated milk. The inside may be more palatable, though all canned Camemberts retain to some extent that lingering evaporated-milk taste.

BRIE

Almost all that has been said of Brie divides itself into roughly two kinds of comment. The first is ecstatic. No cheese has been more celebrated than Brie, and with reason. It is the ultimate cheese, the towering wonder of them all; and even among connoisseurs who decline to speak in absolutes, or whose first allegiance is elsewhere, Brie is surely at the top of the list. For many it is without peer. The second comment that is frequently heard has to do with the difficulty of finding a really good Brie—even in Paris, to say nothing of New York or Chicago, London or Rome.

Yet, like any other kind of pure gold, a perfect Brie is worth searching and waiting for. As Sheila Hibben wrote in the *New Yorker*:

> I can't imagine any difference of opinion about Brie's being the queen of all cheeses, and if there is any such difference, I shall certainly ignore it. The very shape of Brie—so uncheese-like and so charmingly fragile—is exciting. Nine times out of ten a Brie will let you down—will be all caked into layers,

which shows it too young, or at the over-runny stage, which means it is too old—but when you come on the tenth Brie, *coulant* to just the right delicate creaminess, and the color of fresh sweet butter, no other cheese can compare with it.

Brie is often likened to the moon because it is so white, so large and round, and as thin as men in bygone ages imagined the moon to be. Also, one suspects, the sight of a Brie diminishing rapidly—from the full to the half to the quarter, to the merest wedge—gives rise to that atavistic melancholy with which the waning of the moon has always been viewed.

Zola likens it to the moon in his *Le Ventre de Paris:*

> Three Bries, on a round platter, had the melancholy of dead moons; two, very dry, were at the full; the third, in its second quarter, flowed, emptied itself of a white cream, spread out in a lake overflowing the thin platter which sought in vain to hold it.

The comparison is made again in a much-quoted seventeenth-century ode by St. Amant, known in France as the poet of good living. He writes:

> *Brie alone deserves that we*
> *Should record her praises in letters of gold.*
> *Gold, I say, and with good reason*
> *Since it is with gold that one must compare*
> *This cheese to which I now pay homage.*
> *It is as yellow as the gold worshipped by man,*
> *But without its anxiety*
> *For one has only to press it with one's fingers*
> *For it to split its sides with laughter*
> *And run over with fat.*
> *Why, then, is it not endless*
> *As indeed its circular form is endless?*
> *And why must its full moon, eternally appealing,*
> *Wane to a crescent? . . .*

Some Bries, though their diameters may be as much as sixteen inches, are no more than three-quarters of an inch thick. No wonder they are often referred to as pancakes, though they are so delicate that they might better be compared to crêpes. Osbert Burdett writes:

> The very shape of the whole cheese, a vast thin disk of pale and ochreous gold, set upon reeds supported by a circular wooden platter, is an invention of which beauty clearly has been preferred to vulgar convenience. This is a royal circle, as if the cheese had instinctively adopted "the form of perfection" and displayed itself in state, in the manner of a golden coin, with a diameter out of expectation to its thinness.

But even if it were less beautiful, there is little likelihood that Brie would be less beloved. For the taste of this cheese is like no other. It is a mixture: part mushrooms, part cream, part cognac, part earth—as earth smells upon the roots of leeks, with a shade of truffle and with something of the scent of ripe Anjou pears, perhaps.

The texture is more easily described: it is like heavy honey. Satin alone can match its gloss. And it is at its best when it generously spreads itself, and when its honeyed texture is uniform throughout.

More often than not the Bries offered for sale have the same central fault—the same hard, white, caky middle so often found in Camembert. Here is the first thing to look for when you are buying a piece of a large cheese: Is it the same soft glistening yellow at the center—between the top and bottom rind—as it is right next to the rind? Look closely, for your satisfaction will depend largely upon the answer to that question. No matter how good the milk, or how great the skills that went into making it, an open Brie that still has a hard heart of pale curd is unlikely ever to come into its own—for once it has been cut it cannot continue to ripen normally. And despite what cheese sellers may tell you, leaving it out at room temperature will rarely help, for the ripe cheese surrounding that unyielding center may deepen in color, and bulge out over it like a frozen waterfall, but the cheese will never be all of a piece. It will become overripe before the center has yielded one iota. This is the swift passage, with no discernible interval, from youth to what Dryden called "a green old age." Writing of Brie and of "the ineffable way it exudes its pluperfect cream," P. Morton Shand also cautioned: "Good Brie should never separate on being cut into two thick creamy crusts, leaving an even thicker layer of dry white cheese, that looks like Munster, in between. Brie that has not begun to exude is not worth eating."

How to Recognize the Best Brie

The only Brie of course is the French Brie. Other cheeses made elsewhere may be called Brie, but it is not for any one of these that gourmets have thrown down their forks to seize their pens in praise. Though some Brie is made in Normandy and elsewhere in France, the heart of the Brie country is in the department of Seine et Marne, on the outskirts of Paris, to the southeast. By universal consent the very best Brie produced is Brie de Meaux (and, though it is a rarity, the farm-made variety of Brie de Meaux, called Brie de Meaux *fermier,* which is the supreme Brie). But whether farm- or factory-made, Brie de Meaux is *the* Brie—and you can always recognize it by its distinctive shape: large, round and very thin.

Near-Bries

Two others, often called Brie, might more correctly be called *near*-Brie cheeses. Both are smaller and thicker than Brie de Meaux, not nearly so elegant in shape, to say nothing of taste. These are Brie de Melun, which is somewhat stronger and darker than the classic Brie de Meaux, and which is made all year round; and Brie façon Coulommiers, more often simply called Coulommiers, which is younger and less mellow than the other two and which may slightly resemble Camembert in flavor. Coulommiers is in season from November to March. Both can be good, but they are not great—and they are not really Brie. Nor is the so-called Petit Brie, which is hardly larger than Camembert.

Large wheels of domestic Brie from Wisconsin and Illinois also show up from time to time in the cheese shops. Extremely uneven in quality, these can be very, very good (particularly the Illinois Brie) or poor, and so it is essential to taste before you buy. We also import a prepackaged Danish Brie that is the size and shape of a wedge of pie. This has a curiously plastic quality, and we have yet to sample one that is worth eating. But the worst offender of all is the Brie that comes in cans. Everything we said about canned Camembert is true also of Brie. It should be avoided.

SOME POINTERS ON BUYING BRIE

Brie de Meaux should be bought between October and April; its best months are December through March. It should be bought only in the best cheese shops. If you buy a whole Brie, which may weigh from six to eight pounds—and there is nothing better to serve at a party—you will be making a sizable investment, and because it is whole, you will not be able to look into it. This means you must buy where you can put your complete confidence in the dealer, telling him exactly when you expect to use it. And you should plan to use all of it—leftover Brie, like leftover champagne, is at the mercy of time.

If you are buying a piece of an opened Brie, you will be able to see the center. For some reason or other you are more likely to be offered a Brie that is not fully matured than one which is overripe. Only rarely will it be overripe—and this you will easily see because it will be in a state of collapse, with the top crust almost meeting the bottom and the cheese spread out all over the plate on which it rests. A little bulging or running is nothing to hesitate about. Brie that is à point will bulge or run to some extent, so that is a good sign as long as the cheese is not literally beside itself. If you find a perfect cheese one time in ten, you will be striking a fair average. This means that Brie is not really a cheese you can *plan* to buy in advance—unless you have a dealer in whom you can place complete confidence—but it is rather a cheese to snap up when you are lucky enough to see one that looks luscious.

If you should buy, or be given, a Brie that turns out to have a hard heart, some experts say it can be improved by covering it with a damp cloth and letting it sit at room temperature for a day or two, or even three—for however long it takes to come around. It may prove unresponsive, or it may repay your efforts and delight you.

CREMA DANICA

Crema Danica is not merely another make-believe Brie—it is an entirely different cheese with a distinctly different flavor, and the only new kind of cheese of major importance that has been invented in the past forty years. Surely it is the greatest triumph that Danish cheesemakers have ever had. For the first time, Denmark has a great cheese of its own.

Crema Danica made its debut in 1957 or 1958. It was invented by Henrik Tholstrup of Copenhagen, a remarkable man now in his seventies—a prodigious mountain climber and skier, a successful industrialist and the builder of two of Copenhagen's most prosperous hotels. He is also the descendant of three generations of cheesemakers. Tholstrup made up his mind to invent a luxury cheese at a fairly modest price—a cheese that would have the marvelous texture of Brie, without its faults. Crema Danica was the result.

Anyone who likes Camembert and Brie is almost certain to be delighted with this cheese. Its flavor is delicate, decidedly more delicate than either Camembert or Brie, though it belongs in the same range of tastes. And yet it has an earthy quality reminiscent of still other cheeses like the musky Livarot and Reblochon. But its texture *is* like that of Brie at its best. Imagine a Brie without danger of that hard center. The miracle of Crema Danica is that it ripens—or as they say in the cheese trade, "breaks down"—with extraordinary evenness, and after a few hours at room temperature it becomes all glossy throughout. And it comes as a relief to know that the chances of finding a uniformly ripe Crema Danica are almost one in one.

Buying and Keeping Crema Danica

It is tremendously in demand, and is certain to become even more popular as word of it gets around. Already it has moved beyond the gourmet shops and now can be found in many of the better delicatessens and in a few supermarkets as well. It comes in a square chipboard box bearing a label of red and gray with a white crown in the center, two cheeses to a box. Each weighs six ounces, is bar-shaped like an outsize stick of butter and wrapped in gold foil. Usually they can be bought singly for less than a dollar a bar, which makes it a bargain, for it is extravagantly creamy—a luxury cheese if there ever was one.

Just be sure when you buy it that the rind is all pure white, and that the cheese that can be seen on the open rindless sides is pale yellow. The scent should be fresh and sweet, not at all strong or ammoniated. With proper handling and refrigeration its life span is three to four weeks, compared to the three or four *days* at which Brie is at its prime. And be sure to leave it at room temperature—not for an hour, but for three or four if possible—before you serve it. Crema Danica, like few other cheeses, is good even when it comes right out of the refrigerator. For this reason it is often eaten too soon. But forbear for a few hours, and this cheese will demonstrate what wonders a little time will work.

Crème Royale

The Danes have also copied their own Crema Danica. This cheese, whose continuing reliability remains to be seen, is called Crème Royale. It is packaged differently, with four smaller cheeses to the box instead of two, but in all other respects it is the same. Probably the future will bring others—for in cheesemaking too, imitation is the sincerest form of flattery.

12

Cheeses from the Monasteries

It was a monk by the name of Dom Perignon who invented champagne when he found a way of bottling sparkling wines without dissipating their effervescence. Before that, it was the monks of Marmoutier in the Touraine who discovered the art of pruning vines—to the lasting benefit not only of French vintners but of the entire world. But the contributions of monks to the world's gustatory pleasures by no means stopped there. In the Middle Ages the best cooking in all of Europe was to be found in the monasteries. The religious of that time were not only expert farmers, tilling and taming the wild lands which they received from the reigning nobility and transforming them into fertile farms and verdant pasturelands; they also developed formulas for liqueurs and cordials, they preserved and indeed developed the regional character of French cuisine, and they gave the world some of its finest cheeses.

In doing so they ushered in a new era—practically a revolution—in cheesemaking. Until then, cheeses had evolved through the ages into three or four basic types: first came the simple fresh cheeses, made in small quantities from day to day and eaten as they were made.

Then cheeses were pressed to enhance their keeping qualities, and they acquired different and distinctive tastes, partly as a result of the conditions under which they were aged, partly because of the ways they were made and the richness or thinness of the milk that was put into them. This gave us the Cheddar types, and even harder cheeses like the Swiss Sbrinz and Italian Parmesan. A little later came the veined cheeses, which developed, according to folklore, by accident, but in any event by the introduction of a bread mold into the curd.

But until the Middle Ages one great group of cheeses appears not to have been known at all. These were the soft, creamy, rich cheeses—sensuously aromatic—that were the forerunners of the silky Camembert and Brie that were to come still later. Typical of these cheeses are Port-Salut and Pont-l'Évêque, along with a dozen or so others that are similar in their flavor and perfume. The monks had a number of incentives for making such cheeses. So skilled were they in animal husbandry and in the development of pasturage with which to support their animals that they had an abundance of milk to divert to something else. Secondly, they had time—time to experiment with various curds and cultures, and time to await their leisurely development into cheeses. And as many of the monasteries were built of stone, they had excellent cool cellars for curing and storage.

In making cheese it is fundamental that the cheesemaker must remember what he did to achieve a certain effect, in order to repeat it a second time—for cheesemakers recognize that it is not so important (even if it were possible) to understand *why* something happens, as to know *what* they did to make it happen. On this score the monks had another great natural advantage, since they were almost instinctive preservers of knowledge and, as a group, exceptional teachers. Much of what they discovered about making the new cheeses would have been lost to the world had they not been willing to share their learning. And though everything monks make is touted as having been made by "a secret formula," it is more reasonable to think that many of them withheld nothing in their teachings—which included all the ramifications of gastronomy as well as the more exact disciplines. As Waverly Root points out, entire nations are indebted to them for much of their cuisine:

Toward the end of the Merovingian era, say about A.D. 750, cooking, like learning, took refuge in the convents and monasteries, the only places where you could find a book or a decent meal, a fact that accounts for the stock characters of the jolly friars and rollicking abbesses. The monasteries raised their own grapes and made their own wine. They brewed their own beer; many of them still do. We of the Lighter Ages still follow a meal with Benedictine and Chartreuse without stopping to consider the meaning of those names. When the fallow period was over, literature emerged from the monasteries, and so did cooking. No international ecclesiastic flavor had been added. From the cloisters of each country the cuisine proper to that country came forth.

There are also notable examples of individuals—like Grimod de la Reynière, more commonly known as Grimod, whose *Almanach des Gourmands* is one of the classics of gastronomic literature—for whom monasteries served virtually as finishing schools in the art of eating.

Among the Benedictines (a religious order which, unlike others, had no severe restrictions on the kinds of food they could eat), many monks in the more prosperous abbeys had extremely sophisticated palates. They were accustomed to rich and luxurious food and had formidable appetites. But even the Benedictines had a certain number of so-called fast days that had to be got through, when they were denied meat and sought for something more interesting than a diet of vegetables or eggs. We know that they were superb cooks, and many of those who never entered the kitchen directed the orchestra, so to speak, from the refectory. For just as intelligent critics play a role in bringing out the best in artists, many of the Benedictines, accustomed as they were to the best of everything, made most exacting demands of their cooks. One of the most engaging commentaries on their ability to make do—to make the unforbidden fruits as tempting as the forbidden ones—is that of M. F. K. Fisher:

Helped by a hundred fast-days, whose strict observance would have reduced every priest in Europe to a stringy skeleton, the plump brothers spent much time and thought on making delicious dishes appear frugal.

The best ecclesiastical brains on the continent studied the egg, and discovered the formulae for making it appear on Lenten boards as a rose, a cabbage, or a roasted duck. And roasted ducks, and kids and pigs and even tender bulls, were made to look like nothing that ever breathed and walked about under the All-Seeing Eye. Juices dropped from every convent spit, and were metamorphosed into the best of all disguises, sauces infinitely elaborate.

This, she writes, is how "abstinence begot kitchen trickery and good eating survived with holy blessings. . . ." On all those days of abstinence, we may be sure that the monks' cheeses, rich as any venison or partridge, were brought forth—and because they were so good, on the other days as well.

There is no way of knowing whether great cooks and kitchen masters make great cheesemakers or vice versa, for greatness in either calling leads to concentration upon it. But it is fair to assume that knowing how to cook—and how to eat—probably gave the monks a head start in knowing how to make good cheese.

The two that most perfectly typify the kind of cheese they made are Port-Salut and Pont-l'Évêque (whose names mean Port of Salvation and Bishop's Bridge, respectively). And there are a host of other cheeses, some of them bearing saints' names (St. Paulin, St. Nectaire, St. Rémy), and others with names that have a religious association, such as Abbaye de Citeaux and Curé. Though most of these cheeses were invented in monasteries, what really links them is a particular taste—and a corresponding aroma—which is stronger and more pervasive than that of Camembert or Brie, but not aromatic to the point of being smelly. Neither mild nor ultra-strong, these cheeses are somewhere subtly in between.

There are also a few cheeses that happen to have been invented in monasteries but whose flavor is not typical of cheeses the monks usually made. One is the Tête de Moine, or Bellelay, that originated in the Abbey of Bellelay near Moutiers in the Bernese Jura. This cheese, which is not imported here, is decidedly milder than most other monastery cheeses. Another example is the light, sour Wensleydale that was invented by monks in England. In flavor it is similar to Cheddar, and it is discussed in Chapter 9. Still another is sapsago, the sage-green, clover-flavored cheese that was invented by some Irish monks in Switzerland. But since sapsago is essentially a condiment cheese that gets its odd flavor from the admixture of herbs, it is treated in Chapter 16. It is not one of the worldly monastic cheeses that we shall move on to now.

PORT-SALUT

Surely one of the greatest of these—and one that is still being made with variations in some Trappist monasteries—is the yellow, creamy Port-Salut, a cheese as soft in texture as Bel Paese, but decidedly more robust in taste. It represents the perfect meeting place between the buttery cheeses and those whose strength is almost electrifying.

There is a good deal of understandable confusion about the relationship between Port-Salut, Port-du-Salut and St. Paulin, and many people use the names interchangeably. Perhaps we can clarify the confusion by telling how Port-Salut came into being and what later happened to it.

Port-Salut first saw the light of day at the Trappist monastery in the commune at Entrammes, a few miles from the small town of Laval in the Mayenne department. In 1233 this became the site of a priory of monks of St. Geneviève, who were driven out during the French Revolution. In 1815 the old priory was given as a place of asylum to a group of Trappist monks who had just returned from exile, and in honor of that event the priory was renamed the Abbey of Notre Dame de Port du Salut. The time these monks passed in exile had not been lost, for it had been spent in the Swiss Alps where they had had ample opportunity to observe the making of Gruyère and Emmenthal.

They started out with twelve cows, whose milk they used in making cheeses for their own consumption. After a few years, the size of the herd increased and they were able to make enough cheese to sell some of it to neighbors and to visitors at the Abbey. In 1850 they enlarged their dairy, and within a few years the demand for their Port-du-Salut cheese had grown so that they had to buy additional milk from neighboring farmers.

Port-du-Salut made its debut in Paris in 1873. An old manuscript at the abbey gives this account of it:

> The Reverend Father Dom Henri left Port-du-Salut on September 10th, 1873, to attend an Ecclesiastical Conference. In Paris he stopped at the house of M. Mauget, 13 rue Cardinal Lemoine, and with this worthy merchant he was able to place his confidence. M. Mauget was entrusted with the selling of our cheese at a low price to bring us in a modest profit. Three times a week we sent up supplies, and a certain vogue for these cheeses started and everyone rushed to buy them. So much so that as soon as the cheeses reached M. Mauget, he put up a sign saying "cheeses arrived" and instantly all the customers flocked to buy, so that in less than an hour it was all sold.

In 1878, the name was registered as Port-du-Salut in order to protect it against infringement. In 1909 a commercial cheesemaker, impressed with the quality of the monks' cheese, entered into a business agreement with the Trappists of Entrammes in which they gave him the right to manufacture it and even sent a few monks to his creamery to oversee its making. The monks then withdrew from direct participation in the manufacture, but the cheese had made its name—as well as its fortunes—and other makers approximated the formula and appropriated the name as well.

Port-Salut is simply a contraction of Port-du-Salut, and French cheeses known by either name are the same. According to a court settlement in 1936, the Trappists claim sole legal right to the use of both names. Some cheeses made under other auspices in France still call themselves Port-Salut nevertheless. But the only French Port-Salut (or Port-du-Salut) that may be shipped into the United States is the "authentic" one—the cheese made by the commercial manufacturers to whom the Trappists subsequently sold the rights. This is the only brand of Port-Salut we are likely to see here, and its name is Abbey.

The flavor of Port-Salut varies tremendously with its age, so that at its various stages it is several different cheeses. At the strong end of the spectrum it is authoritative and as far removed from its younger self as deep yellow turnips are from summer squash; and Port-Salut at full strength may not be for you.

Port-Salut may be so mild that it closely resembles the bland and buttery cheeses. The miniature Port-Salut weighing only about five or six ounces (normally Port-Salut comes in rounds weighing about six pounds) imported into the United States under the Abbey brand is so mild as to be almost tasteless. Its makers recognize this fault, however, and are working to overcome it. From what Edward Bunyard wrote of the genus Port-Salut it appears that the very mild kind was the only type he knew. For he described it as "a round, firm-skinned, rather dreamy cheese . . . a maidenly cheese, tender and delicate, a thousand leagues from the Rabelaisian Roquefort, nearest in character, perhaps, to the Bel Paese of Italy. A little gelatinous in texture and Dutch in flavor, it will offend none and please some, but it is a little too idyllic for my taste."

"A very subtle cheese," adds Hilaire Belloc. And by and large, the French Port-Salut we import into the United States is on the mild side. It is an eminently agreeable cheese, creamy though firm, and never, however mild, without a little edge that sets it apart from the bland cheeses. The French Port-Salut is also quite dependable, largely because it is still far from fully ripened when it reaches here, and since it is relatively slow-ripening it thus enjoys a long prime—a prime ten times longer than that of Camembert or Brie. It has a long way to go before it can become overripe.

DANISH PORT-SALUT

Danish Port-Salut, of which we import a good deal, is another matter. Many stores stock it, and the leading brand by far is Esrom—a name by now so familiar that the cheese is often identified as Esrom rather than Port-Salut. It comes in a long, almost oval loaf weighing four or five pounds and is stocked by many stores that do not carry the French Port-Salut, which costs approximately twice as much. Danish Port-Salut is also sold in small, individually wrapped blocks, which can often be found in supermarkets.

Danish and French Port-Salut, though related, are different cheeses. The French, if it is typically on the mild side, is a fine, mellow and indeed subtle cheese, by far the safer cheese to serve to guests if you are not sure of their tastes. If it is served for dessert (it goes very well with port, and the fuller-bodied red table wines), it will blend with any sweets or fruits you may serve with it. Danish Port-Salut, on the other hand, is decidedly stronger. It has an earthy quality, and if you are not careful about choosing it, it may be too strong. But it is a splendid cheese, and the difference between it and the French is comparable to the difference between steak and veal. But why choose between them when we can have both? Still, if we *had* to choose, it would be the Danish Port-Salut, whose flavor gives more of a run for your money.

If you buy the individual package, be sure you buy it in a store that appears to have a good turnover. The wrappings should be fresh, never sticky, and the cheese mild-smelling while it is still cold. It is always safest to buy it in bulk, because then you can sample it first.

AMERICAN PORT-SALUT

The United States makes a good deal of Port-Salut, principally in Wisconsin. Ours tends to be milder and a little less unctuous than the Danish, but it is closer to the Danish in flavor than it is to the French. This also comes in long loaves for sale by the piece—it is not sold in individual packings so far as we know—and the best brand we have come upon is Lion Brand from Wisconsin—an excellent, excellent cheese.

St. Paulin

St. Paulin is almost identical to French Port-Salut, though the name is not controlled by one maker, and therefore the quality may be uneven. And the name is different only because many cheese-makers in France (both lay and religious) hesitated to use the name of Port-du-Salut *or* Port-Salut for fear of possible legal complications.

Providence

Another, even closer-to-the-original version of Port-Salut, made by the monks of the monastery of Bricquebec in Normandy, is named Providence in the interests of brotherly peace.

Tilsit

Very close in flavor to Danish Port-Salut is Tilsit, a German cheese (also made in Switzerland) that has been around for a long time, but which for some reason is not much in evidence these days. It does turn up in some specialty cheese stores and in German and Swiss restaurants. It is a typical Port-Salut type—on the sharp side, firmer than either French or Danish Port-Salut, and well punctured with tiny holes. We also make a Tilsit in the United States that is milder than the original, and rather like a well-aged American Munster or a young brick cheese in flavor.

Oka

One of the most delicious of all the cheeses of the Port-Salut type is no more—at least for the time being. This is the Canadian Oka, made by Trappist monks, who suspended all commercial cheese operations in 1964 because they had to give up their property. It is rumored that they may set up business again at some future time. Meanwhile, most stores that sold Oka are now offering another

Canadian cheese called Anfrom which is supposed to be "just as good" but isn't. Anfrom is very shallow in its flavor—and its flavor seems to glance off the palate, leaving bitterness behind.

PONT-L'ÉVÊQUE

On the list of France's most important cheeses, Pont-l'Évêque is a mere fourth from the top, the first three being Roquefort, Brie and Camembert—and like Brie and Camembert it is difficult to find in its perfect state, but much too good ever to give up searching for.

It is a cheese of respectable antiquity, dating back at least to the thirteenth century under its own name, and even earlier under another. For in a document dated 1230, Guillaume de Lorris, author of the *Roman de la Rose,* speaks of a cheese then called *Angelot* (which even then was regarded as ancient) and which later came to be called Pont-l'Évêque.

Pont-l'Évêque, which preceded Camembert by several hundred years, is made in the same vicinity—the Pays d'Auge district of Normandy, in which the small crossroads town of Pont-l'Évêque is to the north, and Camembert to the south. Camembert undoubtedly bears some lineal relationship to Pont-l'Évêque for they have a certain flavor in common, a flavor decidedly more assertive in Pont-l'Évêque, which of the two cheeses "is the less romantic," says Edward Bunyard; "it is more apt to dry into a horny cake than run into tears."

A perfect Pont-l'Évêque is a beautiful sight to see. This small, plump, square cheese (it weighs about seven ounces) is the color of golden bantam corn in mid-August; serrated and cross-hatched by the mats of rye straw on which it has lain, the soft crust, like corn, rises into plump golden beads.

The cheese inside is a paler yellow, with countless tiny glistening holes throughout. No cheese could be more French. It is soft, and though it does not run, it may nevertheless so cling to the knife as it is withdrawn that it may remain bound to the blade by a soft, taffylike string. Left at room temperature for a number of hours, its eyes will tend to fill up.

Pont-l'Évêque has a deep, sonorous flavor which is by no means as outlandish as its scented rind may suggest. Edward Bunyard declared Pont-l'Évêque "a cheese quite by itself and in my view the best of the small French cheeses." Certainly it is one of the most satisfying.

FINDING A GOOD PONT-L'ÉVÊQUE

None of us today can simply run down to the cellar and pick a Pont-l'Évêque that is perfectly ripe, exactly at its prime, as we can be confident its makers did. In fact it is a matter of great good luck to find one in the stores—not in France, but here—that is at that ideal stage. If a Pont-l'Évêque is unsatisfactory, it is most likely to be because it is overripe, and that fault at least is very easy to detect. For when it is overripe, the skin—sometimes indeed the entire cheese—becomes hard and rough. Its paper clings to it, and the ooze between the paper and the cheese congeals and darkens into angry splotches. More often than not the Pont-l'Évêque you see in American shops looks this way, or gives every evidence of moving in that direction. And somebody must buy it. For if the many Pont-l'Évêques and other cheeses displayed in this sad condition eventually had to be thrown away by the shopkeepers, they would soon stop keeping them. To be good, Pont-l'Évêque should look good—plump, golden, as pleasing to the eye as it is soft to the touch. Even so, you may occasionally get a Pont-l'Évêque that looks beautiful in its wrappings and also when it is cut into—and whose aftertaste is curiously bitter, instead of sweet as it should be. Unfortunately we know of no way to detect this condition in advance.

Pont-l'Évêque, like most cheeses of this type, goes particularly well with any sturdy, full-bodied red table wine. A jug of fresh cider is also a perfect companion for it. This is not surprising, for Pont-l'Évêque comes from Calvados, the heart of France's apple country. And if Pont-l'Évêque is good with cider, it is also good with Calvados, or some other applejack. At its best in autumn and winter, Pont-l'Évêque is a unique cheese in every sense of the word, for it has never been imitated with any success.

MAROILLES

Maroilles (or Marolles) is only rarely found in the United States, and then it is often so ripe that it clearly belongs with the ultra-strong cheeses, with which it is discussed in Chapter 15. But before it achieves its full strength, Maroilles is like a somewhat more pungent version of Danish Port-Salut. A square cheese resembling Pont-l'Évêque, only larger, Maroilles was first made around A.D. 960 by monks at the abbey of Thiérache and it takes its name from a village in the Avesnes district.

OTHER MOUNTAIN CHEESES

REBLOCHON

Reblochon is, without doubt, one of the most satisfactory of all cheeses. It has been made for hundreds of years in the mountains of the Haute Savoie from what the natives call the "hard milk of the Alps"—a milk of exceptional character provided by the cocoa-colored Tarentais cow. Reblochon means "second milking," and the name derives from the early practice of making the cheese from the day's second yield. It is round and flat, soft—though not so soft as Camembert or Pont-l'Évêque. The outer skin may range from reddish chestnut color to deep orange, and the cheese within is a pale cream. Reblochon comes in two sizes: a small round about five inches across and an inch and a half high, and a larger cheese of almost the same thickness and about eight inches across. Reblochon should not be too old, because like the other cheeses in this group it turns bitter. But at its prime the flavor is beautiful.

BEAUMONT

Another mountain cheese that is very good, though not quite on a par with Reblochon, is Beaumont, also made in the Haute Savoie. It, too, has a bright orange rind, a light paste not unlike that of Reblochon but mellowing to a light beige with age. A large cheese, it is usually sold by the piece. Girod is the brand we see most of here, with the name Beaumont printed in blue on the paper that adheres closely to its rind. When ripe, Beaumont has a decidedly rustic—which is to say barnyardy—flavor, though when young it may be so pallid as to be indistinguishable from the mild, buttery cheeses.

TOMME DE SAVOIE

The word *tomme*—which is also spelled *tome* and *tamie*—simply means "cheese" in the local dialect of the Haute Savoie, and the tomme we most frequently encounter here, and which belongs with the monastic cheeses, is Tomme de Savoie. This too has a reddish rind and light flesh, and its flavor is somewhere between that of an American Munster at its best and Danish Port-Salut. For those in search of a good substitute for the vanished Oka and who agree that Anfrom is not good enough, we recommend Tomme de Savoie—or St. Nectaire, which follows.

ST. NECTAIRE

St. Nectaire is one of the finest cheeses of the Auvergne, and it has been made since the Middle Ages throughout the vicinity of Mont d'Or, Mont Sancy and the mountains of Cantal. Like Reblochon, it is made from the milk of Tarentais cows and also of Salers cows, both of which André Simon called "the aristocrats of milk-givers." This uncommonly rich milk, perfumed by the grasses of the Auvergne, makes a cheese of exceptional flavor after it has had a leisurely period of maturation in the cool, deep cellars of the district, where it develops a bright red-white-and-yellow crust. St. Nectaire and the other mountain cheeses that are closer in character to Port-Salut than to the Alpine Emmenthal and Gruyère have nevertheless just enough of the Swiss lightness to combine well with dry white wines and rosés, as well as with the more full-bodied red table wines.

LESSER-KNOWN MONASTIC CHEESES

Although cheeses of this type are made in Canada, the United States, Denmark, and other parts of the world, most of them are French, because it was in France that the cheesemaking monks established and left enduring traditions. Their legacy will not have been fully explored without mention of three other monastic cheeses: Curé Nantais, made in Brittany, and St. Rémy, from the Vosges valley, both strong cheeses, rather like Pont-l'Évêque but often stronger (and not imported here); and Grand Murols from the Auvergne, which has only recently become available in the United States. Grand Murols, when you can find it, is very good. It is firm, and the flavor suggests how a French Port-Salut might taste if it were aged longer. It has a reddish, smooth skin and in shape resembles a French raised doughnut, complete with hole.

KERNHEM

The last in this group is a Dutch cheese that is distinctly monastic in its flavor. This is Kernhem, a new cheese developed only five or six years ago, which can take its place with the old ones, including some of the best, for Kernhem is smooth and full-bodied, a cheese the monks themselves would have been proud of.

13

The Blue-Veined Cheeses

Their beginnings could not have been more humble, nor their history more distinguished. If one were to trace the genealogy of the foods most prized by gourmets today, none—not even the truffle which must be mined by pigs before it can be eaten by princes—originated in such barrenness and came to be associated with such bounty as that group of cheeses which are the bluebloods of all *fromagerie:* the great blue-veined cheeses, of which there are now more than fifty varieties.

The oldest blue cheese of all, Roquefort, came into being centuries ago on the limestone wastelands of the Causses in Aveyron—a land too barren to be cultivated or used for the grazing of any animal less durable than the sheep, which can go for days without water, endure extremes of climate, and search out, as few animals can, such short grasses and herbs as tuft the Causses' stony floor. Yet Roquefort would never have come into being in a less harsh and barren land, for it owes its unique character to sheep's milk and to the limestone caves in which it is ripened. While many of the blue-veined cheeses that came later were "invented" by people who had never heard of Roquefort, others represent deliberate attempts to duplicate or at least imitate some of its excellences. But each is different in its own way—as indeed all cheeses must differ, if they are made in different places. Often the differences seem so subtle that only a connoisseur could tell one from another. Indeed many of them, like minor characters in a Russian novel, are impossible to keep straight unless you know their relationship to the major ones—in this case, Roquefort, Stilton, and Gorgonzola, the models for most blues. However, as you try different blues, the distinctions become apparent. Thanks to our enterprising cheese importers, we are having more and more opportunity to do so, as they vie for the honor (not without profit) of introducing new cheeses to the United States. Thus the Septmoncel that today you can sample only on location may be on its way here tomorrow; and the Yorkshire-Stilton that is ripening at this moment in Cotherstone may finish its days in Cos Cob—because so many Americans returning from abroad are creating a demand for the cheeses they discovered in their travels.

FRENCH BLUE CHEESES

ROQUEFORT

According to legend, Roquefort was discovered centuries ago—possibly before the Christian era (for Roquefort was known to Pliny, who wrote of it as "the cheese that bears away the prize at Rome, where they are always ready to compare and to appreciate good things from every land"). The legend has it that a shepherd boy in the rocky country of the Causses left his lunch of bread and ordinary curd cheese in one of the cool caves of the district, thinking to come back for it later in the day. But it was weeks before he returned to find his abandoned lunch. Then, with the morbid curiosity of those who cannot throw anything away without peeking first, he looked, he smelled, and then he tasted. At which there may well have followed one of the greatest *Aha's* in gastronomic history. In any event, thousands upon thousands of Roqueforts have since been made by inoculating the cheese curd, made from sheep's milk, with *Penicillium roqueforti*—a mold-producing substance made from rye breadcrumbs—and ripening it in the damp, cool, drafty limestone caves that are peculiar to the district. Other blue cheeses may be made with sheep's, goat's, or cow's milk—chiefly the latter—or a mixture of all three, and ripened in a variety of ways, but the use of the mold-producing penicillium is almost universal. And since 1411 when Charles VI issued a decree restricting the name Roquefort to the cheese made in the Roquefort district of the Causses, no other "bastard cheese made in bastard caves" (as the people of Roquefort jealously referred to their competitors' products) could be called Roquefort.

To all cheesemakers, these caves are one of the natural wonders of the world, and it is their unusual formation and mineral composition that so largely account for the unique flavor of Roquefort. Like other wonders they have been described many times, but Osbert Burdett gives the clearest picture:

> These caverns end in a natural cleft which communicates, like a chimney, with the open air. As this upper air is cooler than that in the caves, presumably from the presence of hot springs in the rock, a current of air, humid and cool, is available in these naturally warm cellars which enables the cheeses to ripen without evaporation and shrinking. So valuable have these natural conditions proved that, when the fame of Roquefort had nursed a great industry for export, vast cellars, often several floors deep, were excavated and tunnels made to the ventilating shaft, to multiply the advantages of the caverns. With Roquefort, in sum, the conditions for ripening are more important than the method of making the curd.

It is these caves that make the difference, that are the reason Roquefort—probably the most imitated cheese in the world—has never been duplicated.

Next in importance is the sheep's milk from which it is made. As Waverly Root points out, "Almost alone of modern cheeses it is made of sheep's milk. There are a number of French cheeses which formerly used sheep's milk but most of them have shifted to cow's milk in these hurried times, for reasons that will be clear to anyone who has ever tried to milk a sheep." And even if it were easier to milk a sheep it is doubtful that much of the milk would go into other cheeses, for almost all of France's sheep's milk is earmarked for Roquefort, and the demand for it far exceeds the supply.

Roquefort is made in Roquefort-sur-Sulzon in the province of Rouergue, a little town of fewer than 2,000 inhabitants and of a size that could not possibly be expected to yield all the milk needed to make the 25,000,000 pounds of Roquefort produced there annually. This milk comes from surrounding areas strictly designated by law, which extend well up into the Auvergne and south into the Pyrenees. A more distant but important source for Roquefort milk is Corsica, which, like the other suppliers, converts the milk to curd, inoculates it with the mold, and after it has "worked" for a week or so, ships the unripened cheeses to Roquefort for aging in its incomparable limestone caves.

The resultant cheese, with its incomparable flavor, has been prized for centuries. In France they tell a story about a certain Gascon who was delighted to see a whole Roquefort set before him at the table. He asked his host, "Where shall I broach it?" "Why," said his host "anywhere you please." "In that case," replied the ruthless guest, "I'll broach it at home." And he signaled his valet to bear off the cheese.

A more princely response to Roquefort is attributed to Charlemagne. According to the annals of the monks of St. Gall, Charlemagne, while an overnight guest at their monastery, was found picking the blue-green bits out of the cheese he had been served for his dinner (because it was a Friday and the monks had no fish to offer him). The monks protested that he was wasting the best part, whereupon the King tasted it as it was meant to be eaten and pronounced it excellent. In fact, he was so taken with it that he commanded two *caisses* of the cheese to be delivered each year to his palace at Aix-la-Chapelle. He further designated that each cheese be cut open before it was sent, to make sure that the blue veins were there in quantity, after which they were to be bound together with wood fastenings and dispatched to him. Let us hope that the monks were able to time the deliveries for arrival between November and May, which are the prime months for almost all blue-veined cheeses.

The blue veining—also called *persillé,* which suggests the resemblance between parsley and the tiny flowerets of blue mold with its threadlike stems—this delicate marbling that Charlemagne came to admire so much is common to all blue cheeses but somehow is at its best in Roquefort. In fact, no cheese on earth can surpass a really fine Roquefort, ripened and seasoned just as it should be—and as it almost always is when you eat it in France.

In writing of its "pleasant prickly flavor," Osbert Burdett gets to the essence of this cheese—as does Bunyard in referring to "the tingling Rabelaisian pungency of Roquefort"—for it does indeed have the tingle of champagne bubbles to the tongue, and the same refreshing piquancy. It is effervescent, almost, and it would be redundant to serve Roquefort with a sparkling wine. It is at its best with a fine claret, but it will enhance the flavor of almost any wine. Indeed, as Edward Bunyard reports, "it is said that wine buyers [i.e., tasters] are not allowed in their contracts to use this cheese to cleanse the palate, so flattering is it to the meanest of wines."

Unfortunately, we don't invariably get perfect Roquefort here, because Roquefort that is exported is salted more liberally than that made for French consumption—possibly as a means of prolonging its life for travel—and as a result those we get here are extremely uneven. Often they are much too salty; sometimes they are only a little too salty, which can be corrected by serving with unsalted biscuit or mixing with some sweet butter; and once in a while you come upon a Roquefort that is perfect. These variations make it essential to sample Roquefort before you buy—because the appearance gives no clue whatever to the taste. Once you have tasted a perfect Roquefort you will be inclined to sample it whenever you see it, just in the hcpe of repeating the experience. One taste of a really good Roquefort explains why it has been so widely recognized as the King of Cheeses. It may be your impression, as it was once ours, that Roquefort, though indeed an excellent cheese, doesn't merit the superlatives heaped upon it. If so, we urge you to sample more of it until you find one that is at its best. When you are in France, make room for Roquefort among the unfamiliar and exotic cheeses you may be trying, for it is almost unfailingly good there, even in the most modest bistro.

BLEU DE BRESSE

Among other important French blues that have become rather widely available here are Bleu de Bresse, a rich, darkly veined blue made from unskimmed cow's milk, which is distributed in individual packages weighing about a half-pound.

Buying Bleu de Bresse here is a real gamble, for more often than not it is overripe and consequently strong, dry and salty; and because it is prepackaged it is difficult to tell in advance whether a cheese has reached this stage. Therefore we cannot recommend buying it anywhere but in a shop in which you have complete confidence, and even then it may be risky. But this is a cheese you should not fail to eat in France—and it is to be hoped that importers and cheese shops here will eventually take steps to bring cheeses of similar quality here. Bleu de Bresse in France, particularly in the early spring, is a cheese unlike any other: its paste is not a paste at all but has the consistency of a thick cream, like the honey-textured cream within a ripe Brie, and the little lumps of blue are suspended in that cream like nuggets of caviar. It is the softest veined cheese we have ever tasted, and one of the best.

PIPO CREM'

Another blue that can frequently be found in the delicacy shops of large department stores and in gourmet and specialty cheese stores is Pipo Crem', an exquisitely delicate blue that comes in a long, cylindrical form about four inches in diameter. Pipo Crem', which in France is called Grièges, is made at Grièges in the Ain. It is higher in cream content than most other blues, and its body is a very pale yellow as compared with the whiter body of Roquefort and many other blues, probably because of the extra cream. It is very moist, more so than most of the others, and when it is cut into it falls into soft glistening pieces, like outsize curds of cottage cheese. The veining in Pipo Crem' is a light, "true" blue—so delicate that a heavy slice of it looks almost like a piece of Wedgwood in reverse. The cautions that apply to Bleu de Bresse are not necessary here, because Pipo Crem' is sold in bulk, which means that you can see and taste it before you buy.

Pipo Crem' is almost certain to appeal to anyone who does not insist that every blue cheese have the sharp bite of Roquefort or the pungency of Gorgonzola. It will also appeal to lovers of mild cheeses who have found other blues a bit too tingly. For Pipo Crem' has something reminiscent of the uncured double-crèmes—seasoned, but most delicately, by its azure mold.

OTHER FRENCH BLUES

A decidedly sharper blue is Fourme d'Ambert (sometimes called Fourme de Cantal for the place where it is made), another cylinder-shaped blue cheese several inches larger in diameter than Bleu de Bresse, which is rather salty, densely veined, and as crumbly as shortbread.

Another sharp blue is Saingorlon, which represents France's attempt to imitate Gorgonzola. Like Gorgonzola, it is creamy and its veins are greenish rather than blue, and it is very good—but it is not Gorgonzola. This cheese has not been imported here yet.

Another, and splendid, French blue that does turn up from time to time is Bleu d'Auvergne (or Bleu de Salers), which is made in the Auvergne department, not far from the home of the Roquefort which it is intended to approximate. It is made exclusively with cow's milk, which may account for its being less piquant than Roquefort, though superb in its own way. Its size and shape are the same as Roquefort's.

Still other French blues that you are more likely to encounter in Europe than here, but which are worth investigating wherever you find them, include: Septmoncel and Bleu du Haut-Jura (Jura department), Sassenage (Isère), Bleu de Basillac (Limousin), Mont Cenis (Mont Cenis region in southeastern France), Bleu des Causses (central France), Persille de Savoie (Savoie), Bleu de l'Aveyron (Aveyron), Bleu de Laqueuille (Puy-de-Dôme), Olivet (Loiret), Tignard (Tigne Valley, Savoie), Laguiole or Guiole (Aveyron), and the delicately veined Gex (Ain department), which P. Morton Shand likened to fine Cippolino marble, and which some British cheese connoisseurs prize even above Stilton.

ENGLISH BLUE CHEESES

STILTON

Stilton is one of the great cheeses of the world. "Roquefort, from the English point of view, is Stilton without a college education," wrote Bunyard. "There are, of course, those who prefer other cheeses but we wait with a serene confidence for the day when they shall see the error of their ways." And again, "Stilton: the noble word comes as easily to an Englishman's tongue as the word Shakespeare, and a touch of pride accompanies both."

Burdett adds, "Stilton is happily still strongly entrenched in its native home, and, so long as its quality is maintained, need fear no competition. It survived a generation ago a passing threat from Roquefort. It has no fear of Gorgonzola. The Dutch have tried and failed to imitate it. The original Stilton reigns supreme."

Stilton has been immortalized in the poetry of Pope, the prose of Jane Austen, and the letters of Charles Lamb, who wrote to thank his friend Thomas Allsop in 1823 for a gift of Stilton: "Your cheese is the best I have ever tasted. Mary has sense enough to value the present; for she is very fond of Stilton. Yours is the delicatest, rainbow-hued melting piece I have ever tasted." And John Jay Chapman recalls "a morsel that was like Agincourt. It was sonorous, undying."

To Englishmen, Stilton is appropriate at any meal, and Sir John

Squires, for example, in observing that Stilton needs no accompaniment except bread, added: "The delicacy of crisp celery is permissible with it, particularly if one is making a breakfast of it."

Stiltons are accustomed to receiving a good deal of attention. So much time, skill, and care goes into making them that, as Mrs. Musson of Wartnaby, a dairywoman famous for her cheeses, remarked to Rider Haggard, "Except that they make no noise, Stiltons are more trouble than babies." They have to be turned more often than other cheeses while they are ripening, and at the later ripening stages they have to be brushed each day to keep them free of mites. Of those who do the daily brushings Sir John Squires has said, "The job is one in which a man should take as much pride as a groundsman takes in his wicket at Lord's." And Burdett calls their work "Blessed labour!"

Stilton appears to have come upon the scene in the early part of the eighteenth century, and its discovery is variously attributed to a Mrs. Orton of Little Dalby, a Mrs. Paulet of Wymondham, and a Mrs. Stilton who worked for the fifth Duchess of Rutland in 1800. There is no evidence, in any case, that Stilton cheese was first made at Stilton, but it probably originated somewhere in Huntingdonshire, Leicestershire or Rutland—the three counties which are famous for it—and derives its name from the fact that it was first sold at the Bell Hotel, in Stilton. "You used to see a great pile of them in front of the house," wrote the Reverend T. E. Grillon in *Memory's Harkback* (1889), "and a smart traffic was done with the travelers and coach passengers."

Made of the richest of milk, to which the cream of other milk is added, Stiltons—unlike Roquefort, Gorgonzola, and many other blues that are ripened in cool caves—mature without refrigeration, natural or otherwise—and Stilton is decidedly different in flavor and appearance from the various blue cheeses we have been discussing. It is set apart from all other blues by a distinctive flavor which is a blend of the characteristic blue-veined taste and the clear undertone of Cheddar. Whereas some blues can be almost shrilly pungent, Stilton is mellow. Whereas some are soft with butterfat, Stilton retains, even at warm room temperature, the pebbly consistency of aged Cheddar. Its rind is dark, crusty and wrinkled, and the cheese itself is off-white, deepening almost to amber around the edges. In England Stilton is most commonly eaten with biscuits and port—a classic combination—but if you want the best of two worlds, serve it for dessert with very tart apple pie.

Two widely propagated notions about the preferred way to eat Stilton are (1) that the cheese should be scooped out with a spoon or cheese scoop; (2) that it should then be moistened, or the resulting cavity filled, with port, or possibly beer, to enhance its flavor for the next serving. But the people who make Stilton, and others who prize it, deplore this practice. Osbert Burdett termed it high treason—because the scooping of a Stilton causes good cheese near the rind to be dried out and wasted; and soaking it with spirits is viewed as something of a desecration. "A drenching with Port will mask the faults of an imperfect cheese," declares André Simon, "but there is not a vintage in the world that will improve a good one."

This is true of the mixture of any cheese with wine or spirits. If the flavor of a particular cheese, when mixed with spirits, appeals to you, good enough. Or if you have a leftover piece of blue cheese that you do not expect to eat at once, you can preserve it indefinitely by combining it with an equal amount of sweet butter, dousing it generously with brandy, covering it tightly and refrigerating it. But do not heed the commercial cheese packers who claim to put top-quality cheese into the cheese-and-spirit mixtures that are popularly sold in crocks. For if they do, they are either unscrupulous or as wasteful as the restaurant chain whose advertising boasted that no beef other than prime filet mignon went into its hamburger.

BLUE CHESHIRE

At one time the blue Cheshire was a sport among all blue-veined cheeses. It started out to be ordinary Cheshire but mysteriously developed blue veining as it ripened. Those who tasted this maverick blue insisted that it was blue Cheshire's rich, ripe, unusual flavor that made it so prized—and not the fact that it turned up, like the Scarlet Pimpernel, at its own will. It was once estimated that no more than six Cheshires in a hundred turned blue, but recently there have been successful efforts to induce the blue veining by artificial means, and blue Cheshires are much more in evidence than they once were, although none comes to the United States.

BLUE VINNY

Another curiosity is England's Blue Vinny, which is also known as Blue Dorset for its place of origin, Dorsetshire. This blue cheese is not veined irregularly as are most blues, but instead has a horizontal blue streak, a veritable *cordon bleu*, running through its center. The name "Vinny" is a corruption of the old West Country word *vinew*, which derives from the old English word *fyniz*, meaning "mold." Said to be a favorite of Hardy, this strong, hard, skimmed-milk cheese is by no means for everyone, for it is dry and cakey even when fresh; and because it tends to become grainy very rapidly it has not, to our knowledge, ever been exported. In fact the cheese gets so hard that the people of Sherborne in Dorset say that a train once ran on Blue Vinnys instead of wheels.

BLUE WENSLEYDALE

A cheese that is considered the best of all the blues by some English gourmets is blue Wensleydale, the predecessor of the white Wensleydale which has become widely available in the United States. When they were first developed by Catholic monks in Yorkshire, all Wensleydales were marbled cheeses, but as time went on and cheesemaking became commercialized, the blue Wensleydales, which required more time and care to make, became scarcer and scarcer. They are not imported here and are something of a rarity even in England, but are well worth seeking out. For blue Wensleydale is a rich, double-cream cheese, rather like Stilton but more delicate; and it is particularly esteemed for its creaminess and pleasant aftertaste.

OTHER ENGLISH BLUES

There are two other English blue-veined cheeses worthy of note. One is Cheshire-Stilton—a Stilton in which the characteristic Cheddar undertone comes out loud and clear and of which Vyvyan Holland suggests that "it was no doubt a cheese of this sort, discovered and filched from the larder of the Queen of Hearts, that accounted for the grin on the face of the Cheshire Cat in *Alice in Wonderland.*" Another is Yorkshire-Stilton, or Cotherstone, made in the Valley of the Tees in Yorkshire, which with age develops a succulent internal fat that makes it popular with trenchermen with a taste for heavy stout and well-hung beef.

ITALIAN VEINED CHEESES

GORGONZOLA

The third in the great triumvirate of blue cheeses is Italy's Gorgonzola, which, together with Roquefort and Stilton, has dominated the world of marbled cheeses for centuries.

One of the earliest of all veined cheeses, Gorgonzola was first made in the Po Valley in the ninth century, and is named for a village near Milan. According to local lore, Gorgonzolas were originally uncured and unveined cheeses made by farmers who sold them at a market near the town wineshop. Those who didn't have enough money to pay for their wine used to give the proprietor cheeses instead, and he accumulated so many of them that they had to be stored in the cellar, where they eventually developed a green mold.

Gorgonzola is still being produced in the great curing houses in and around Milan as well as in Novara, Lodi, Codogno, Cuneo, Pavia and Valsassina. It is extremely popular all over the Continent as well as in the United States—we import more of it than any other marbled cheese except Danish blue—and the English have imported so much Gorgonzola over the years that many Englishmen think it is an English cheese. The English are so fond of Gorgonzola that even Bunyard, emphatic as he was about Stilton's supremacy, contradicted himself when he wrote: "Gorgonzola towers above all in world esteem, so robust are its virtues and sturdy its traveling powers." One need not travel to Italy to taste superb Gorgonzola, for the quality of the Gorgonzola we import here is excellent. Superlatively rich and creamy, Italian Gorgonzola has a flavor all its own, which is at the same time frankly reminiscent of Livarot, one of the most seductive of the soft-ripening cheeses. Gorgonzola's characteristic veining, pale green rather than blue, is so diffused as to be instantly recognizable (the nickname "Gorgonzola Hall" for London's Stock Exchange came from the mottled greenish look of its marbled interiors). Of all the veined cheeses, Gorgonzola is the softest and most malleable, and it is without doubt one of the finest cheeses made anywhere in the world today. The original, *Italian* Gorgonzola, that is. We do produce a very good blue-veined cheese that looks like Gorgonzola and bears its name, but tasty and satisfying though it is, somehow the special virtues of this exceptional cheese have managed to elude it.

OTHER ITALIAN VEINED CHEESES

Other noteworthy veined cheeses of Italy include Erbo and Moncenisio, both similar to Gorgonzola. And one of the best is the mild Dolcelatte, so green and delicate that it has been compared to parsley in cream.

THE SCANDINAVIAN BLUES

DANISH BLUES

Denmark went seriously into the business of reproducing French and Italian cheeses during World War I, when exports from these countries were cut off. Since then Danish cheeses—and particularly the blue-veined varieties—have developed enormous world markets, and by far the greatest quantity of blue cheese imported into the country now comes from Denmark.

Danish blue (also known as Danablu) was invented in 1914 by a cheesemaker named Marius Boel, who created the mold on a barley bread which he had baked for that purpose. The fact that it is made from homogenized milk, very rich in cream, accounts for its buttery consistency. Danish blue is so buttery, in fact, that one can tire of it more quickly than of the "leaner" blues such as Roquefort, Norwegian, and our domestic varieties. The flavor is strong and rich, and the pencilings of blue are so legible and liberal throughout that you might think the Danes were out to capture honors in penmanship as well as cheesemaking. These cheeses as they are made in Denmark for local consumption are even more densely veined, and their sharper flavor has the tingle of peppermint, which comes through all the more clearly because these cheeses are lower in cream content than those that are exported. By and large, Danish blue is superior in flavor to our blue cheeses, good as they are; and with only one exception it is also the least expensive of the imported blue cheeses, selling here at about the same price as domestic blue.

Another veined cheese that is very popular in Denmark is Mycella, which is midway between a blue cheese and a Gorgonzola.

NORWEGIAN BLUE

That one exception is Norwegian blue, a dark horse among imports, and at this writing it is one of the best bets in blue-veined cheeses today. It has only recently begun to be widely distributed in this country. Lovely to look at, delightful to eat, the pale Norwegian blue emulates better than any veined cheese in its price range the lean piquancy of Roquefort. It avoids the faintly bitter aftertaste of some of our domestic blues and, though not so creamy as the Danish product, it has more character.

OTHER VEINED CHEESES

Besides all of these, dozens of other blue cheeses are being made in various other parts of the world—some of which occasionally find their way here. The list includes Irish Stilton; Corsican Blue;

Sarrazin and Paglia from Switzerland; Cabrales, a goat's-milk cheese from the mountains of Spain; Eremite and Bluefort from Canada; Queso Blue and Gorgonzola from Argentina; Niva and Czech Blue from Czechoslovakia; Tyrolean Blue from Rastadt; Swedish Blue; and Aura from Finland. There is also a Nazareth Blue from Israel, a South African Blue, and Akyrie Blue from Iceland.

American Veined Cheeses

If we seem to give American blue cheeses short shrift it is because there isn't much to say about them. The United States began trying to reproduce Roquefort around the end of World War I (when first we identified and isolated the *Penicillium roqueforti*) and eventually made acceptable blues from cow's milk, but nothing resembling Roquefort. A few of our blue cheeses are cured in caves—as, for example, the Minnesota blue that ripens in caves of sandstone. This and some of the other domestic blues are good but undistinguished.

Some years ago, at the University of Wisconsin, a marbled cheese was developed by ultraviolet radiation that had white veins instead of blue. The whole cheese was white on white and was named Nuworld. At first, commercial cheesemakers were enthusiastic about Nuworld's possibilities because it seemed to solve a vexing merchandising problem: when Nuworld was used in cheese spreads it made a spread that was pure white instead of grayish, as spreads from ordinary veined cheese always are. And many of the people who object to the dark mold in other veined cheeses could be counted upon to find this cheese aesthetically more appealing. But Nuworld turned out to be very expensive to make and commercial cheesemakers lost interest.

14

The Goat and Sheep Cheeses

THE GOAT CHEESES

Ironically, the poor man's cow produces some of the world's most expensive cheeses. Even in France, which produces more than two thirds of all goat cheeses, they are generally regarded as luxury cheeses. Still, nowhere in the world are the prices of goat cheeses as high as they are in the United States. At this writing the three or four goat cheeses available in New York's most reliable cheese store cost $2.50 or more a pound—and are selling very well.

Just why these essentially rustic cheeses can command such exotic prices may be partly explained by the relative scarcity of goat's milk. Not only are there fewer goats than cows, but the average goat gives only two to three quarts of milk each day, while a cow gives somewhere between ten and twenty. Thereafter things become more complicated—starting with the goats themselves. Goats are erratic milk producers. They are physically sturdy and can survive, even flourish, in grazing lands that would not support a cow, but they are far more sensitive than cows. They do not take kindly to abrupt changes in weather, environment, handling or feeding. Intelligent, high-strung, fastidious (despite the slanders against them), they could hardly be less bovine in temperament, and their immediate reaction to unexpected occurrences, of which there seem to be an uncommon number in a goat's life, is to withhold their milk, thereby adding another few cents to the price of goat cheeses around the world.

But what makes a goat-cheese aficionado pay premium prices? Probably the distinctive flavor, which is immediately discernible even in the youngest cheeses. These tend to look like small blocks or rounds of cream cheese, but they do not taste like cream cheese; the flavor is more akin to dry farmer cheese, but with important differences. Whereas the curdy flavors of our pot and farmer cheeses are bland, tending toward sweetness, the curd of the goat cheese tends to be sour. An even greater difference, however, is the presence of a slight but unmistakable hot pepperlike sting. It is this sting that gives the young cheese its zip and character. And it is this same sting, as the cheese ages, that deepens and, it seems, acidifies, until in a very few months it takes over completely, suffusing the cheese with an ammoniated essence that can leave strong men gasping.

As with all cheese, the younger it is the more innocuous; a chèvre at four weeks has more zing than one five days old (which you will have to go to France to get anyway). But for those who have never tasted *any* goat cheese before, the soundest approach, we think, is to start with the youngest you can find and work your way, step by step, into the maturer cheeses—and as you reach the three-month category, you will also be struck by the humanity of this advice.

Goat Cheeses in France

To the American eye the array of tiny goat cheeses one finds in any good Paris *crémerie* between April and November is a fetching, if misleading, sight.

Side by side the classic goat shapes—the cylinder, the pyramid, the *crème caramel*, the small plump oval—seem to suggest a dessert tray of pastries and puddings. These little cheeses are seldom more than four inches across, and usually smaller. With the exception of the pyramid, they are never more than an inch and a half high.

Some are exquisitely wrapped in chestnut leaves (to keep the cheese moist as long as possible) and tied with a strand of dried grass. Some are rolled in herbs—rosemary, anise, fennel—and some are dusted with the ashes they've been cured in, a disconcerting sight to most Americans, as are the thick strands of straw that frequently appear in the center of some cheeses.

These cheeses will appeal to all who are nostalgic for the homespun and authentic, who feel that we are too removed from nature and have become machine-tooled and mass-produced in everything, including our cheeses. At least the young goats will have such an appeal. The old goats may be another matter, for as we move toward the strong end of the goat-flavor spectrum, few may have the stamina to hang on to the end. Dusty-gray, lavalike and unlovely in appearance, looking more like five hundred years than five months old—hard and brittle in texture, ammoniated in flavor—the mature goat cheese is largely an acquired taste. The fact remains, however, that French connoisseurs not only prefer the aged, acid goat cheeses, but this preference has become a measure of connoisseurship. At the very least the sophisticated French palate will choose the medium-ripened goat cheese about two months old, rather than the fresh. These carry a good deal of authority and are certain to startle the uninitiated American palate—but compared to their seniors they are mild as May.

Of course the connoisseur wasn't born with an ardor for the aged goat cheeses—he probably moved from milder to stronger in easy stages, lingering for a while in the middle ranges, his palate already bored with the very young cheese, until at last he made that ultimate leap.

Notes on a French Goat-Cheese Tasting

Without question a goat-cheese tasting can be numbered among life's memorable experiences—particularly if it covers about fifteen cheeses ranging in age from two weeks to five months and if it takes place in the early morning before one has eaten and while the palate is fresh. Following are some notes on just such a tasting. The time, early autumn; the place, Paris.

Little fresh nameless goat, two or three days old.

Very white. Like an unfried potato cake dipped in flour—or a flat, white dumpling. About the texture of marzipan. Delicate sourish flavor, like a sour cream cheese.

Poivre Ail Vin Blanc, a few days old.

Soft and young, beautifully wrapped in light-green leaves and tied with brown gift-wrap string. Very much like Boursin Fines Herbes and almost as good. A nice little cheese for cocktails.

Poivre d'Âne, three weeks old.

Young, thick, white paste, covered with needlelike herb that has a flavor difficult to place; pleasant and prickly (the name means, literally, "donkey's pepper"). Shaped like a *crème caramel*. Pleasing fresh taste. Those who want to learn to like goats might well start with this one.

Sarriette, three weeks old.

Shaped like a *crème caramel*. Rolled in a fine olive-colored powder that tastes like bitter pepper. A young goat, white, moist, yet firm. So far it has a fresh goat's-milk taste with a bite; but there are already evidences that in time it will become quite disagreeable.

Romarin, three weeks old.

Again, shaped like a *crème caramel*, but this time covered with a powder of what tastes like a finely ground turkey seasoning. Much like Sariette, except for its dustings. Dry, curdy Roquefort-like texture.

Feneuil, three weeks old.

Looks like a Romarin. Yeastlike texture, nice clean white paste. Rolled in powdered fennel and has a definite licorice taste. A nice young goat.

Provence, three weeks old.

Looks very provincial indeed, rather as if it had been dropped in the dust and dung. Rolled in crushed herbs. If you can get past the strong acid smell, the flavor isn't bad.

St. Maure, one month old.

Small cylindrical shape; looks more or less like a rigid manicotti. Gray, ancient, and evil-looking already. Crust about ¼ inch thick around cheese. The crust stings to the taste but has the flavor of a blue cheese about it. Has a tight crumbly body, and flakes as you eat it. Reminiscent of the body and base of Roquefort, but the texture is drier. Good with bread and butter.

Camembert de chèvre, one and a half months old.

Looks like a small, golden-crusted Camembert. Pretty, but it is a goat masquerading as a cow. The crust is typically Camembert, but inside one finds the unyielding, compact paste that is the hallmark of the goat cheese. Definitely tastes like a goat cheese and might as well have kept a goat shape. Very salty.

Crottin de Chavignol, three months old.

Like one of Satan's caramels. Small (1½ inches in diameter and ¾ inch high), hard, wrinkled, looks like an artifact. Not surprising to learn that *crottin* means dropping. Strong prolonged acid aftertaste. Not pleasant.

Berry, three months old.

Sour. Crust: light yellow mixed with pale gray. Like an ossified wrinkled triple-crème. Strong aftertaste with overtones of soap.

Cendre de Vendôme, five months old.

Hard as a rock; flat pancake shape (3½ inches wide by ¾ inch high). Looks like a piece of child's pottery that has just been fired in the kindergarten; all the ashes must be knocked off and this ill-made piece cleaned up before it can be glazed.

Inside looks like a petrified soap eraser. Uncuttable. Tastes like butterscotch and dung.

Chèvre au Marc, three months old.

Cylindrical and wrapped in an autumnal green leaf turned brown in places. A piece of stiff straw runs lengthwise through the center of the cheese as if to keep it in shape. Hard caramel texture to cut through. A definite acid butterscotch flavor. Flaky and dry.

Le Pouligny, age unknown, but clearly not young.

Pyramid shape, a good 4 inches tall, heavy gray crust mottled with white. Flesh near the crust is very gray and heavy. Gets whiter as you go deeper into the cheese. Very salty.

Dieux. Old.

Small, flat; petrified inside. Discolored: rust against greenish white. Intense acid smell. Couldn't bring ourselves to taste it.

Sancerre. Old.

Strong, acid smell, hard disagreeable crust. Didn't taste.

Rocamadour. Old.

Looks like a small, flat, lightly fried croquette. So acid it was necessary to spit out the bread used to clear the palate.

Young Cows Disguised as Goats

The French government is harsh on those who try to sell a cow's-milk cheese under the pretext that it is the higher-priced goat cheese. However, there is no law against making a cow's-milk cheese in the shape of a goat cheese. Although many of these are labeled, they still look like goat cheeses and through some alchemy of manufacture also manage to taste like them. Here are notes on two of them:

Romans Vache, eight days old.

Covered with long, brownish-green, needlelike herbs, pleasant and prickly to bite down on. Similar to Poivre d'Âne.

Definitely a goat flavor. Tight yeasty-white body, sour paste, sharp clean sour taste, quite pleasant. Shape and size of a pancake Camembert. A very sour creamy cheese.

Piment, ten days old.

Round, flat and small, wrapped in pale-green leaves and tied with dark-green strings. Very soft. Looks like farmer cheese with paprika on it, but the paprika turns out to be extremely hot pepper. A good cheese, very sour, very fresh and curdy, soft and moist. Slight banana taste.

The Better-Known Varieties

Goat cheeses are made in many parts of France, but most of them are made in the west-central area, in particular in the departments of Deux-Sevres, Indre-et-Loire, Vienne, Charente, and also in the Indre and Chèr. The best-known goat cheeses are the three pyramids: Levroux, Pouligny Saint Pierre and Valençay; the cylindrical St. Maure; the plump oval Selles-sur-Chèr; and the well-named little Crottin de Chavignol.

Other goat cheeses well known in France and among cheese connoisseurs throughout the world are La Mothe-Sainte-Héraye, Chabichou and Jumeaux from the Poitou area; Le Cabecou from Béarn; Rocamadour from the Causse Mountains; Le Pelardon from the Roquefort area; Le Banon, Le Poivre d'Âne and St. Marcellin from Provence; Le Roman from the Dauphine; Le Chevrotin and La Tomme de Praslin from Savoie; Rigotte de Condrieu and Chevroton from the Lyonnais district; and Le Thoissey from Bresse.

Some of the more expensive *crémeries* in Paris receive these cheeses and many more. But even they do not receive them all. Like wines, many of them are local cheeses and if you want them you must go where they are. But many of the best do in fact, find their way to Paris. When the mayor of St. Maure gives an important civic dinner, for example, he does not obtain his St. Maure cheese locally, but instead orders it from the fashionable cheese shop Créplet-Brussol on the Place de la Madeleine.

GOAT CHEESES YOU CAN BUY IN THE UNITED STATES

By and large, we get only the young goat cheeses here in the United States. They usually go by the generic name of *chèvre*, and are between two and four weeks old—that is, relatively fresh. Some stores, especially those with a substantial French clientele, carry particular cheeses which have established reputations for excellence—such as, for example, Valençay. Valençay comes in a pyramid, usually weighs about nine ounces and costs about $1.75. One New York cheese store has commissioned the Valençay makers in the department of Indre to make it in four-pound pyramids.

Another frequently found here, in the stores that carry goat cheeses, is Le Banon, a little round cheese about four to four and a half ounces in weight. Le Banon comes from Provence, and it is first dried in leaves and then dipped in a blend of brandy and marc, a spirit distilled from the husks of grapes after the wine has been made. Finally it is wrapped in chestnut leaves which have also been dipped into the brandy.

Then there is St. Marcellin, which, though it is almost never made entirely of goat's milk these days but of a mixture of cow's and goat's milk, nevertheless retains a goaty taste. In this country St. Marcellin is often sold as "100% goat cheese," though not by reputable cheese stores. St. Marcellin is soft and creamy, and in France it is about three quarters of an inch high and two inches in diameter. Here you will often see it larger—about six inches in diameter and two inches high. At the urging of American importers, the French are increasingly tailoring their cheeses to American cheese-dealers' needs; and the dealers seem to feel that it is easier and more profitable to sell cuts from a larger cheese than to sell individual small ones. Some shops also carry the small St. Marcellin sprinkled with pepper or covered with the herb *sarriette*. In each instance, however, the St. Marcellin takes on the flavor of the additional ingredient and becomes a rather different cheese.

Chabichou can also be found in some stores here. It is cylindrical in shape, about two and a half inches across, two inches high, and it weighs about three and a half ounces.

Goat Cheeses from Other Countries

Goat cheeses are produced in a number of other countries besides France, but they rarely reach these shores. They include Belarno, Fontini and Caprian from Italy; Bifrost from Norway; Caprino from Argentina; and Beckenried from Switzerland. When you do find them here, it is usually in a store that serves a particular nationality. An inexplicable exception, however, is Gjetost from Norway, which can usually be found in any well-stocked cheese store. The caramel-chocolate colored Gjetost is quite unlike most other goat cheeses in flavor, and in its own way it appeals to a rather specialized taste. Twenty-five years ago Edward Bunyard summed up our view of this cheese: "A taste for goat's milk cheese, a chocolate block of most unusual aspect, is perhaps only to be acquired in the fjords; one tries it and is glad to have extended one's experience, but personally I shall not pass that way again."

The French eat goat cheese the way they eat all cheeses—with bread at the end of the meal. But there's no reason for not eating the young cheese as an appetizer, just as Middle Easterners eat the not too dissimilar Feta that we'll be discussing shortly. As an appetizer, or for lunch with bread (and butter if you choose), young goat cheese goes particularly well with Greek olives and small, hot peppers, or sprinkled with paprika, fennel, thyme or any other herb or spice you're fond of. This is what French cheesemakers do—and it is one reason why there are about seventy-five "different" French goat cheeses.

THE SHEEP CHEESES

The most famous of all sheep cheeses is, of course, the incomparable Roquefort, which gets its singular texture and flavor directly from the sheep's milk from which it is made. But Roquefort's distinction comes from its blue veining, and so it is discussed in Chapter 13. It need only be repeated that almost the entire French output of sheep's milk that goes into cheeses goes into Roquefort—which means that an area whose milk has been designated as "Roquefort milk" generally has little left over for other cheese-making.

Most sheep cheeses are local cheeses that seldom travel beyond their home territories where, in countless peasant dwellings, they often take the place of meat. Because of its high protein content, we often hear cheese spoken of as substitute for meat; but of all cheeses, these are the only ones that, in fact, do *taste* like meat. The snowy-white, creamy Ricotta Pecorino, for example, has a flavor decidedly reminiscent of milk-fed lamb, while a sheep cheese in its early maturity seems distinctly muttonlike in its flavor. The comparison ends abruptly when we reach the well-aged sheep cheeses. These make as rigorous demands upon the American palate as the older goat cheeses do.

Upon reflection, it is not surprising that the countries where these are the principal cheeses are also poor lands. For the peasant, the sheep is an invaluable beast. It can find nourishment where a cow would find only slender grazings, and in return for relatively little it gives wool, milk, and in due course, mutton. In the areas where sheep cheeses predominate—Portugal, Greece, Turkey, Italy, Yugoslavia, Hungary, Romania, and throughout the Balkans, the Carpathians, the Caucasus and the entire Middle East—the kinds of sheep cheese made (there are about a hundred in all) seem to fall roughly into these types:

First is the fresh cheese that looks like a cross between cream cheese and hard-pressed farmer cheese, but which, like the fresh goat cheese, has a mild sourish taste. This cheese must be eaten immediately—it will keep without refrigeration for a day in the summer, or two days in the winter, but not beyond that. Obviously it doesn't travel well. Bricotto from Corsica, for example, is made in small quantities mainly for domestic consumption, and there are innumerable others. This same fresh cheese is also heavily salted to preserve it for longer periods. The amount of added salt determines the flavor. The less salt, the better you can taste the fresh curd—but also the shorter the life of the cheese. The firmly pressed Ricotta Pecorino found in Italian-American neighborhoods falls into this group.

Next there are the pickled cheeses that abound in the Middle East. Greek Feta is an example, as is Romania's Brândza de Braila, and Eriwani, a cheese that travels under a number of names throughout the Caucasus. These cheeses may be salted first but they are thereafter preserved in brine. The brine is a simple mixture of salt and water, or, as in the case of Feta, milk and salt and water.

Another type is the hard-grating sheep cheese used chiefly as a condiment. In the United States the best-known variety is the hard-grating Pecorino Romano, which is used on pasta and other foods by our large Italian-American population. In this same group, and popular among some Italian-Americans, are Asiago and Sardo, grana-type cheeses with a pungent aroma. Originally sheep cheeses, Asiago and Sardo are now made from cow's milk, but somehow they retain their sheepy taste.

Then there are the table cheeses that are sharp and pungent but decidedly milder than the grating Pecorinos. A notable example is the Italian Pecorino da Tavola. Others are Greek Kasseri and Kefalotyri, and Bulgarian Kashkaval.

Though they are usually made of cow's milk, two table cheeses that increasingly resemble sheep's-milk cheeses as they age are Cacciocavallo and Italian provolone (unsmoked). These two cheeses are made in almost the same way and are similar in flavor. When well aged, they both have the hot sting that is characteristic of sheep and goat cheeses, and they are both salty—as are almost all cheeses eaten in the hot Mediterranean countries. Their shapes, however, differ. Cacciocavallo looks like an outsize vegetable marrow and weighs between four and a half and five and a half pounds, and its honey color, to Osbert Burdett, is reminiscent of the travertine stones of Rome. Provolone comes in a variety of shapes and weights. It may be round, pear-shaped, or salami-shaped, and can weigh from one pound to two hundred.

Finally there are the Portuguese sheep cheeses, which are considered by many connoisseurs to be among the best of all. The Portuguese cheese (Quejo de Serra is the generic name) is almost a category in itself because of its texture, which is soft, oily and rich.

SHEEP CHEESES IN THE UNITED STATES

Obviously, you will not find the very fresh cheeses here. You will find Feta and the similar Bryndza in most well-stocked cheese stores, along with Kasseri, Kashkaval, and Pecorino Romano. Ricotta Pecorino and the Portuguese cheeses will usually be found only in stores that serve Italian and Portuguese customers.

With the exception always of Roquefort, Pecorino Romano—more often called Romano—is perhaps the easiest of all to find in some of our major cities. Almost 50 per cent of Italy's production of this cheese comes to the United States, and more Romano is bought by Italian-Americans than by Italians in Italy. (Many northern Italians there look down upon it as they do on other southern Italian specialities, and probably a great many Italians in the south can't afford to buy it.)

The pickled and salted cheeses go beautifully with Greek olives, California ripe olives, hot peppers, and with caponata, an Italian hors d'oeuvre made with eggplant, tomatoes, onions and a little olive oil—an hors d'oeuvre also eaten in the Near East. The table cheeses—Pecorino Romano, Kasseri, and Kashkaval—should be served in small pieces or thin slices—the older the cheese, the thinner—on a bread that has enough character to stand up to them, with or without butter as you prefer. Ricotta Pecorino is excellent by itself, with a few grains of fresh-ground pepper, or on Italian whole-wheat bread. The Portuguese cheeses, which should be left at room temperature until they spread easily, are eaten without butter on sturdy bread or unsalted crackers. Finally, if you like it, the hard-grating Pecorino Romano is best used sparingly as a condiment on pastas and other foods on which you would sprinkle Parmesan. A domestic "Romano" is made in considerable quantity in Wisconsin and is sold in most supermarkets and neighborhood stores already grated, in shakers. This Romano is made from cow's milk, not sheep's, is much milder than the original, and is for all practical purposes an entirely different cheese.

15

The Strong Cheeses

No cheeses have such loyal supporters and such vociferous critics as the very strong cheeses such as Limburger, Liederkranz, Livarot and a half-dozen others, which have in common an aroma as unequivocal as a thunderclap. People who like them extol as virtues the very qualities that others deplore. Looking at a Liederkranz that is *à point,* an enthusiast will see below its russet mantle the creamy, smooth cheese within—a cheese with something of the flavor of a Camembert or Brie intensified many times over. To him the flavor is robust, the aroma awe-inspiring. But to his opposite number, that aroma, in the words of Osbert Burdett, can "cling and penetrate with the tenacity of cigar smoke. Perhaps for this reason," he adds, "the puritan nose twitches in indignation."

This, of course, is a matter of taste and of conditioning, not only to a particular kind of flavor but to a particular kind of smell; for while flavor and aroma always go together, in no other group of cheeses are they so closely united. As a result they are often confused with each other. Aficionados do not apologize for the aroma, but they often reassure the neophyte who is hesitant about trying a strong cheese that its bark is indeed worse than its bite.

To the person who likes bland foods—the conservative who likes his steaks grilled medium, who chooses white meat instead of dark, who wants to be able to recognize exactly what is in a dish, who will never be found eating sweetbreads or shad roe, who would like game if it weren't for the gamey taste—such assurances are in vain. He is not likely to cultivate a taste for these cheeses, at least not until he has had a few reassuring encounters with a Port-Salut or a Tilsit or one of the other cheeses with the same worldly overtones.

By and large, people of German, Swiss and Austrian descent, and from elsewhere in middle Europe, are partial to strong cheeses. The French also favor them, and many cheeses in Paris *crémeries* bear rinds so dark and heavily encrusted with mold, with the over-ripe cheese oozing out wherever it can, that an American accustomed only to bland and quiescent cheeses would be undone by the sight—to say nothing of the smell. And these, strong as they may seem to us, are mild in comparison to some of the cheeses made and eaten by farmers from the French provinces—cheeses so starkly pungent that a ripe Limburger, placed beside them, would seem as mild as Devonshire cream. The matter of strength is relative, even though some cheeses at the extremes of the olfactory scale seem as absolute as anything known to mortals. So it must have appeared to one Parisian lady—a woman of delicate sensibilities, who did not deny her husband and his friends the outrageous cheeses they preferred, but who simply threw away the dishes they had been served upon.

Aside from those that are not well known outside the rural communities where they are made, the ultra-strong cheeses are few in number. There are nine principal ones, all of which can be found in this country: Limburger, Liederkranz, old brick, Bierkäse, hand cheese, Romadur, Livarot, European Munster and Maroilles. The last four are by no means commonplace, but they do turn up in shops that carry a large variety of cheeses. If this group seems small, it is because we have all no doubt been assailed by the smell of other cheeses that would seem to belong with them. But many are only the erstwhile good cheeses that have fallen upon evil days. More often than not they are imports which, through indifference and neglect, have been allowed to decline into an unrecognizable state. They smell bad because they are long since overripe, not because they were made to be aromatic cheeses to begin with. And they taste bad—nothing at all like naturally strong cheese at its prime, as it was intended to be.

Unfortunately it is not always possible to tell instantly whether a cheese is a once milder cheese that is over the hill, or a good naturally strong one. But if it is prepackaged, as it almost always is, the outer wrappings should be clean and fresh-looking and should adhere loosely to the cheese. If the wrappings are stained and sticky, watch out. Similarly, the aroma may be strong, but it should not be rank. T. A. Layton, an expert on cheeses, once wrote the Belgian minister of agriculture for a phrase descriptive of the aroma of Limburger, to which the minister replied, "It is something between a bouquet and a stink." But as a general rule, if the "bouquet" leaves you pale and shaken, forget about the cheese. As for appearance, each of these cheeses *looks* appetizing when it is in good condition. Some salespeople will open the wrapper to let you look at a cheese if you express doubt about its condition, and if it is plump and yielding, not sunken and hard, it will probably be all right, even if there is a little mold on the rind. But more often they will not unwrap a cheese to let you see it. And the buyer is well within his rights to complain about—and, better still, to return— cheeses found to be in poor condition once he gets them home. The common retort that "that's the way they are supposed to be" is sheer nonsense. This assurance has moved more bad cheeses into the hands of hapless customers, and caused them more disappointment, than any other single practice in the business.

The disappointment is not confined to the single purchase that turns out to have been a mistake; the buyer who experiments with a new cheese and is sold a poor one will probably never try it again. He may indeed believe that that's the way the cheese should be, and he may wonder what other people can possibly see in it and whether his own taste is somehow deficient for not being able to appreciate it too.

LIEDERKRANZ

Many people assume, because Liederkranz bears certain similarities to Limburger, and because of its name, that it, too, originated in Germany. And indeed it is rather curious, in view of the American taste for bland cheese, that the only two cheeses native to this country (the other is brick) are both ultra-strong. In any event, Liederkranz, for all its seeming Germanic characteristics, first saw the light of day—quite by accident—in Monroe, New York, in 1882. There a cheesemaker by the name of Emil Frey was attempting to duplicate a popular German cheese known as Bismarck Schlosskäse, having been commissioned to do so by a New York City delicatessen owner who had more requests for this imported cheese than he could fill. Frey did not succeed in this, but he did come up with something that everybody liked even better.

Frey was a member of the singing society of Liederkranz Hall in New York, a group that loved good food as well as song, and they were soon introduced to his new cheese. They liked it and bought it regularly, and it was in their honor that it was christened Liederkranz, which, roughly translated, means "wreath of song." Liederkranz quickly caught on, and after it was bought up by a large dairy company, it became available all over the country. Small quantities have also been exported to Europe, where it is warmly accepted and thought of as more European than American. During World War II, when much of European cheesemaking was at a standstill, a fair amount of Liederkranz was shipped to Europe, and the family of one Midwestern G.I. received an ecstatic letter about a cheese that he had discovered abroad and was sending home to give his family a real European treat. Thus at least one Liederkranz took the grand tour from the Middle West (where it is now made) to Europe and back again.

Liederkranz comes in small oblong loaves weighing four ounces each, and like Camembert it is never sold in bulk. The rind is soft and moist, a light orange in color, and often still bears the faint impression of the straw mats on which the new cheeses drain and mature.

To be enjoyed at its very best, Liederkranz should be fully ripened—that is, the cheese should be soft and glossy, with the texture of heavy honey through and through. When it is not quite ripe the crust is very light rather than deep yellow, and the cheese even at room temperature is rather firm to the touch instead of very soft, as a fully ripened Liederkranz always is at room temperature. These slight differences in color and texture may be hard to judge until you are familiar with it, but if you cut into it and find in the center a firm, rather chalky curd, paler and decidedly tighter-textured than the surrounding cheese, it means that the cheese is not quite ripe, and it should be closed, rewrapped and returned to the refrigerator and allowed to ripen for another five to seven days. If, on the other hand, the cheese is overripe, the rind will be brown-orange, rather sticky, a little shrunken, and strong and acrid in smell and taste. But, it must be added, we have never got such a cheese from any store that had reasonable turnover, for Liederkranz is also above average in dependability. The large company that makes and distributes it has its salesmen check the coded dates on the wrappers and replace old cheeses with new ones, much as bakers' routemen do. Thus the retailer is relieved of any incentive to unload cheeses that are past their prime, and, for the company's part, the reputation of a valuable brand name is protected.

Liederkranz should always be eaten at room temperature (virtually every cheese should be, but with soft-ripening cheeses such as Liederkranz the texture of the cheese absolutely depends on it). Delicately flavored crackers are lost under it, but good pumpernickel or sour rye bread is not, and the combination is wonderful. It is also very good on matzos, and if you like a nice mild raw onion now and then, you may be sure that no cheese takes more kindly to it than Liederkranz. It goes best of all with cold beer or hot coffee, but if you prefer wine, a light Moselle or other simple white wine, well chilled, will be more refreshing than a red.

A final word to the fainthearted: Liederkranz is by no means as strong in taste as it smells. Even the rind, unless the cheese is very, very ripe, is delicious, and as for that creamy center—we make no other cheese that is quite like it, and not too many imported cheeses, in the condition we get them here, can compete with it either. Emil Frey probably had no idea how much he was contributing to the sum of human happiness.

LIMBURGER

In comparison, Limburger—which is the first name people usually mention when they speak of very strong cheeses—is a little heavier in taste, less piquant and decidedly stronger. Though it has many loyal champions, we do not put it in first place by any means, but of course that is a matter of preference. As Lincoln remarked in a different context, people who like this sort of thing will like this very much. In any event, it is not the very first strong cheese you should try if you've never taken the plunge before.

This cheese, too, is popularly thought to have originated in Germany. But it was first made in Liége and marketed in Limburg, Belgium, though it is now made in Germany as well. It is also made in the United States, and the domestic is probably the safer variety to buy because it is less likely to be overripe. The imported kind is recommended only to those who know exactly what they are doing.

A process Limburger is also made here, which is available in almost every supermarket in the country. This is a homogenized blend of Limburger and other more neutral cheese foods, "stabilized" against further ripening. Because it is packaged in screw-topped jars, it is innocent of all smell until you open it, and even then it is subdued in comparison to the strong natural cheeses. The Limburger overtones are there, but they are muffled and somehow not the better for having been suppressed, so that the taste slightly resembles that of an old yeastcake. We don't like it; but it has so long been a staple at dairy counters that there must be people who do.

The strong smell of natural Limburger is credited with having caused the Limburger Rebellion in Green County, Wisconsin, where a good deal of Limburger is made (as well as in upper New York State). One hot afternoon the local residents threatened to stage a Boston Tea Party when a caravan, loaded with cheeses, was parked in front of the town bank, leaving hundreds of Limburgers to ripen in the sun. Order was restored only when the offending cheeses were granted asylum in somebody's cellar. A few years later Green County was also the site of a postal crisis, again precipitated by the aromatic Limburger. Here is an account of it by Emory A. Odell, then owner and publisher of the Monroe *Evening Times*:

> A rural carrier in Iowa reported that he was made ill because of the odor emitted by a parcel containing Limburger. Warren F. Miller, acting Postmaster at Independence, ruled against the cheese because of an old regulation, and the old question of whether Limburger radiates fragrance or fetor was warmly argued. Postmaster Burkhard of Monroe, Wisconsin, accused Iowa postmasters of lack of appreciation of Limburger's aesthetic value. He declared that Limburger creates its own exclusive atmosphere and asks no odds of anyone.
>
> "Green County folks do not judge books by their covers, people by their faces, or a good cheese by its smell," he wrote in a challenge to Postmaster Miller to a Limburger duel. The challenge was accepted. The duel took place in the Julian Hotel at Dubuque in March, 1935, with press and public represented. The Limburger was sampled, to the delight of all permitted to share in the delicacy. Limburger came out victorious by the unanimous decision of the judges.

Limburger enthusiasts like it best with pumpernickel and other whole-grained dark bread, crackers, pretzels, onions and beer. As Marye Dahnke sums it up, "it goes with barbershop harmony."

BRICK

Brick is the second cheese, besides Liederkranz, which is a native American. Although it is rather little known along the Atlantic seaboard or the West Coast, brick has been very popular in the Midwest ever since it was first made in 1877 by a cheesemaker of Swiss descent, John Jossi, of Dodge County, Wisconsin. Jossi's specialty was Limburger, and he observed that when the curds for making Limburger were kept to a lower moisture content, a cheese with a different texture resulted. This was brick. Old brick is strong indeed, though not so strong as Limburger, and the cheese is firmer and more elastic.

Its name is thought to derive either from its shape or, more likely, from the bricks originally used to press the whey out of the unripened cheese. Old brick is cream-colored and perforated by numerous small holes. The rind is caramel-colored, strong and bitter—much more bitter than the cheese—and it should be removed before eating. The flavor is not dissimilar to Limburger, but is even closer to very well aged Tilsit or Danish Port-Salut. People who like strong cheeses, but who draw the line at Limburger, will find old brick comfortably within their range.

Like others in this group, it goes best with sour rye or dark pumpernickel, followed by the familiar retinue of onions, beer, ale and whatever else you like that will stand up to it. Wine, the classic accompaniment to cheese, yields its customary place to beer as the best drink to serve with strong cheeses. As Edward Bunyard has pointed out, "the reason underlying the marriage of wine and cheese is, of course, the alkalinity of the cheese; but with the non-acid beer the effect is not so much a contrast as a blending, the slight bitterness of the hops being the chief contrast to the malt and the cheese." Many of these cheeses seem to have a taste of the hops themselves, and it is perhaps principally for this reason—as well as the fact that they are thirst-making—that beer and ale go so well with Liederkranz, Limburger, old brick and the rest.

BEER CHEESE

Another cheese that is all but indistinguishable from old brick, and that goes equally well with the same kinds of food and with beer, is in fact named Bierkäse (or beer cheese). This is a little easier to find on the Eastern seaboard than old brick, particularly in German communities, and it is even more popular in the Middle West. Bierkäse originated in Germany, where it is also known as Weisslacker because of its lustrous white appearance. The American version, made largely in Wisconsin, is a little firmer and a little milder than the original, but no one who likes the taste of a good strong cheese will feel that the Wisconsin product has failed to deliver.

ROMADUR

Romadur is still another cheese that is much like Limburger, but it is smaller than Limburger, with a milder aroma, and it contains less salt. Romadur is made in southern Germany and the little that is imported here can be found chiefly in German communities and in a few shops that carry a very large variety of cheeses. Similar cheeses—and ones even less likely to turn up here—are Schützenkäse, made in Austria; Schlosskäse, made in Austria and Germany; Harracher, Hochstrasser and Kremstaler, from Hungary; and Hervé, from Belgium.

HAND CHEESE

Hand cheese gets its name from having originally been molded into its final shape by hand, as it still is in some parts of Europe. It is a small, conical cheese that will fit easily into a man's palm. The smell is arresting to say the least, and even lovers of ripe Limburger may feel that strong is strong, but this is something else again. Hand cheese is popular among German people and is known by a variety of local names. In Germany, Mainzer Handkäse or Harzkäse, Alte Kuhkäse or Berliner Kuhkäse, Ihlefeld or Satz; in Austria, Olmützer Quargeln or Olmützer Bierkäse; and in Russia, Livlander. In the United States, cheese of this type is made by farm families of German descent in Pennsylvania and in a few factories in New York, Wisconsin and northern Illinois. It has a heavy, dark-gray rind, and the cheese—of the several samples we've tasted here —has a translucent, gelatinous look, almost like cartilage. Even those who like it concede that it is an acquired taste.

LIVAROT

Livarot is a cheese that has hardly been surpassed by any other in strength, and yet, with the exception of Liederkranz, it surpasses all others in this group in quality. It is named for the tiny town near Caen where it is made, and it is one of Normandy's most important cheeses. The flavor of Livarot is not unlike that of Pont-l'Évêque, though it is decidedly stronger—so strong that it defers to no cheese we have discussed in this chapter. All the same, it has a certain finesse that is not to be found in the heavier Germanic cheeses like Limburger and Bierkäse; and in fact, in France Livarot has been described as the very Verlaine of cheeses.

Like two other cheeses in this group—Munster and Maroilles— Livarot is aged in cellars or ripening rooms where fresh air is not allowed to enter. Frequently the walls are covered with mortar mixed with chopped hay. "The smell of one of these rooms," writes T. A. Layton, "where lie on either side mountains of ripening and browning cheeses, is hard to describe. Overpowering, certainly; it is like the odour of slowly rotting apples combined with ammonia, a whiff of ripe Camembert and a soupçon of seaside ozone, or if you want to be less kind, of town drains running into the sea."

The crust of Livarot is a dark, reddish brown, and it is rolled in sedge leaves or wrapped around with dried reeds to restrain the soft, ripe, yellow cheese within. In France, Livarot is nicknamed "Le Colonel" because the five reed bands usually seen around it correspond to the five bands denoting this rank on a French Army officer's uniform.

Livarot is in season during autumn and winter and is best eaten in France, simply because a cheese that is exported has more time to age, and in the case of Livarot, excessive ripeness would indeed be a matter of piling Pelion on Ossa. Nevertheless, it is occasionally possible to pick up a good Livarot here—and if it is appetizing and sound-looking, despite the smell, you will be glad you bought it. The crust should be removed and the cheese eaten with Melba toast, crisp breadsticks or a good French bread. It goes well with Calvados, or with any cold dry wine you like, and it's excellent with coffee.

EUROPEAN MUNSTER

Munster cheese as we know it in the United States is as bland as butter and completely unrelated, except by name, to European Munster—which is a very strong cheese, powerful when it has been well aged, and highly aromatic. Indeed, Munster, which was first made in the Alsace, is considered by many to be one of France's finest cheeses. It is semisoft, rather like a strong but not overripe Pont-l'Évêque in flavor, and at its best from November until April.

MAROILLES

Recently the French Brotherhood of Cheese Tasters gathered in the medieval village of Maroilles, near Lille, to celebrate the thousandth anniversary of Maroilles (or Marolles), which has long and affectionately been known to French gastronomes as Vieux Puant, or Old Stinker. Maroilles was first made around A.D. 960 by monks at the abbey of Thiérache, and it has long been the most important cheese of that district.

Maroilles' aroma lives up to its nickname. But here again, the strength that may at first seem excessive is only skin deep: Under Maroilles' formidable reddish rind is a heart of gold. Like Livarot, which it resembles in flavor, Maroilles is representative of French cheesemaking at its best, and if you have the opportunity to try it—small quantities are occasionally imported here—you will be rewarded for your fortitude.

Maroilles is at its best from November to July. It is square and looks like Pont-l'Évêque, only larger. Maroilles' distinctive flavor is derived in part from frequent brushing of the rind while it is aging, followed always by a rinsing with beer. Like Livarot, it is particularly good with crisp breadsticks, French bread, or any good salted cracker. Appropriate wines include Beaune, Châteauneuf-du-Pape, Côte Rôtie, or any other full-bodied dry red wine.

Cheeses almost identical to Maroilles and made in the same district, but not imported here, are: Sorbais (nearly as large but less thick), Mignon (thinner still), and Quart (three-quarters as large). A Maroilles that is specially made for long aging is known as Vieux Gris, Gris de Lille or Vieux Lille.

For most people, a liking for these strong cheeses is an acquired taste, arrived at by degrees. For those who do not already have it, the first step may be taken by getting to know Camembert and Brie as they deserve to be known. The next step would be the monastery cheeses like Pont-l'Évêque or aged Port-Salut. And anyone who stays with them for a while will not be undone nor will his palate be at all astonished by those strongest of all cheeses that we have been considering here. For if cheese can be called the wine of foods, the aged and ripened varieties are the brandy of cheese. To those who have come to love them, many other cheeses seem shallow in comparison.

16

The Spiced
and Flavored Cheeses

*I must have novelty—even if there is none left
in the world.*

—*La Fontaine*

Consider the mashed potato. Though there are those who love it
for itself, its true vocation is to serve as a vehicle for other things—
gravy, or simply more butter, or additions ranging from a little sour
cream or grated cheese to the meat and onions that make it a hash.
So with the cheeses which have "something added." These are with
few exceptions cheeses virtually as bland as mashed potatoes and as
able to assume the character of what is added to them, forsaking
their own identities and almost becoming the thing to which they
have given their hospitality. And it follows that people who like
the cheeses to which pineapple or bacon or curry or kirsch have
been added eat them because at that moment they want the taste of
pineapple or bacon or curry or kirsch, and not the taste of cheese.

This is not to denigrate these cheeses that travel in so many
different guises. With only one exception we can think of—the
French Boursin or Boursalt Fines Herbes that has not yet been
successfully imported here—they are not great cheeses. But every

cheese need not be great, and many of these are extremely good and we can be glad to have them.

Adding things to cheese is as old as cheesemaking itself. Herbs with medicinal value were often added in ancient times, as were other things having nothing to do with taste preferences. Sometimes they were added to protect the cheese itself. In Elizabethan England, for example, dairymen used to make something called "nettle cheese"—a cheese that was rolled in nettles, sheathed in them top and bottom, so that, protected by the stinging hairs, the cheese could ripen unmolested by mites, flies and other pests; and the nettles on the bottom formed a kind of trivet that served as a draining board for the cheese.

In addition to things added to protect the cheese and the eater, others were added to deceive him as well. Colorings, for example. Before annatto was discovered in the eighteenth century as a safe coloring for cheeses, many other colorings were used—wild pot marigold leaves, carrot juice, saffron and ordinary household dyes, many of them toxic—particularly in cheeses of poor quality, to impart a richer look. And holes were added to ordinary yellow cheeses that used to be sliced and sold as Swiss.

Then too, there were many "filled cheeses"—cheeses into which animal fats were introduced to make up for deficiencies in milk and cream content. These must not have tasted very good, and it is likely that they were also spiced to mask the poor taste. This is one of the oldest uses of flavorings. Sometimes masking flavors were added not to deceive the buyer but to salvage a mess of curds that had not come out right but could not be let go to waste. These were often mashed and flavored with sugar, nutmeg and rose water, which not only delayed spoiling but made the cheese reasonably palatable as well.

Finally, there were the special spices and brines that are still used, as they have been for hundreds of years, as a means of preserving or literally pickling them.

Cheeses with "something added" are of two major kinds. The first is the natural cheeses, of which there are a considerable number.

The base is almost always mild—a young Munster, Samsoe or Cheddar, or some other bland natural cheese. And the something added ranges from the spices and herbs, wines, liquors and cordials that we might expect to find mixed with cheese to more surprising additions—such as, for example, the Fondue du Raisin, which is covered with grape seeds and pips; or the special variety of mozzarella (called Manteca) which has at its center a yolk of sweet butter.

The second kind is the process cheeses, most of them the bland white spreads that were made to be dominated by something else. That something may range from the conventional pineapple, pimentos or relish to mushrooms, lobster, shrimp, herring or wood smoke. The something added may even be *cheese*—for example, a blue cheese, which thus makes a "blue cheese spread"; or even Limburger, for those who are not daring enough to eat it straight. As between the natural and the process types, not surprisingly the natural cheeses with something added are generally older and more interesting.

NATURAL CHEESES WITH SOMETHING ADDED

Caraway and Cumin Cheeses

Caraway and cumin seeds are among the most widely used additions to bland natural cheeses. Caraway is the familiar small crescent-shaped seed (minutely yet perfectly striped in alternating shades of brown and beige) that seems to impart a pleasant sourness to other foods even though it is not itself sour. Cumin looks like caraway except that it is lighter in color and is perfectly straight rather than curved, but it has a strong, pervasive, almost turpentiney taste. Of the two, caraway seeds are the better known in the United States, certainly among lovers of rye bread, while the less familiar cumin has its largest following in northern Europe, where it is used for seasoning meats and vegetables, liqueurs and, of course, cheeses.

Cheeses seasoned with these are popular in Scandinavia, Germany and the Netherlands (whose islands in the East grow most of the caraway we import). And many of these cheeses are named after the seeds: Kummelkäse, Kuminkäse, Cuminost, the names and spellings varying slightly from one country to another. The cheese itself may range from a buttery cheese like a young Munster to a brittle yellow cheese so dry that it cannot be sliced thin without splintering. Other cheeses are not named for the seeds—for example, the Danish King Christian IX, which is a rich, soft Samsoe that differs from the others in being large and cylindrical rather than loaf-shaped as most seeded cheeses are.

In the United States in the past ten years, Munster with caraway has become very popular, and one large New York supermarket chain now sells as much Munster with caraway as process American—which is saying a great deal. The popularity of this particular cheese is probably due to its excellence, for the Daitch Supermarket cheese is easily the best Munster with caraway we have tasted—creamy and studded throughout with plump, moist seeds. When the seeds are plentiful in a Munster, as they are in this one, you can eat the cheese by itself and enjoy the illusion of eating it on a good sour rye bread, without the calories.

Once a specialty to be found in only a few shops, Munster with caraway can now be bought in supermarkets from coast to coast in prepackaged slices. Some house brands are better than others, but if you can find a good one freshly sliced and packaged—or better still, if you can have it sliced to order from the loaf—this is preferable to those outsize slices of tasteless cheese that are sold everywhere in vacuum bags.

CLOVE CHEESE

The Dutch and Scandinavians particularly like cloves in their cheeses, for reasons best known to them. The presence of cloves, excellent as they are for hams, somehow doesn't do a thing for cheese, in our view—but North Europeans obviously feel differently, as witness the popularity of the Dutch Leyden or Komijne Kaas and Friesian clove cheese, and the Norwegian Nokkelost (made also in combination with cumin or caraway, or with all three) and other similar cheeses that are made in Sweden and Denmark. Nagel (which means "nail") is another popular North European cheese which gets its name from the clove whose flavor completely dominates it.

Gjetost

In our opinion, no cheese is more unnerving than the fetid, sweetish, brown, sticky Scandinavian favorite called Gjetost. This cheese, which is particularly popular in Norway, is made from the whey of cow's milk to which at least 10 per cent goat's-milk whey has been added, together with caramelized lactose (milk sugar), or sometimes a small quantity of brown sugar, as well as fats. When it is made from goat's-milk whey only, it is called Ekte (genuine) Gjetost; and when it is made exclusively from cow's rather than goat's milk, the name becomes Mysost. This cheese stands apart from all others, and in fact it hardly seems like a cheese at all. An Australian couple described the taste. The lady called it, "that awful sweet brown cheese they served us for breakfast in Norway." She was quite exact in observing that the texture was grainy, rather like polenta, and she suspected that, because of the fishy taste, the cheese must have contained fish roe. "Yes," her husband added, "and probably a little kerosene."

Sage Cheese

The very agreeable sage cheese, sometimes called Vermont sage, is like an extremely young and therefore bland white Cheddar that is mottled throughout by what appear to be sage leaves, whose flavor is dominated by the sage taste. The combination of the sharp, clean, head-clearing sage flavor with the bland cheese is a good one, assuming that you like sage—though it may be an acquired taste. We were not taken with it at first, but liked it on the second or third try.

Sage cheese originated in England at least three hundred years ago, and was considered one of the best cheeses of Derbyshire, a district known for its flavored and herb-streaked cheeses, where it was commonly called "green cheese." This was because an infusion of sage "tea" was mixed into it together with the leaves, which imparted a pale-green color throughout, accented by the darker green of the herb itself. It was considered as beneficial to health as camomile, for sage (*Salvia officinalis*) derives its name from the Latin *salvus* which denotes the healing virtues that have been imputed to it since antiquity. Sage has a natural affinity for pork, not only for cooking but in making sausage, and it is also used for chicken, duck and goose, and in poultry dressing. This dates back to the eighteenth century, when sage was depended upon to help make meats and other foods safer to eat. People also added it to cheese, in hopes of making it more digestible. Whatever the therapeutic effects of sage may be, it is safe to say that as it is infused into cheeses nowadays, the effects are nil. For sage cheese, as it is made now in the United States, does not contain real sage leaves, gently bruised to release the flavor, as it once did; instead it is flavored by diluted Dalmation oil of sage, mechanically sprayed over the curd. The mottled-green-leaf effect is then introduced by mixing in either chopped pressed alfalfa or green corn cut fine. Nevertheless today's commercially made sage cheese remains a good cheese, even though all the romance has gone out of it.

SAPSAGO

Sapsago, a cone-shaped, light-green, hard grating cheese, has been made in the canton of Glarus, Switzerland, since at least the fifteenth century and perhaps much longer. It is also made in Germany and is known by various names including Schabziger (of which the name sapsago is a corruption) Glarnerkäse, Grünerkäse, Krauterkäse and Grünerkrauterkäse. Its unique pungency results not so much from the sour skim milk, buttermilk, and sour whey used in making it as from the addition of large quantities of a dried aromatic clover, *Melilotus coerulea*, which has a sharp and indeed most distinctive flavor. This clover is said to have been first put into it by some Irish monks who were in Switzerland to propagate the faith a few hundred years ago and who put four-leaf clovers into their cheeses for old times' sake. They were heedless of the consequences, apparently, because sapsago has a very funny taste.

Other Herbs and Condiments Added

Other additions include many kinds of herbs besides the ones mentioned here. For example, among the French goat cheeses alone, at least twenty different herbs are added, usually to the surface, and the cheeses look and taste as though they may have been rolled in anything from pine needles to barn sweepings. Other cheeses carry an admixture of seasonings throughout the cheese itself—a classic example of which is Hungarian Liptauer, a soft and rather oily cheese with a finely granular texture, to which may be added any number of condiments, including paprika, capers, chives, garlic, onions and hot peppers.

Smoked Cheeses

The most important of these is Provolone Affumicato, which is kept in brine from one to three days and then is suspended by twine or rope (which gives the cheese its characteristic grooved surface) to drip until it is dry. The wood-smoking of the cheese often takes place in rooms with open hearths. The Italian Provolone Affumicato we get here is often too salty and is so heavily smoked that the smoky taste completely dominates the cheese. In Italy, to meet the growing demand for bland cheeses, cheesemakers are making provolone milder and milder, and are reserving the strong ones for export to the United States, where they are sent, in the words of Osbert Burdett, "to console Neapolitan exiles."

Other smoked cheeses include an ivory-colored cheese with a dark, baconlike rind which is found all over the United States under a variety of brand names, and some process and cold-pack cheeses of undistinguished character which are usually sold in small casings like sausages.

CHEESES WITH WINES AND SPIRITS

Many cheeses, usually Cheddars, but sometimes Stilton and other blues, are mixed with brandy, port, sherry and other spirits. These blends can be very good, and a few drops of brandy or wine will often lend to an otherwise drab cheese a distinction it would never have had on its own. But an excellent cheese should be left alone. Commercial packers of cheeses generally respect this dictum, and for the most part they use only indifferent or inferior cheeses in those cheese crocks with wine or liquors added.

MANTECA

One of the most unusual and felicitous additions to cheese is the lump of solid sweet whey butter to be found at the center of a special kind of mozzarella called Manteca. This has been made in Italy for many years, and for a very practical reason. Until recently mozzarella was made exclusively in southern Italy, which is very warm and where little or no refrigeration existed. This climate, combined with the frugality of life in the south and the fact that poor people could not afford to waste good food, led to the ingenious storing of the whey butter, a by-product of cheesemaking, inside the cheese itself. Thus the cheese protected the butter against spoilage, and the butter in turn suffused the cheese with its flavor and helped keep it moist as well. Cut open, Manteca is a beautiful cheese to see—and to eat, with the butter spread first on a cracker or bread, then the cheese, sprinkled if you wish with fresh-ground black pepper. The flavor of the butter is closer to the celebrated Danish butter than to ours, and the taste is more pronounced.

THE FONDUE CHEESES

Not process cheeses, and yet not completely natural cheeses either, are a small group of pasteurized cheeses—that is, cheeses that have been cooked after they have been made—of which two in particular are outstanding.

Fondue du Raisin

The first is Fondue du Raisin, also called La Grappe or simply grape cheese. This is the soft white cheese that is distinguished from all others by its blue-black covering of grape seeds (and sometimes grape skins). There are some who maintain that it should be eaten seeds and all, although this makes hardly more sense than eating a lichee nut shell and all. The grape seeds are, in fact, a nuisance and messy to remove, though even more troublesome to leave on. But perhaps because of its exotic appearance this cheese has begun to enjoy a popularity that cannot be accounted for by its flavor or quality. The cheese inside is a nonentity compared with its covering. Fondue du Raisin has a kind of emulsified creaminess, and its sweetish flavor is distinctly that of the process Gruyère from which it is made. If it is possible for a cheese to be exotic and undistinguished at the same time, this is it.

Gourmandise

The white and even creamier Gourmandise is very similar to the grape cheese, though it wears no seeds. As made in France, Gourmandise is flavored with kirsch, but the cheeses to be exported to the United States must, by law, be flavored with cherry extract instead. In consequence ours is even sweeter than the French and is not so much a dessert cheese as a dessert. To our taste, its ultracreaminess seems somehow contrived, like the whipped cream that comes out of a squirt can. But many people who are discriminating about cheese do like Gourmandise, and it appears to be a favorite particularly among those who like sweet fruit wines.

PROCESS CHEESES WITH SOMETHING ADDED

In addition to all these natural cheeses with something added we have the process cheeses that do yeoman's service in carrying every conceivable kind of food around with them wherever they go—which is everywhere. But nowhere are they more popular than in the United States. Commenting on our predilection for these "cheese canapés" as they are called in France, a journal published by the French Ministry of Agriculture has this to say about them:

> . . . [In America] there exists an infinity of cheese canapés, made with vegetables, radishes, celery, salad and olives, and also with fruit: pears, raisins, pineapple, etc. Their preparation is left to the free imagination of the cook who is never disturbed by the incongruousness of the mixture.
>
> The popularity of "le snack" can be explained thus: Americans live very much in their homes and often entertain their friends and relatives. Instead of cooking a meal, they are satisfied with various little preparations to accompany bottles of Coca-Cola or beer. Television also encourages this, and they have developed a manner of eating that requires neither cooking, nor a table, nor any table service . . .

This prompted us to pay a call on one of the department heads at the French Ministry of Agriculture to sound out the French view on American tastes in cheese, particularly the crazy, mixed-up kinds. He conceded that the French are consuming their share, but mostly of the process kind—not fine natural cheeses that are best left alone.

Picking up a trade journal he pointed to one news item. "A

terrible thing has happened in Brooklyn," he said. And the terrible thing was that a food demonstrator in a department store had put some Roquefort, some cream and cognac into a blender, and then, unable to stop, had added Camembert, cream cheese, a little Swiss, some Worcestershire, some Gruyère, some Cheddar. . . . The demonstration, according to the article, had been a huge success.

17

---∘∞∘---

What Happened to Cheese
in the Process

Process cheeses are the TV dinners of the cheese world. Many of the same arguments can be marshaled for both: they are convenient, neat, inexpensive, and can always be found at the corner store. Kept in the arrested state in which they reach the consumer, they can easily survive him, and sometimes do. They belong to the present, and equally to the past and future, because time has stopped for them.

Few people have subsisted exclusively on TV dinners all their lives, but to millions of Americans process cheese has come to mean cheese itself—all cheese, every cheese. They know nothing else. The number of different kinds we make or import is stunning. There is a variety for every imaginable taste, as long as it is not a taste for cheese. Process cheese comes studded with bits of onion, bacon, ham, shrimp, mushroom, pineapple, herring. It is infused with garlic, cognac, spices, wine, celery, curry, tomato and smoke. And these are only a few of the special kinds. Whether it is simply called "American cheese" (the omnipresent filling in every drugstore "cheese sandwich" that comes in slices from a pale-orange or light-yellow loaf), or "cheese spread," or "cheese food," process cheese comprises more than half the cheese made in the United States today.

The package of a popular process spread tells us that it is made of "American cheese, condensed whey, water, nonfat dry milk, sodium phosphate, salt, cream and artificial color." According to the U.S. Department of Agriculture's guide to cheeses and cheese-making, *Cheese Varieties,* "Process (or Pasteurized Process) cheese is made by grinding fine, and mixing together by heating and stirring, one or more cheeses of the same or two or more varieties, together with an added emulsifying agent, into a homogeneous plastic mass. Lactic, citric, acetic or phosphoric acid or vinegar, a small amount of cream, water, salt, color and spices or flavoring materials may be added."

Cheese Varieties goes on to describe the heating process that gives the cheese its homogeneous, plastic quality: "Steam-jacketed kettles, equipped with mechanical agitators . . . stir the cheese. . . . As much as 30 minutes is required to heat the cheese in a large kettle. In most large factories . . . live steam injected directly into the cheese heats it in from 3 to 5 minutes. The cheese is heated to a temperature of at least 150° F., and usually 155° to 160°, and it is held at that temperature for at least 30 seconds but usually for about 5 minutes. . . . When long, thin strings of hot cheese can be drawn from the batch with a spatula and the cheese is smooth, homogeneous, glossy and creamy it is ready to be packaged. . . . The high temperature attained in heating, together with the heat retained during the several hours required to cool the cheese [in its package] to room temperature, makes the cheese practically sterile; it keeps well and does not ripen further."

The cheese is now in a state of permanently arrested development and what little flavor it has is all it can ever hope to have. Of such cheese Edward Bunyard wrote, "Economy has been pleaded for it, and quite justly. Peter Pan, no doubt, kept on with knickers all his dream life, and wore his pre-school ties well into his second childhood. But the very essence of cheese lies in its maturity, how it stands up to life and faces it, so away with all such artificially produced cheese childhoods."

Much process cheese is sold in prepackaged slices, which initially posed a manufacturing problem because the slices tended to stick together. This necessitated still another operation, in which the same liquid cheese is run onto a roller that forms it into ribbons of even width, and the ribbons in turn are run onto a conveyor and automatically stacked, cut and packaged in a continuous operation. Thus the processed product, by the time we get it, has been through a lot—and rather a lot has been through it.

The ratio of real cheese to the weight of the finished product varies. Of the three kinds of process cheeses made, process blended has the most real cheese; process cheese food has less; and process cheese spread—in which no more than 51 per cent must be cheese—has least.

Most of the real cheese that goes into process cheese, like fruit that has been picked green, will never come into its own. And it is its underripeness that largely accounts for process cheese's pallid flavor. Cheese that has been aged for a few months is sometimes mixed in, particularly in those designated as "sharp" or "Old English style." But the mix is generally made up of young and indifferent cheeses.

Cheeses with defects such as imperfect rind, pinholes, gassiness and open texture, as well as some flavor defects, are also grist for the mixing vats. Makers of process cheese always emphasize the quality of the cheese that goes into their product and the care and skill required to get the right blend. But these same makers will take you through their curing rooms for real cheeses—their Cheddars and Swiss—and in extolling the virtues of *these* cheeses will point out that imperfect ones are always spotted by inspectors and that the rejects—"grinders" as they are called—are destined for processing.

Process cheese does have certain advantages over real cheese, in addition to being economical. The question is whether these advantages are worth the cost. A process cheese need not be refrigerated until it is opened, it melts easily and evenly, and has extraordinary keeping qualities. Grocers like it because it is waste- and trouble-free, and has been promoted to the point where it sells itself. Individually packaged portions of process cheese travel well and can double for candy as a source of quick energy. As a food, process cheese is nutritious and otherwise perfectly wholesome. It has a taste all its own—and many people who appreciate real cheese enjoy eating process American once in a while.

Two other kinds of cheeses are often confused with process cheese because special steps are involved in their making which natural cheeses do not undergo. These are the coldpack cheeses and cheese foods. They are usually sold in crocks (or as refills for the crock the customer has already bought), and the word "club" is often part of their name—for example, Kaukauna Club and Mac-laren's Club Imperial. Coldpack cheeses are a combination of two or more natural cheeses, usually Cheddars or blues, blended without heating. A number of ingredients used in process cheeses are also included, but they are not cooked as process cheese is. Cold-pack cheeses are longer-keeping than natural cheeses in their original state, are softer and more spreadable, and they can be quite good.

Today the varieties of process cheese are almost endless—it comes in every conceivable shape or form except (as far as we know) in an aerosol spray can. It is being ground and oozed out at a furious pace, not only in the United States but all over the world. Consumers on the Continent, with the single exception of the English, have never cared for Cheddar and therefore do not like the various orange "American"-type process cheeses, which are all Cheddar-based. Instead, the great majority of process cheeses being made in Europe today are a creamy white or ivory and are, if anything, even blander than ours. The Scandinavian countries are making a great deal of this type from their own already bland natural cheeses, and so is Holland. Switzerland, the first to process cheese, is producing its little triangles of "Gruyère" by the millions and selling them all over the world, as it has for decades. Despite its name, it contains more Emmenthal than Gruyère, and it is one of the best of all process cheeses. It is so well known here and abroad that countless people think that the name Gruyère *means* these little foil-wrapped triangles of process cheese, rather than the holed natural cheese of the Alps that is the real Gruyère. The United States also makes this process Gruyère, as do Austria, Germany, Denmark and many others. The Austrian has always been cheaper than the Swiss (though it is not as good), but recently it has had stiff price competition from a newcomer—process Gruyère from, of all places, Ireland.

Countries all over Europe are even busier making a second type of process cheese. This is the very soft white or ivory process spread, glistening and elastic, that is, in its extremely mild way, agreeable in taste but even less like cheese than the triangles of process Gruyère. It comes in little foil-wrapped loaves, in metal crinkle-cups, in glass and plastic jars, and (from Denmark) in toothpaste tubes. The individual portions may take the shape of triangles, checkerboard squares, chips the size of a silver dollar, or tiny "cocktail bites" that exactly resemble bouillon cubes. They have been coated with colored pull-off plastic and shaped in the images of little pigs, shepherds and shepherdesses, and Snow White. But whatever the shape or the country of origin, these pale, soft cheeses are all quite similar.

France makes rather little process cheese, and few Frenchmen will own to eating any of it themselves, though they buy it for their children. They also export it—some of it to Italy, for example, under the name of Tost, which is described as French melting cheese of the Chester variety (the French have never learned to spell Cheshire). This is stiffer, drier and more lacking in flavor than process American. The Italians also import a process Limburger from Germany that looks like our white process American loaf cheese, but has a starkly evil taste. It is purported to have some buyers who use it for melting instead of mozzarella.

Italy also makes a variety of soft white process cheese spreads, and one very popular type is a creamed process version of Bel Paese. This is hardly different from the host of other soft white spreads that are everywhere, except that it comes in three "styles." The first is called Bébé and the box bears the photograph of a toothless, smiling infant, into whose warm cereal or milk the cheese is to be dissolved. The second, also called Bébé, shows a boy of about seven, still smiling and in possession of all his teeth and a full head of hair. This version of Bébé is meant to be spread on bread. The third style comes in the same package as the others, and bears the name Crema Bel Paese, but since it covers all the subsequent ages of man, it has no photograph. The odd thing is that after repeated sampling of all three we were still unable to distinguish one from the other.

The popularity of process cheeses throughout the world cannot be denied. And it cannot be completely attributed to the special virtues—their durability and convenience, and all the rest. The fact is that they have gained favor, not despite, but because of, their tastelessness.

We could make process cheeses that taste like real cheese if we wanted to, and one big distributor in fact has done so. This is the United States Government, which buys countless tons of Cheddar every year under its price-support programs. Much of it sits in government warehouses long enough to acquire a good age—and in consequence, an excellent flavor. But what to do with it? Much of it is processed in the end, because it is easier to handle in that form. The resulting process cheese has much more flavor—and tastes much more like real cheese—than the commercial products on the market, not so much because it has more real cheese in it (though it does) but because it is made of much better and older cheeses.

This government cheese never goes to market. It is distributed to schools, to people receiving public assistance, to prisons and other government institutions, and you can't get it unless you become indigent or throw a brick through a window.

Why doesn't some commercial cheesemaker put a cheese like

that on the market? Walter V. Price, of the Dairy Marketing Department at the University of Wisconsin, one of the deans of dairy research in the United States, had one answer: "You might make an intensely cheesy process Cheddar with flavor enough to delight any cheese connoisseur—and go broke." He cited the example of one cheesemaker who made and tested a "cheesier" process cheese on a number of consumer panels. They were asked to decide which of two cheeses they preferred: the improved cheese that had what any cheese connoisseur would call an excellent flavor, or a second process cheese that was utterly drab, with practically no flavor at all. The latter won hands down.

People seem to want blander and blander cheeses. This is why the Italians have deliberately muted the flavor of provolone for consumption in Italy and have toned down the sharpness of their wonderful Gorgonzola; and it is why a number of very bland cheeses have over the past few years gained such popularity in France—one of the last strongholds of great cheese.

During a recent trip to Vienna, one of the authors was invited to Grinzing to spend the evening in an arbor, sampling the new spring wines. The custom is to have pitchers of wine served at your table, but to bring your own wurst and cheese, or whatever you like to eat with it. The daughter of the family was dispatched to one of the most elegant delicatessens in town, while we sat in the soft evening, sipping our wine and waiting. She finally arrived in a state of excitement about a special treat she had found for us: it consisted of three cellophane-wrapped packages of Kraft American slices.

Process cheese is indeed leaving its mark on Europe, but we Americans eat more of it than the rest of the world put together. The garden varieties are to be found in every grocery store and are served at the counters of every drugstore, luncheonette, five-and-ten and diner in America, and in a good many otherwise respectable restaurants. In Madison, Wisconsin, for example, at one of the best hotels frequented by professors of the University of Wisconsin's Dairy Department—any one of whom will tell you what great Cheddars we are capable of making—the "Cheddar cheese" in the chef's salad turned out to be tiny strips of rubbery, tasteless process American.

Even the better shops cannot afford *not* to stock process cheeses; and they appear in those so-called "gourmet gift assortments" that are offered by every department store and mail-order house in the country. Generally these include a young baby Gouda, some cocktail sausage or Iceland shrimp in tiny jars, liver pâté—and enough little rounds and squares of sticky process cheese to keep your jaws glued together till next Christmas.

This is a matter of taste, but it raises a serious question: is a kind of Gresham's law of cheeses operating in the United States? Will the bad ones drive more and more of the good ones out of circulation? And will we have to look increasingly to imports, few of which can survive the journey in good condition, to get real cheese?

III

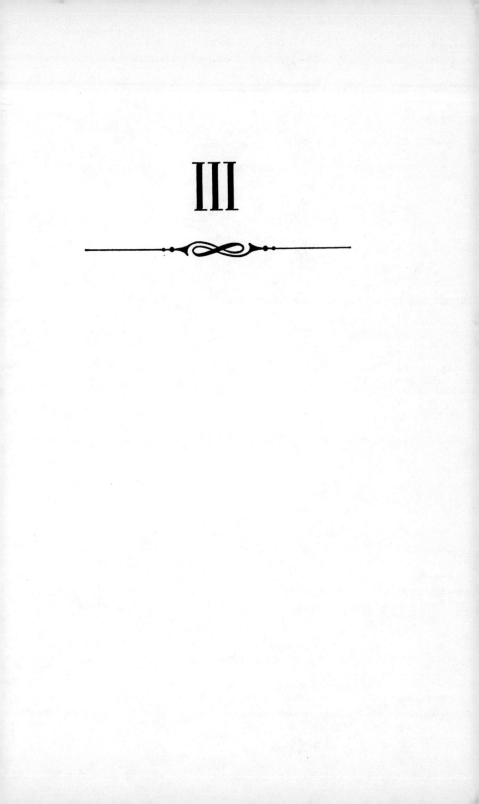

18

---∾---

The Art of Cheese Tasting

The only way to learn about cheese is to eat it.
—*Ernest Oldmeadow, English gastronome*

The only way to get to know cheeses is to taste them—not simply trying unfamiliar cheeses picked at random (though this can be interesting at first) but tasting them according to some plan that will enable you to keep them all straight—to discern the subtle differences between cheeses and discover your own preferences.

The best and quickest way of going about this is to approach it in the deliberate fashion of the professional taster, sampling many seemingly similar cheeses one after another. You can learn far more from sampling and comparing a variety of cheeses selected from the same group than from sampling new cheeses willy-nilly or from reading detailed descriptions of cheeses in this or any other book.

There is an obvious parallel in wine tasting. If you try different and unfamiliar wines at random, and at different times, you may enjoy them all, but your palate will not remember the subtle gradations of dryness or sweetness. If you assemble a half-dozen splits of red or white wine (but not both) and sample them one at a time, clearing your palate between sips, you will be able to compare them, determine which is the drier or sweeter, which has the most pleasing bouquet, which has more body. Similarly, in tasting cheeses you should assemble a half-dozen or more of the same kind. For example, you might start off with a half-dozen different Cheddars or blue-veined cheeses, or cheeses from one of the other flavor groups. Then you will be ready to make some fairly exact comparisons.

Here are a few pointers—drawn from the experience of professional tasters of wines, teas and foods—that can be useful in tasting and comparing cheeses.

First, plan on two separate tastings of the same group of cheeses. Two tastings are necessary to "fix" the taste of each cheese so that your palate will remember it. A quarter of a pound of each cheese should be enough for two samplings for two people.

Remember that all cheeses should be tasted at room temperature. Keep the cheeses refrigerated until a few hours before you sample them, and then remove only the amount you think you are going to use. No cheese takes kindly to a series of abrupt changes in temperature, and the true flavor of most cheeses is often not realized because the cheese has not had enough time at room temperature to come into its own. An executive of a prominent French cheese company says that whenever she offers samples at food shows, people say that they are familiar with the cheese but have never before had this quality. But, she says, the sampled cheese is the same as the cheese they buy. The difference is temperature. She always keeps the cheese at room temperature for three hours before serving.

Don't distract the taste. This means avoiding bread or crackers that have assertive flavors. A good French or Italian white bread is best, or, if you prefer, a plain unsalted cracker or water biscuit. Onion rye, sesame-seeded crackers, or celery- or cheese-flavored crackers will only divert your taste from the business at hand. The same with beverages. Drink whatever you like, but bear in mind that beer will drown the flavor of delicate cheeses (and will also be as filling as any food). Wine, of course, is a classic companion to cheese and will usually enhance its flavor, but wine will not help you judge the cheese on its own merits since any cheese tastes better with wine; however, if you want wine, choose one that is dry and light. Don't drink it while eating the cheese; instead, wait until the aftertaste of the cheese has "set"—then sip the wine. Thereafter, clear your palate with a small piece of unbuttered bread before you go on to the next cheese. The same applies if you're drinking coffee.

Many experts maintain that no one should smoke or drink hard liquor for at least half an hour before tasting. Professional tasters of wines and fine teas go even further—they don't smoke at all, and they do their tasting early in the morning, when their palates are freshest. But it's up to you. Smoke or drink if you will—up to the moment you start tasting. Just remember that you'll taste more if you skip the cigarette or drink *while* you're tasting. We have found that tea is ideal for cheese tasting—both as a foil for thirst and as a palate clearer. The tea should be taken without lemon because the acidity in citrus fruits collides with the aftertaste of some cheeses.

Be deliberate. Sample small amounts of cheese slowly and deliberately, so that all your tasting faculties can help you comprehend the flavors fully. The taste apparatus is not concentrated in one place: sour tastes are perceived at the tip of the tongue and inside the cheeks; bitter tastes are largely experienced at the underside of the tongue, and sweet tastes on the flat of the tongue. This means simply that if you eat a cheese too quickly, you will not taste it fully.

Repeat the tasting later the same day or the following day—with the same cheeses, breads and beverages. At the end of this second tasting you will have fairly definite ideas about your preferences and reservations.

Above all, remember that too much of *anything* can pall, and that appetite is a necessary concomitant to taste.

Cheese Tastings

What might you find, for example, if you were to assemble half a dozen cheeses from the blue-veined family? Let's say you have samples of Danish and domestic blue, Roquefort, Pipo Crem', Stilton and Gorgonzola.

You will probably observe that both domestic and Danish blue are more liberally veined than the French Roquefort. And that the nonveined areas of the Roquefort are decidedly whiter than those of the Danish or domestic blue. As between the Danish and the domestic blue, the pencilings of the former are more "legible"; in the domestic product they tend to blur. Other differences among these six blues are easily seen. The markings of the Pipo Crem' are a paler and truer blue than the others, while the Stilton has an ivory background that deepens into gold around the edges, and the Gorgonzola, which may be either white or cream-color, is also rather blurry in its markings and is notable among all these cheeses for its particularly soft, malleable look.

As for texture, the Danish blue is likely to seem the creamiest. The Roquefort, in contrast, will seem lean. To make an extreme comparison: take the texture of Danish blue to its ultimate and you have soft butter; take Roquefort to its ultimate and you come very close to the texture of white meat of chicken. The textures of the other blues fall somewhere between.

As for flavor, obviously there are no absolutes in taste. Tastes do indeed differ, and sometimes the difference is physiological.

Differences in the human taste apparatus are not fully understood, but investigations have shown that there can be wide variations in the way people react to the "same" taste. Most people usually agree, for example, that sweet is sweet, but there are those to whom sweet is actually bitter. Often what is only moderately sweet to one person can be too sweet to another. Differences in taste also derive from differences in experience and background. But in any case no two people experience precisely the same taste.

Fortunately, however, most persons' tastes are close enough for us to be able to reach some kind of agreement on flavors, and a sampling of the blue-veined cheeses may suggest to you many of the same things it suggested to us. In comparison with the other blue cheeses, Danish and domestic blue are rich, sometimes fruity. This fruitiness becomes more apparent when the cheese has been at room temperature for a couple of hours, depending, of course, on the warmth of the room. When soft, these cheeses tend to be a little flamboyant. The Stilton is the mildest, and faintly resembles English Cheddar in flavor. At the other extreme is Gorgonzola, strongest in taste but by no means overpowering—perhaps because of its creaminess. Again on the milder side is the Roquefort, whose flavor has a piquancy bordering on tartness. Roquefort and Danish and domestic blue (which are sometimes offered in its place) do have certain characteristics in common, but Roquefort has a subtler flavor and one can eat more of it without surfeit.

Or take a few cheeses from the Swiss group—say, Emmenthal, Appenzeller, Wisconsin Swiss, Swiss Gruyère, French Gruyère, and Jarlsberg.

In appearance the Appenzeller, the French Gruyère and the Swiss Gruyère are almost identical. All three have a rough brown rind that resembles the skin of a shelled almond; the color is a beige-yellow; holes are about the size of large peas and are fairly frequent. The Emmenthal (or Switzerland Swiss) has the largest holes of all, some of them the size of a walnut, and the holes are invariably smooth and glossy; Wisconsin Swiss, which is made to approximate the Switzerland Swiss as closely as possible, also has very large holes, but their borders tend to be irregular rather than smooth and glossy, and the texture of typical Wisconsin Swiss is different from that of the firm Emmenthal—you have the feeling that if it dropped, it would bounce. Also the Wisconsin Swiss, if it is typical, will be devoid of rind, having matured in plastic wrap. Jarlsberg has the lightest color—more of a creamy off-white than a pale yellow. If they are all left at room temperature for the same length of time, the Jarlsberg will sweat butterfat, while the others will tend to keep to themselves.

The differences in flavor are unmistakable. The Appenzeller is clearly the strongest in the group, with a gamey flavor somewhat like a strong Port-Salut. The Emmenthal is mellow, somewhat nut-like and faintly sweet; the Wisconsin Swiss, which is intended to approximate it, is far less mellow, has less true "Swiss" flavor, and is often bitter. The lean Swiss Gruyère has a flavor that is mildly reminiscent of Parmesan—and so has the French Gruyère, which has, however, a little more tang and subtler nuances of flavor than its Swiss counterpart. Jarlsberg is creamier—and indeed has a little less character—than any of the others.

Of course your own tastings may yield different judgments—if only because cheeses are never absolutely the same from one purchase to the next, varying as they do in age, condition and quality.

In any event, in conducting your own tastings, you will find many cheeses that you will like immediately, others that you will grow to like, and still others that you will never like at all. A cheese lover does not necessarily love all cheeses. As Oscar Wilde observed, "It is only an auctioneer who can equally and impartially admire all schools of art." Perhaps it is only the cheese dealer who can take an Olympian view of all cheeses.

19

---∞---

Selecting
and Buying Cheeses

Gone are the days when people selected a cheese in the leisurely fashion that Osbert Burdett describes:

> One Autumn, in the very old and small-windowed grocery of a little country town, we selected a whole cheese by the deliberate method of inserting a cheese-trier into several. . . . A month later we repeated the trial and, in spite of the grocer's assurance that the Stilton was perfectly mature, we waited a month, tried yet again, and in the end declined to accept the Stilton, which had been chosen in November, until the following February. The perfection of flavour then reached is unforgettable.

Though the buyer today has the advantage of far greater variety and convenience in making his purchases, he rarely has a dealer who is as concerned as he is with the quality and suitability of the cheeses he eventually takes home. The more knowledgeable he is, the better he will fare—but he must fend for himself. Gone too are the times when, as in many English towns, the town crier used to come through, as Henry Steven recalls in *Cheddar Gorge,* and recite "an imposing list of the awful pains and penalties to be visited on anyone selling a cheese not up to reputed weight or standard." But we shall try to present some guides for judging cheeses before you buy them, and discuss the things to look for wherever you do your shopping.

WHERE TO BUY

Naturally, it is important to buy your cheeses at a shop in which you can place at least reasonable confidence. And the less familiar you are with the cheese you are buying, the more important this becomes. Unfortunately we have never found a cheese shop, large or small, whose cheeses, all of them, are invariably in good condition. Even the best stores occasionally have some, particularly among the soft-ripening imports, that are over the hill—which is why you must always watch what you are doing.

Sampling a cheese before you buy it will tell more about it than anything else can. So, if possible, buy your bulk cheeses at a place where you can try a cheese that is new to you or that you may have doubts about. Most department stores with good delicacy departments, and many gourmet shops, are glad to give samples, and people who buy a lot of cheese and know their cheeses often do ask for them. So don't feel like a neophyte—or a nuisance—in asking to sample a cheese. Good stores are obliging about it. Try to take your business to a place that takes an interest, answers your questions and doesn't rush you.

Buy your cheeses at a store that does enough business to suggest that the cheeses do not languish on the shelves beyond their time. Notice how the retailer keeps his cheeses. The shop should be clean and well kept, and the cheeses should be covered, usually with plastic film (Bloomingdale's in New York, for example, uses fifty dollars' worth of plastic film each week just for covering and re-covering cheeses every time they are cut).

Strong and mild cheeses should not be in close association with one another. Nor should a mild cheese like a Swiss be cheek-by-jowl with the ham or boloney, as it often is in delicatessens and butcher shops. For mild cheeses very readily absorb the smells and tastes of other, stronger foods.

Most of the cheese should be refrigerated, and only as much cheese should be out on the counter as may be expected to be sold that day. Parmesans and other equally hard cheeses can be out in the open if the temperature in the store is cool.

Good Cheeses Look Good

The specific things to look for in buying a particular cheese are discussed in the earlier cheese chapters, but here are some general buying guides that apply to all cheeses.

First, the cheese should *look* good to you. This is half the battle in buying any cheese, whether you are an expert's expert or consider yourself completely inexperienced. A few cheeses (such as the older goat cheeses sold in Paris and other far-out cheeses) don't look good by ordinary standards, but they have their own special following just as hundred-year-old eggs do, and doubtless they look good to the people who like them. Countless imported cheeses can be found in deplorable condition, and dealers will sometimes press them on the hapless buyer, arguing that "that's the way they're supposed to be." The fact is that most of these are not fit to eat. Their rusted or brownish looks are matched by their taste. Good cheeses, on the other hand, almost invariably look good.

BUYING CHEESES IN BULK

If you are buying cheeses in bulk, you have less chance of going wrong because you can see the cheese itself, as you also can when you buy pieces that have been pre-cut and cellophane-wrapped in supermarkets. Grocery stores, delicatessens and supermarkets do not encourage their customers to taste before they buy, so asking for samples may be awkward or impossible. So for the moment let us assume that you can see but not sample the cheese.

The Hard-Pressed and Marbled Cheeses

A Cheddar or similar firm, pressed cheese need not look moist but it should not have cracks on its surfaces indicating that it is dry, or flecks of white mold in the body of the cheese. Cheddars and others of the same consistency are good, long-keeping cheeses, and if they show signs of wear and tear you can be sure that they have been around too long and have not been properly cared for.

Blue-veined cheeses should be bought in bulk at small neighborhood stores only if the dealer sells a fair amount of them; usually these are safer to buy at a good supermarket with a faster turnover, and they can be bought with even greater safety in good department stores, gourmet shops, and specialty cheese stores.

A veined cheese, in any case, should look moist rather than granular, and the marbling should be pleasing to the eye, whatever kind of veining it is. Each one, in its way, will look right if it is right. When any one of these cheeses is too old, it gets a dry, cakey, forlorn look; and where the rich veins should contrast with the clean white or ivory body of the cheese, instead there are dry fissures of black streaking its graying or yellowing body. If the cheese within half an inch of the rind of Gorgonzola or Stilton looks dark or faintly disagreeable, try it before you buy; it may be too old.

Of all the blues, however, none is so important to sample as Roquefort, by general consent one of the half-dozen great cheeses. It *is* that good when it is as it should be. But since Roqueforts exported to the United States are likely to be oversalted, every once in a while a Roquefort is just too salty to be enjoyable.

Buying Swiss

Among neighborhood stores the choice will generally be between a domestic and an imported Swiss, either pre-packaged or in bulk. The imported will cost more but it's worth the difference—*if* it's Switzerland Swiss. Imported does not necessarily mean imported from Switzerland, and many a Finnish Swiss that is simply marked "Imported" fetches a fancy price from people who assume that they are getting the far superior Switzerland Swiss. If you are buying the cheese in bulk, look for the word "Switzerland," stamped all over the rind; if you are buying it in plastic packages, read the labeling carefully. Bulk is generally better than packaged Switzerland Swiss, and both are decidedly better than our domestic Swiss —which is often slightly bitter and wanting in real Swiss flavor.

Buying Parmesan

The only Parmesan you will find in neighborhood stores—unless it happens to be an Italian neighborhood—is pre-grated, usually domestic and bearing the familiar name of one of our larger cheese companies. This is better than having no cheese for your spaghetti, but it simply does not compare with the Italian Parmesan, particularly the finest, which is the Parmigiano-Reggiano. Soon these cheeses will have their name stenciled over the rind. Meanwhile, buy Parmesan by the piece, if you can, in the best Italian store or department store or specialty cheese or gourmet shop you have access to. And sample it first. If you buy it in a supermarket—and a few of the better ones do carry high-quality Parmesan—be sure that it is marked "Italian Parmesan" or "Imported Italian Parmesan." Of course you won't be able to investigate it further until you get it home.

Buying Medium-Firm Cheeses

Most of the medium-firm cheeses, such as Munster, Fynbo, Elbo and the other Scandinavian "bo's," French Port-Salut, and Gouda and Edam particularly, are among the safest you can buy as far as keeping qualities are concerned. Almost without exception they will be good if they look good. Munster, however, varies a great deal in its creaminess. The richer ones usually look softer, whereas the less creamy ones have a harder, drier appearance and the cheese, as it is sliced, flops over like pieces of cardboard instead of bending away from the blade.

In buying Fontina, avoid the soft, bright-yellow substitute that is currently being marketed in a red rind. The genuine Fontina d'Aosta has a rind the color of an almond skin, and the cheese is the same ivory shade as a Switzerland Emmenthal or Gruyère.

BUYING BRIE

Of all cheeses, Brie is the most difficult to find at its peak. This, however, is one of the few soft-ripening cheeses that you can buy in bulk, which means that you can see what you are getting. The best Brie is Brie de Meaux, which comes in a large white pancake, very thin, hardly more than a half-inch high. Be sure it is glossy throughout and that it does not have a hard, cheesecakey center, for it is unlikely to ripen, if it ripens at all, in time to catch up with the rest of the cheese. Buy a whole uncut Brie only from a dealer to whom you would entrust your own mother, and tell him a few days in advance when you expect to use it.

PACKAGED CHEESES

Packaged cheeses present special problems because you can't see them. But here's what to look for: the wrapper should be fresh and clean and adhere loosely to the cheese; if it is gummy or sticky or stained, don't take it, and don't take it if it smells when it shouldn't, or smells more than it should. Don't take it either if the paper is broken anywhere and the cheese is exposed.

But the look of the paper is not by itself an unfailing indicator of the condition of the cheese inside. Here is what a guide, written for retailers by a group that promotes French cheeses, has to say about outfoxing the customer who buys "with his eyes":

> If owing to a previous accident in the temperatures successively undergone, and even by the consequence of the ripening fermentation inside the boxes, the paper wrapping the soft cheeses like Camemberts or Carrés, seems under the lid to be sinking into the crust of the cheese by excess moisture or sticking to its moulds (*natural and indispensable*) but likely to put off the customer who buys first "with his eyes," *take off this paper.*
>
> And re-wrap the cheese with the same paper to be obtained from the wholesaler who is supplied by the French exporter of the brand, then put it back in its box.

And here is another piece of advice to the dealer from the same source:

> For soft cheeses "caught" by the heat during the delivery, seeming to sweat in their boxes, take them out of their boxes, take off their wrapping paper, put them direct on rye straw on the shelves, turn them over twice in 3 days and repack as said above.

SPECIAL POINTERS ON SOFT-RIPENING CHEESES

The shape of the cheese is another indicator of a cheese's condition, and one that cannot so readily be doctored. All but the hard cheeses should be pleasingly plump. They should fill out their wrappings perfectly and feel smooth and yielding to the touch, not rough and wrinkled.

Soft-ripening cheeses like Camembert and Pont-l'Évêque should fill up their boxes, and the centers of these cheeses should not be sunken, nor the outside edges be standing up in ridges. The cheese should not be hard or brown, but golden and soft. Its paper will be sticky but the stickiness should be uniform and moist, and the paper should not be glued down in little hard blotches. French Camembert, Pont-l'Évêque and other similar imported soft-ripening cheeses should be avoided, by and large, during the summer months.

At this writing, Liederkranz cheeses are dated, and it is usually best to buy a Liederkranz that has a few days at least to go before its expiration. Sometimes cheeses with different dates will be found in the same refrigerator case, and if you poke around you will often find the newer cheeses to the rear and at the bottom of the stack. Lift off the lid anyway and take a quick look to be sure that the paper is fresh and the cheese upstanding, even though soft. It should not be mushy or sticky.The smell may be strong, in a kind of direct barnyardy way, but it should not be rank. There is a real difference.

The world is divided between those who take back things that are bad, and those who simply throw them away. Time permitting,

we are takers-back. There are a number of advantages in taking
back. One is that you get the measure of your retailer. Another is
that you avoid feeling that you've been had—a feeling well known
to those of the throwing-away school. A third is that you may get a
decent cheese in exchange for the bad one. And finally, if you
know in advance that you will not accept a bad cheese, you can
avoid the disappointment *and* the trip back this way: we always
open any doubtful cheese we have bought before we are a dozen
steps away from the premises. If it's no good, it goes right back.
And if any dealer will not permit you to take the lid off a boxed
cheese and look at it without unwrapping it—and some won't—he
does not deserve your business and his cheeses are probably suspect
anyway.

There are a number of kinds of stores in which to shop for
cheeses; each has its advantages and limitations.

What You Can Get at the Corner Store

The chief advantage of the corner grocery store is its convenience, although its selection of natural cheeses is usually limited. But suppose you had to put together a buffet quickly for
unexpected guests. Assuming reasonable turnover, you could probably find there the ingredients for assembling a respectable, if not
exotic, cheese tray: a wedge of young, medium, or more-than-six-
months-old Cheddar (the wedges sold prepackaged by two large
cheese companies are all good); a wheel or half-wheel of domestic
Camembert in the little sections; a Liederkranz; a fresh cream
cheese; and, if you are lucky, some Switzerland Swiss. The store
may also carry little wedges of blue or Roquefort cheese, and
though these can be good they are often dry and in need of a little
sprucing up with cream and cognac.

The Neighborhood Delicatessen or Supermarket

Neighborhood delicatessens and supermarkets usually carry a
larger assortment of cheeses than do small grocers, and the variety

is growing all the time. Thus, in addition to the cheeses carried by the grocer, you are likely to find: Munster, in bulk or freshly sliced and packaged—with or without caraway; natural Limburger; Danish blue or Roquefort in wheels or cut freshly from whole cheeses; the dependable and delicious Bel Paese; Port-Salut perhaps—Danish, or the domestic; the bland and creamy Baronet or Gold-N-Rich; and of course the ubiquitous Edams.

Nowhere is the growing American taste for cheeses reflected more clearly than in the refrigerator cases of supermarkets and delicatessens all over the country. One is likely now to find many cheeses that were unknown to such stores a few years ago—for example, Crema Danica, the luxurious dessert cheese from Denmark, or the Hablé Crème Chantilly, the exquisite mild cheese from Sweden. Often the condition of their packaged cheeses, particularly the perishable imports, leaves a good deal to be desired. But by and large the cheeses sold by the piece, wrapped in cellophane or plastic, are good cheeses and usually in excellent condition.

Department Stores and Gourmet Shops

There are advantages in buying cheeses in the fancy pantries of large department stores like Macy's and Bloomingdale's in New York, and Marshall Field in Chicago. These stores rate among the most dependable sellers of cheese we know. Their selections are wide, from time to time including cheeses that are difficult to find anywhere, and they keep their cheeses well. The prices are a little higher than elsewhere, but worth it because you get what you ask for and you can rely on the quality.

Stores Specializing in the Foods of One Country

If the cheese you are looking for is Feta, you may find it in a large cheese store or—though rarely—in a supermarket, but the one place you are certain to find it, and probably at its best, is in the little neighborhood Greek store in any city with enough Greeks to support one. Similarly, if you are looking for Gorgonzola or imported Parmesan or ricotta, your best bet is a little neighborhood Italian grocer. Proprietors of the small stores devoted to the foods of a particular country—the little *salumerias* or *bodegas* or *wurstwarrens* and other such stores that are to be found in so many cities—are usually obliging with samples because they appreciate your interest in the specialties of their country. You may be well rewarded if you give them a try, and also take the opportunity of tasting some cheese that looks good and that you may not have known before.

Cheeses in these stores are often good because many of them have little bands of devoted customers who know their Gorgonzola or whatever it happens to be. Most of these stores buy their cheeses in small quantities as they are needed, because imported cheeses are usually not cheap. This means that they are usually fresh and otherwise in good condition. Do not be put off by what may seem to be a poor storefront, for the proprietor may feel it is more important to put his capital into quality products than into paint and chrome.

THE SPECIALTY CHEESE SHOP

Specialty cheese shops have only rather recently come into being, at least on a national scale. Now such shops have grown up in cities all over the country and in many smaller communities as well. They offer a large variety of cheeses, in many cases at prices below those of department stores and delicacy shops. Some of them are good places to shop in, others are not.

We know of one chain, for example, with branches throughout Westchester, New Jersey and Connecticut, where high standards are scrupulously maintained and where customers are not rushed out before they have had a chance to think of what they want.

On the other hand, there are two independent cheese shops we know which are both renowned for the variety of cheeses they sell and crowded at almost any hour you walk into them. Here you are not encouraged to sample, and your first question may be answered so summarily that you will feel disinclined to ask any others. If the clerks happen to be in a jocular mood they will call you "honey." One August afternoon we paid a visit to one of these shops, whose much-publicized assortment boasts an extraordinary number of imported as well as domestic cheeses. Some of them were in refrigerator cases, but more than two-thirds of them were out—almost out on the street, because the store had removable doors as many vegetable stands do, and the doors were off. The afternoon was leaden with heat. We were surrounded from floor to ceiling by cheeses glistening with sweat. Tears were running out of the Swiss's eyes while the others sweated down their eyeless, hardened faces. Many by now were misshapen and squat. A Munster was bulging as if it might explode; even reasonably firm cheeses were oozing, glued to their places by their own heavy juices. What must the softer cheeses have been doing under their discreet wraps?

The purpose of the visit was to return a Bresse blue that had been bought there the day before. When cut into, this cheese had all but struck back. Obviously it had been bad for many weeks—so bad that it did not bear close examination.

The clerk took one look, rewrapped the cheese, and put it back on the refrigerator shelf with other Bresse blues he had on sale. "All right, honey," he said, "pick out anything else you want." Clearly some else was destined to get that same cheese. "But that cheese has been cut into," we objected. "It's okay," he said, "pick out anything else you want."

This store's catalogue is impressive. It even lists cheeses which cannot be imported into the country: English farmhouse Cheddar, Italian Stracchino, Swiss Sbrinz, Piora, Bellelay, and Vacherin du Mont d'Or.

Some of the cheeses sold in these two stores, particularly during the cooler months, are perfectly good and in good condition. But others are not, and the clerks will not hesitate to improvise—to give you a substitute for the cheese you want without telling you it *is* a substitute. Thus in one of them we were simply given an Argentine Sbrinz when we had asked for Swiss Sbrinz. The two are entirely different cheeses.

The cheese buyer of a large and reputable department store was puzzled when one of his customers told him that he had seen loaf Camembert sold by the pound in one of these stores, and at a surprisingly low price. A spy dispatched to the spot ascertained that the "Camembert" was a Danish Port-Salut—for Camembert is never made in loaves or sold in bulk.

This is not to discourage people from shopping in stores of this kind. But they are not places in which to relax. You must be alert every moment, and the more you know about cheeses the better. The less you know about the cheeses you are buying, and the less you want to struggle, the better off you will be in the hands of a dealer in whom you can place confidence. But he is a rarity, and only trial and error will turn him up.

Buying Cheeses by Mail Order

The same applies to mail-order business. Specialty cheese shops often have extensive catalogues. But if you can't be sure of what you are getting when you go there, how will your order be filled in your absence? Nevertheless there are department stores, cheese and delicacy shops, and mail-order houses specializing in cheese, many of them in Wisconsin, with thousands of satisfied customers. You should know their reputation before you give such an establishment your business.

In general, the harder the cheese the more likely that it will arrive in good condition. Cheeses like Cheddar, Swiss, Gruyère, Parmesan, American Munster, Edam, and Port-Salut (if it is not too ripe) travel well. Soft cheeses like Camembert, Pont-l'Évêque and Brie are risky to mail, even by air. With luck, and a dealer who can be depended upon to select one properly green for shipping, the cheese may arrive in its prime.

One mail-order catalogue features a gift assortment of cheeses at $15, more than half of which are soft-ripening and ultra-perishable. Even assuming that these all arrive in good condition—which is unlikely—imagine the consternation of the recipient who has to use up all those cheeses before they are overripe, say within twenty-four or forty-eight hours. What goes into a gift assortment should be balanced between perishable and longer-keeping cheeses. It is safer to pick such gifts yourself rather than to send for them. Assortments that are padded, as many are, with process cheeses, are best avoided unless you know that the recipient's tastes run that way.

Some mail-order houses specify the minimum orders they will handle, and they will not cut bulk cheeses in quantities of less than one pound or over. Some add a flat sum, such as twenty-five cents per pound on cut cheeses as a "delivery charge," which may or may not include postage. Many reserve the right to substitute other cheeses for any that are "not ripe or ready." A reputable dealer, if he does this at all, will try to make as close a substitution as he can. But his idea of a close substitute may not be yours, so this is a situation to be aware of; and obviously those dealers whose catalogues list cheeses that are never imported here must always be making substitutions because the cheeses aren't "ripe or ready."

To sum up, no one store, if it has hundreds of different cheeses to worry about, is likely to have them all in good condition. In a store with an imposing variety, including some obscure cheeses for which there cannot be consistent or heavy demand, the likelihood is that some or many of these cheeses will be off. As a general rule, it is better to sacrifice some of the variety for a smaller selection in a store that keeps its cheeses well than to have hundreds of cheeses to choose from—many of them real gambles.

20

---◦∞◦---

Serving Cheeses:
What Goes with What

Making do with what she had, the eighteenth-century dairy-woman used to set out her new-made country cheeses on fresh green cabbage leaves, sprinkling them with water from time to time to keep them moist. No way of arranging them could have been simpler or more appealing.

In France, even today, cheeses are often displayed in shops on woven rye mats or wrapped in chestnut leaves, ice-green in early spring, russet in October, changing with the season but always reminding us that cheese, like wine, is a fruit of the soil and is most in its element with natural things. And if you have ever bought *formaggio fresco* in a small Italian store that makes its own cheeses, one reason they may have looked so inviting is that they were shown in the rustic little wicker baskets that have been used for draining fresh country cheeses for hundreds of years.

In serving cheeses you will find that no crystal or china, however beautiful, can be more harmonious with it than natural things—the grained wood of the cheese board, the more simply shaped the better, with no other decoration than perhaps a few leaves for the cheeses to rest upon or a garnish of fresh cress or parsley; or instead of the wooden board, a slab of fine marble. This matter of harmony enters into everything that has to do with the serving of cheeses, for a certain natural harmony determines what goes with what; it is the final arbiter not only of the serving equipment, but of the foods and wines and other drinks that accompany the cheeses, and of the choice of the cheeses themselves.

In Europe, no food is so popular at all hours as cheese, which makes its first appearance on the breakfast tables of the Dutch and is enjoyed throughout the day and into the night until the last steaming bowlful of onion soup has been given its sprinkling of Parmesan at Les Halles in Paris. In England, cheese has for centuries been the lunch of draymen—of the workman who, according to Edward Bunyard, "had his meal of bread and good cheese and good beer or cider out of a stone jar under the hedge." Except that they drank their ale out of silver tankards, whole public schools full of English boys daily partook of the same lunch, as Evelyn Waugh recalls in his autobiography; and the combination remains a favorite at most London clubs. For, as Bunyard wrote, "Any Englishman whose heart is in the right place will be quietly content with a lunch of beer and cheese and bread." And men all over the world would agree.

In addition to serving cheese as a snack, as an hors d'oeuvre with drinks, or as part of a buffet, Americans increasingly are honoring the European custom of serving cheese as a last or next-to-last course of a meal. At the cheese and wine tastings that are becoming popular here (after having taken hold in Britain, where they are viewed as an answer to the high price of whiskey), cheese occupies the center of the stage, with the entire meal consisting only of cheeses, with a variety of breads and garnishes, and wines and beers to go with them.

POINTERS FOR SERVING CHEESE

Serve all cheese at room temperature. If the weather is hot, they will need to be out only half an hour; if it is warm, an hour on the average will be enough; otherwise allow two or three hours or more. Soft cheeses like Camembert warm up in a third of the time it takes for a hard cheese like Gruyère to come into its own. This means that you may have to put out cheeses at different times, starting with the harder cheeses and ending with the softest ones.

Cut and serve only as much cheese as you expect to use. Though a wheel of cheese looks more handsome than a wedge, no cheese, not even a hard Cheddar or Gruyère, will benefit from re-refrigeration after it has been out in the open for a number of hours.

Leave enough room around each cheese so that it can be cut easily. A board too closely covered with cheeses gets messy quickly, and makes it awkward for guests to help themselves.

Do not place strong and mild cheeses next to each other. These should be placed well apart, or served separately.

Have enough knives and other cutters so that the same knife need not be used to cut more than one cheese.

Be careful about overpowering delicate cheeses with strongly flavored breads and beverages.

Vary the accompaniments to strong cheese. A strong cheese may be supported by beverages and foods that are equally hearty, or their strong taste may be contrasted with light wines and beers, and with sweet butter and plain breads.

Offer a choice of beverage. Though wine is the classic accompaniment to cheese, there is no cheese that is not good with tea or coffee, and many, particularly the soft-ripening cheeses, have a natural affinity for tart cider.

Vary the cheeses. Unless you are familiar with the tastes of each of your guests—and even then you would have to anticipate their moods—have an alternative, even if it is only one other cheese, to the strong cheese you may be serving. If cheese is one of the main foods, try to strike a balance between strong and mild cheeses, old standbys and cheeses that may be new to your guests.

Avoid a tricked-out look in serving cheeses. This applies to most arrangements involving toothpicks, bits of cherry, pineapple, sprigs of parsley, and stars and hearts cut out of vegetables. Likewise, all suggestions for serving cheeses with "gaily decorated" little anythings should be ignored. Good cheese is beautiful in itself. It shows off best on plain wood or other natural materials, or plain white plates and platters.

CHEESE AT THE END OF A DINNER

For centuries it was believed that "cheese digests all things except itself." There are adages and couplets to that effect in many languages, dating from the seventeenth century to as far back as medieval Latin. But cheese has long since been proved digestible, and the belief has no carryover into our time save one: some people think it is responsible for the custom of serving cheese at the end of a meal.

This custom is largely European. Especially in Italy and in France (where the *pâtissier's* art is unsurpassed), diners sometimes have the best of two worlds—having cheese and fruit as the penultimate course, followed by the sweet. And sometimes such fine matters of taste are not at issue, as in the case of Jorrocks, who cheerfully announced after his supper, "I'll fill up the chinks wi' cheese." In any event, if you are serving cheese at the end of dinner, it is always a good idea to have some little sweet on hand for those who may prefer it.

Cheese harmonizes with many kinds and combinations of foods, and as a last course it will enhance almost any dinner or luncheon, with these broad exceptions: it is not suitable following extremely rich meat or poultry, such as pork or roast duck. It should be introduced sparingly if at all following a rich creamed main course (or, obviously, a cheese dish like a soufflé). It should be avoided in menus to which it naturally seems alien—particularly with dishes from a part of the world where little cheese is eaten. For example, cheese would seem wrong following a Chinese or Japanese dinner, a paella, or a hot Indian curry.

Conversely, it goes particularly well with the foods and cuisines of countries that are big cheese producers and consumers. It is difficult to imagine an Italian dinner, for example, without some cheese during or after it—and the same is true of a French or Viennese or Swiss menu.

Generally speaking, dinner cheeses are of two kinds. Some are called dessert cheeses, though they may not be sweet and may in fact be eaten at any other time. Very delicate creamy cheeses like Hablé Crème Chantilly, and the double- and triple-crèmes are examples—all of them very luxurious and meant to be eaten as a sweet, in small dollops, as the final touch to a perfect dinner. The French often serve them, particularly Petit-Suisse and Fontaine-bleau, with a light sprinkling of sugar and, in season, with straw-berries or raspberries.

Not so delicate as these are Brie and Camembert, which together with Roquefort are the traditional after-dinner cheeses of France, just as Stilton (with its inevitable glass of port) is the dessert cheese of England. These are all cheeses which may be followed by a sweet.

The rich and delicate crèmes are best served at luncheon or after a light dinner, for as Edward Bunyard has so correctly observed, "The meal that they end must be of pastel shades; an omelette, chicken in aspic, and wood strawberries, for instance. Any rough red meat or loud-spoken wine would be disastrous in the theme of things." And a "rough red meat" demands a cheese of equal charac-ter to follow it—a cheese not especially rich or creamy but almost astringent, like Stilton or one of the other blues.

Some cheeses, on the other hand, somehow do not suggest them-selves as suitable for after dinner. These are the eating cheeses that primarily serve hunger rather than appetite—cheeses like Cheddar and Swiss and Gruyère, which also may form the basis of dishes that are themselves the meal. And the same is true of very bland and buttery cheeses. The only cheese we can think of that is used primarily in cooking and that also serves admirably as a dessert cheese is Parmesan—if it is your good fortune to get a well-flavored piece that is moist and chewy.

CHEESE AS AN HORS D'OEUVRE

The choice and variety of cheeses to serve as hors d'oeuvres depends upon whether you are serving cheese with the drink that immediately precedes dinner or at a cocktail party that may last for several hours before any thought is given to dinner.

In the first instance, the cheese is just a little something to set off the drink, but it should not dull the appetite. Accordingly, it should be a cheese of definite flavor and piquancy so that a little goes a long way—like Roquefort or Brie. It should not be a cheese like Cheddar or Swiss, or bland cheeses that people can eat a lot of very easily and that are more filling.

At a cocktail party, particularly if it goes on and on, cheeses that give some sustenance are welcome and sometimes necessary. For a large party, we recommend selecting three or four good cheeses in different taste ranges and sticking to them, with enough of the same to keep replacing them as they are eaten. For example, a big slab of Fontina, a half or whole Canadian Cheddar, a large piece of a select, creamy Gorgonzola (this spreads and manages better, when guests are helping themselves, than the more crumbly marbled cheeses, and it looks better longer); and perhaps some bars of well-softened Crema Danica or, for the ultimate in elegance, a half or whole wheel of Brie de Meaux.

Every taste will be served with this balance of one mild firm cheese (instead of Fontina other good candidates would be French or Swiss Gruyère, Appenzeller, or French Port-Salut); one choice Cheddar or Cheddar relative such as Caerphilly or Leicester; one marbled cheese; and one luxurious soft-ripening cheese (alternates might be a whole Reblochon or Kernhem, a Triple Crème Parfait, Four Seasons, Caprice des Dieux or any number of others, including Camembert if it is in whole rounds rather than individual portions).

Sticking with the same three or four cheeses you start out with not only avoids needless complications, it avoids the familiar frustration of large cocktail parties at which various foods are served once and disappear never to be seen again—if they have been seen at all—by some guests. It is also frustrating to have just a taste of a cheese one finds spectacular and, after completing the long circuit of the room, to return to find it replaced by something entirely different.

Strong cheeses like Limburger and Liederkranz are not for cocktail parties because after an hour or so at warm temperatures they will all but clear the room. Also they demand beer, onions—and understanding friends.

WHAT TO DRINK WITH CHEESE

Wine is of course the classic accompaniment to cheese—countless kinds of cheese—followed in popularity by beer and ale, which are not appropriate to as many different cheeses but are traditional to some. As Edward Bunyard wrote, "For lovers of wine or beer, cheese would have *had* to be invented had it not grown up with these two drinks." Which cheeses are better with wine and which with beer? Though this is a matter of taste, there are certain broad divisions established by custom, from which we can make a few generalizations.

CHEESES WITH ALE OR BEER

Cheeses that go particularly well with ale or beer fall into two main groups: the first is Cheddar together with the large family of cheeses whose flavor has something of the Cheddar taste about it—cheeses like Cheshire, Double Gloucester, Dunlop and Caerphilly. The second group consists of the very strong cheeses—Limburger and Liederkranz and others like them.

It has been recognized for centuries that cheeses in the Cheddar group have a natural affinity for beer or ale, and the marriage survives to this day, not only in pubs all over England but in the form of the Welsh rabbit—which was not originally made with ale, but washed down with such quantities of it that recipe writers eventually put the ale into the rabbit itself. Though the British prize their glass of claret or port with cheeses of other countries, many experts strongly favor beer or ale with all British cheeses except Stilton. Ambrose Heath, discussing his favorite Wensleydale, says: "Port, I think, is too powerful an ally; besides it is pledged to Stilton by use. . . . Wine drinkers must forgive me if I point out what is really the only possible accompaniment: Beer. Our English cheeses are brawny, hearty creatures that really need English fashions. A glass of beer comes naturally to the mind when cheese is being discussed; and if your meal is simple . . . there is no reason why beer should not after all be best."

And Osbert Burdett goes so far as to say that English cheeses have no place at the kind of elegant dinner where course succeeds course, and carefully chosen wine follows wine. English cheeses, he says, "are plain fellows, better suited to a plain oaken table, a clean cloth, and a tankard. We shall do no good by trying to dress them up in fancy clothes."

As for the strong cheeses that also go best with beer or ale— surely there are no plainer fellows than these, no cheeses more conducive to thirst or more compatible to the equally plain onion, whose closest ally has always been beer or ale, not wine.

Cheeses with Wine

Edward Bunyard gives us a useful generalization: "It has been noted that the native cheese is usually the perfect complement to the native drink. These earthly essences, long separated in their transmutation through the cow or the vine, or perhaps our native barley, seem to rejoice at their meeting, as old friends long parted."

Throughout France, districts noted for their wines usually do not produce much cheese, and vice versa. But compatible wines and cheeses are often produced in neighboring districts, and the generalization that local wines are good with local cheeses holds true if you interpret it broadly. Often a wine will go extremely well with a cheese from a distant locality, if they both come from places with similar climates.

The cheese itself will often suggest what to drink with it, and more often than not it will be a drink natural to its own background. Emmenthal or Gruyère, for example, seem to call for a cool white mountain wine—light and undisposed to overpower the cheese—rather than more southerly and heavier wines like sherry or port, which somehow seem alien to it. A well-aged, rustic goat cheese, which has something of the taste of a mutton chop about it, does not call for a velvety wine but for a hearty, coarse vin du pays whose sting will cut through that rich meaty taste, and refresh the palate. A fine Roquefort, on the other hand, made with sheep's milk, which is more delicate than goat's, has a certain delicacy under its tingling flavor. It calls for a velvety wine—a full-bodied Burgundy (possibly even a white one like a Meursault), a Rhône, or one of the full-bodied clarets like St. Emilion or Pomerol.

Probably the best known rule for the selection of wines is the familiar injunction: serve red wines with red meat, and white wines with chicken or veal, fish or other seafood. Widely respected as it is, there is nothing sacred about it, but neither will it ever lead you astray. A variation can be applied to the selection of wines to go with particular cheeses. The lightest dry white wines should be served with the cheeses that are lightest and most delicate in flavor; and the heaviest, fullest-bodied red wines should be served with cheeses that are the strongest and most definite in character. Cheeses in the middle ranges should be served with wines that occupy a corresponding place in the range of wines.

Many specific lists of wines and their appropriate cheeses have been put out by the wine and cheese trades, but as T. A. Layton observes, these have generally been "wildly hit-or-miss affairs: caseous and vinous marriages based solely upon how much money each had at the time as a dowry." To be useful, such lists would have to be much more detailed. For example, if they recommend a Port-Salut, one should know if it is very young, middle-aged, or ripened and highly aromatic. For at each age the cheese has a different character that calls for a different wine.

Much more useful are the general guides to the kinds of wines usually preferred with various courses or kinds of foods. One of the best of these has been compiled by André Simon, the widely respected authority on wine and food. We have adapted his list to serve also as a wine guide for cheeses:

For delicate foods such as oysters, and the correspondingly delicate cheeses such as the uncured double- and triple-crèmes: a dry white wine such as Moselle, Alsace, Graves, Pouilly, or a Tavel Rosé.

For fish, poultry or veal, and such cheeses as Gruyère, Dunlop, young Parmesan, young Port-Salut: the fuller white wines, such as white Burgundy or hock, or dry champagne.

For beef, lamb or mutton, and such cheeses as Camembert and Brie, medium Port-Salut, aged Cheddar: Médoc, Beaujolais, Touraine or other rather light, red wines.

For duck, goose, pork or venison, and the strong soft-ripening cheeses such as aged Port-Salut, Pont-l'Évêque, Livarot and Maroilles as well as Roquefort and other veined cheeses: St. Emilion, red Burgundy, Côtes du Rhône or other full-bodied red wines.

The list is by no means complete, and some people may argue with this or that classification, but it does suggest a way of looking at cheeses and wines. In making your selections, you can be as flexible as you wish, despite the orthodoxies of the many experts. And for ordinary purposes, any dry wine you happen to be drinking at dinner will be perfectly good to finish off with your cheese.

Simon's list is built almost exclusively around French wines which, though they are the world's best, are not necessarily the best with all cheeses. Italy, for example, produces many fine wines and some of these are especially good with Italian cheeses. The Italian wines that go best with bland fish and chicken dishes include Soave, Lugana and Verdicchio, and any one of these, particularly the Soave, is excellent with the mild Fontina or Bal Paese. Italian Bardolino, Valpolicella, white Chianti and Orvieto Secco go well with cheeses, Italian or otherwise, that are on the mild side, like young provolone or Parmesan, or Friulana. Italian red Chianti, Frecciarossa Rosso, Barolo, Barbera and Barbaresco—all wines that can hold their own with rich or highly seasoned foods—are recommended for correspondingly strong cheeses such as Romano or Gorgonzola.

Also good with cheeses are the Rhine and Moselle wines of Germany, the not dissimilar wines of Alsace, and the less celebrated wines of Switzerland, Spain, Chile and a few other countries—as well as the wines of California, New York and Ohio. They are all well worth experimenting with, especially because the great wines, like France's clarets and Burgundies, have become not only increasingly expensive but also, in the case of vintages earlier than 1957, increasingly scarce. But when you can get them, great clarets and Burgundies may more than repay their cost, for no other wines have been so universally revered by cheese lovers, and these are wines that go with all kinds of cheeses except the very mildest. Port is also highly praised—possibly because so much of what has been written about cheese has been by Englishmen, who recognize no other wine as a fit companion for Stilton.

BREAD, BUTTER AND GARNISHES

The question has long been debated whether butter should be eaten with cheese. And though the French have always maintained that it should not, some experts attribute their view to parsimony. This is clearly another matter of taste. We have found that sweet butter will have a most pleasing effect upon a very strong Gorgonzola or a Roquefort that is too salty, and it will improve many other cheeses that have no such fault. The rich, soft-ripening cheeses don't seem to need it, but the leaner and drier ones do. Some people go further and eat cheese with cheese. The proprietor of Créplet-Brussol, one of the finest cheese shops in Paris, confesses that he usually eats a little Petit-Suisse with his Roquefort; similarly Stracchino which unfortunately you get only in Italy, is delicious with Fontina, Gorgonzola, or Parmesan.

As for breads and crackers, many unlikely combinations can turn out to be great discoveries; nevertheless some of the most conventional combinations can hardly be improved upon, for they have a natural compatibility. Thus a good rye bread or pumpernickel can't fail to be good with cheeses that are characteristically Swiss, German or Dutch; and the French and Italian breads are always good with French and Italian cheeses (and most other cheeses, too); even our own white bread, soft as foam rubber, seems to have been created for process American cheese.

Crisp crackers (without celery or other strong flavorings) are good with almost all cheeses, but they should be salted only lightly, if at all, and one of the best American crackers—one that goes particularly well with the soft-ripened cheeses because of the contrast in textures—is Triscuits, those little squares that are rather like Shredded Wheat. But some unlikely combinations can be excellent too, as for example, Canadian Cheddar on a buttered graham cracker.

Almost any fruit that is juicy is good with cheese. And so are all kinds of crisp things: watercress, celery, cucumber, and with the English Cheddar-like cheeses particularly, gherkins and sweet mixed pickles. These cheeses are also excellent with a touch of mustard, particularly Dijon or English. This list would be incomplete without one more entry: Liederkranz, with a thin slice of onion.

21

Storing and Restoring Cheeses

Most Europeans view the American practice of keeping cheeses in the refrigerator as just another example of our morbid fear of germs. Indeed, before giving a customer a brochure listing the cheeses he sells, M. Le Febvre, proprietor of Créplet-Brussol on Place de la Madeleine usually crosses out the sentence, "To store cheeses, keep them in the refrigerator." That it should be there at all is surprising, for the French connoisseur rejects the refrigerator, insisting that cheeses should be kept in some cool corner of the house.

If one lived abroad it would make sense to follow the European example, for in the absence of central heating, cool corners are easily come by, and many are not much warmer than the 38° F. one finds on the top shelf of almost any American refrigerator. We know one Parisian family so devoted to good living that it set aside an entire room for food storage. But finding such a room in a centrally heated American house or apartment is a problem. Cellars have long since yielded to insulated basements, and the few remaining pantries are as cozy as a baby's bunting. Cool larders are in short supply, and most of us have to rely upon our refrigerators, which, by and large, do a good job—as long as the temperature dial is properly set.

For most storing purposes, the desirable temperature range is from 35° F. at the bottom of the refrigerator directly above the vegetable crisper to 38° F. on the top shelf just beneath the freezer. In a kitchen where there is a lot of activity and where the refrigerator door is opened frequently, this 35° to 38° F. range can be maintained by setting the control dial at its middle point. This allows the refrigerating mechanism to adjust for the warm air that rushes into the box each time the door is opened. If the door is not opened during the day or over a week-end, the dial should be set for a higher temperature—about 20 per cent higher. (If you have ever opened the refrigerator to find that the lettuce in the crisper had frozen, even though you had not altered the dial, it probably was at a time when you had not opened the refrigerator door for a day or two.) Unless this adjustment is made, the concentrated cold, with no warm air to dissipate it, will drive the temperature down below the freezing point. Obviously this is harmful to cheeses and to most foods. In general, all cheeses fare well when they are well wrapped and kept on the top shelf of the refrigerator—or in the butter or cheese compartments found on the inside of many refrigerator doors. But these were clearly not designed by a cheese lover, because they are too small.

A cheese is well wrapped when it does not lose moisture. The amount of moisture in a cheese depends on its type, and so it becomes useful here to think in terms of firmness rather than flavor. Hard cheeses like Parmesan and firm cheeses like Cheddar have had more moisture pressed out of them than semifirm cheeses like Port-Salut. Soft-ripened cheeses like Camembert and fresh cheeses like cottage cheese, on the other hand, have been allowed to retain a good deal of moisture. But hard or soft, a cheese needs whatever moisture it has, and improperly wrapped refrigerated cheeses soon lose their moisture and become dry and hard, as do cheeses that are left exposed at room temperature long after the party's over. And even when they are well wrapped, a high temperature will cause firm and semifirm cheeses to sweat their fats away, and soft-ripened cheeses to spread and run, then harden and dry.

Storing Hard, Firm and Semifirm Cheeses

The more moisture a cheese has, the shorter its life. A Munster can't be expected to last as long as a Cheddar or a Parmesan. Munster may keep for three weeks, or perhaps longer, if well wrapped, but Cheddar will last for months, and Parmesan even longer.

The best wrappings for these cheeses are plastic wrap, aluminum foil or a damp cloth. Although a damp cloth won't adhere as closely as plastic wrap, it does restore moisture as the cheese loses it. Some connoisseurs dampen the cloth in a mild brine (a half-cup of water, a half-teaspoon of salt and a teaspoon of vinegar) but water alone will do if the cloth is dampened frequently. One further way of preventing moisture loss is to seal the pores of a cheese by running the flat of a knife over the cut surface.

Firm and semifirm cheeses have a longer life than softer ones, and you can buy them in larger quantities—if you buy them in one piece, cut off what you need, and return the rest to the refrigerator. No matter how splendid it looks, don't put a ten-pound wheel of Cheddar on the table each time you serve it. Repeatedly returning it to the refrigerator after it has been at room temperature for several hours will eventually affect its flavor. Nevertheless, if a firm or semifirm cheese has been left at warm room temperature until it is sweating, you can restore it by wiping it with a cold, damp cloth, wrapping it carefully and putting it into the refrigerator. Hopefully, this won't be necessary often; even the firmest cheese can take only so many temperature changes.

Finally, don't be dismayed to find that a cheese has developed a slight mold. If the cheese has been carefully wrapped, this is unlikely, but it may happen. Just cut off the mold; the cheese underneath will still be untouched and perfectly good.

Storing Blue-Veined Cheeses

Before blue cheeses are refrigerated they should be wrapped in a damp cloth or covered by a glass or plastic cheese dome. The damp cloth replaces the moisture the cheese loses but still permits some air to reach it. A dome keeps the cheese from losing too much moisture while giving it the air it needs. The need for air is a peculiarity of the blues; it is the interaction between cool air currents and bacterial spores during the curing stage that brings about their singular blue veining.

This veining, or mold, gives the blues their flavor, and it continues to develop slowly even while they are refrigerated. Therefore a blue cheese will be slightly sharper in flavor after a lengthy period of refrigeration. If you prefer a milder blue, buy a little at a time and eat it quickly. If you like a stronger blue, leave it in the refrigerator for a few weeks.

Cutting some blue cheeses presents special problems. In cutting a whole Danish or French blue, any sharp knife will do because these are creamy, and unlike the drier Roquefort, they do not crumble. For Roquefort, Norwegian blue, and some of the drier American blues, it is best to use a very thin, sharp knife or a fine wire cheese cutter.

Because of a Stilton's height—nine inches compared to a Roquefort's five—it can not be cut in one straight forward motion. This is probably why so many people over the years have scooped Stiltons. Stilton scoopers plunge their spoons or scoops into the center, digging up bits and pieces of the middle until they eventually tunnel their way down through the heart of the cheese, leaving a wide rim to dry and harden. The more dedicated scoopers pour port into these unsightly craters to restore the moisture—a practice all connoisseurs deplore, and with reason. Port goes superbly with Stilton, but when it is mixed with the cheese itself it adulterates Stilton's unique flavor and turns its creamy texture into a sodden mass. Scooping and port-pouring have a large following, however, and many people are convinced that this is the only way to deal with a Stilton. Once, when Ambrose Heath was dining in "a well-known foreign restaurant in London," he was urged by the waiter to have some of their Stilton in the real English style. "After much summoning by waiter and headwaiter," Heath writes, "there was borne to me half a Stilton, encased in a kind of bloodstained cloth, as well it might be; for inside the rind was a strangely lurid pulp, which the waiter stirred vigorously with a spoon. It was 'the real English style,' and what had made that caseo-vinous mash was Port."

The scooping practice is indeed wasteful. A Stilton weighing approximately fourteen pounds will yield, if scooped, probably no more than seven pounds of really good cheese—whereas if it is cut properly there is very little waste. A whole Stilton should first be cut in half—horizontally across its middle. This will give you two cheeses, each about four and a half inches high. Wrap one half in a damp cloth or plastic wrap and store it in the refrigerator until you've used the other half. (Or buy a half Stilton in the first place.) To cut a half Stilton, place the point of a long, sharp knife about half an inch below the exposed surface of the cheese and, keeping the blade horizontal, sink the point into the cheese until you reach the center. Hold the point of the knife firmly at the center and move the handle around the circumference. Then cut out small wedges of this half-inch layer for each serving. When you have used all the cheese on this level, you'll still have a Stilton four inches high. Then, following the same procedure, cut another half-inch layer. The point is to move down the cheese horizontally and in orderly stages, leveling the surface of the cheese as you go. In this way you expose less of the surface and keep the Stilton moist until the last morsel is gone.

Storing the Soft-Ripening Cheeses

There are three kinds of soft-ripening cheeses: free-flowing ones like Camembert, Liederkranz, and Brie; relatively firm ones like Pont-l'Évêque and Reblochon; and thick, creamy, cured double- and triple-crèmes like Monsieur Fromage and Triple Crème Parfait.

Of the three, the free-flowing ones are the most perishable and short-lived, and the only sure way of keeping them in good condition is to buy them in small quantities. Obviously what constitutes a small quantity varies with the occasion and depends on how many people are going to eat the cheese. A whole wheel of Brie de

Meaux, for example, is a reasonable amount for ten people but not for three, unless they can be counted on to do away with all or most of it at one sitting. The only thing to do with leftover Brie—or any free-flowing soft-ripening cheese—is to wrap it in plastic wrap or aluminum foil, leave it at room temperature overnight and eat it the next day for lunch, or breakfast, for that matter. But once it is flowing freely, don't stop the action by refrigerating it. It will never be so good again.

All whole uncut soft-ripening cheeses like Liederkranz, Brie, or even triangles of foil-wrapped Camembert, should be left in their chipboard boxes and stored in the refrigerator until several hours before you serve them. Even in the refrigerator they will ripen a little each hour—refrigeration retards the ripening process but it can not stop it.

The stages a Liederkranz goes through as it ripens are more or less the same as for all free-flowing soft-ripening cheeses. At the time it is shipped from the factory in refrigerated cars, its crust is white-yellow, its center is hard and chalky, and it has little flavor. After about ten days it ripens to the stage at which the crust is slightly yellow and the flavor is beginning to develop character. After another seven days, the crust is moist and full of yellow, the core is golden yellow, and the cheese has considerable flavor. Within the next seven days the crust, still moist, acquires a deep red-yellow color, the core has disappeared and the full interior of the cheese is a semifluid with a golden yellow color and a pronounced flavor. The cheese is now at its peak. From this point on, the flavor steadily deteriorates, becoming harsh and ammoniated.

Other soft-ripening cheeses may differ from Liederkranz, and from each other, in the color of their crust, but the progressive development of the interior and flavor is common to all. A soft-ripening cheese tends to ripen in direct ratio to the increase of temperature. We say "tends" because in trying to speed up the ripening process too quickly you can end up with a cheese that is ripe and flowing throughout except for the core, which remains hard and chalky to the end. This, unhappily, happens all too often with Brie.

The firmer soft-ripening cheeses like Pont-l'Évêque and Reblochon also mature steadily even when they are refrigerated. They too have their point of no return when flavor begins to deteriorate. They are not quite as short-lived as the free-flowing cheeses but you have to watch them carefully. These cheeses can be marvelous one day and terrible the next. The best thing here too is to wrap a leftover portion in plastic wrap or aluminum foil, leave it at room temperature and eat it as soon as possible.

The cured double- and triple-crèmes, although short-lived compared to firmer cheeses, seem to hold their flavor and their texture longer than any of the other soft-ripening cheeses. They can be opened, brought to room temperature, partly eaten, then wrapped and returned (in their boxes) to the refrigerator for several days before being brought to room temperature again—and still they can survive with no apparent deterioration of flavor. A possible reason for this is their extremely high cream content. Heavy cream, even though the container has been opened, will often last several weeks in a refrigerator, as will sour cream. Skim milk, however, sours quickly. The cream in milk appears to act as a stabilizer, and it may well serve the same function in the double- and triple-crèmes.

Storing the Fresh Country Cheeses

These cheeses too, should be bought in small quantities and kept away from foods with strong odors. Put cottage cheese in plastic cartons; wrap cream cheese and mozzarella in plastic wrap to seal in the moisture. Don't use a damp cloth, because these high-moisture cheeses lose moisture faster than a damp cloth can replace it.

Storing Odds and Ends of Cheeses

Ends or pieces of hard and firm cheeses that have become dry can be grated, kept refrigerated in a tightly covered glass jar, and used as a condiment. Blue cheeses can be mixed with an equal amount of butter, moistened with brandy and worked into a very good spread. Stored in a small crock, this will keep indefinitely.

IV

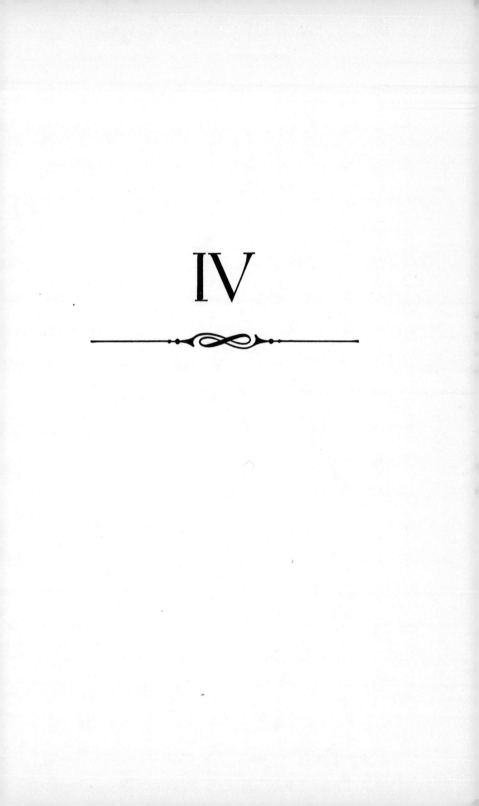

22

---◦◦◦---

Recipes

COOKING WITH CHEESE

The important thing to know about cooking with cheese is that too much heat or prolonged cooking tend to make cheese stringy or leathery. This can be avoided by shredding, stripping, grating or breaking up cheese into small pieces to cook more quickly; by blending it with other ingredients, such as a cream sauce, to reduce its density; by using a double boiler rather than direct heat for melting; and by keeping the heat moderate. And cheeses will take less time to cook if they are at room temperature beforehand.

The better-aged the cheese the more flavor, and the less you will need of it for seasoning; the younger and milder the cheese, the more you will need. Use well-aged cheeses particularly for dishes such as soufflés, which must be light.

Note: Four ounces of cheese, when grated, will fill, or slightly more than fill, one standard measuring cup.

Cheese Pastries

GALETTES AU FROMAGE
Cheese Wafers

These featherweight wafers are often made of Swiss cheese, but you can use other cheese or a mixture of cheeses if you wish, and thus employ leftovers. The dough contains just enough flour to hold the galettes together while they bake, and ¾ cup of flour is usually right for Swiss cheese. You will probably need more if you are using soft cheeses, and should always bake one as a test.

For about 30 wafers.
Preheat oven to 425 degrees.

½ pound (about 2 pressed-down cups) grated Swiss cheese or a mixture of cheeses
½ pound softened butter

¾ cup sifted all-purpose flour, more if needed
¼ teaspoon pepper
pinch of Cayenne pepper
salt to taste

Knead all ingredients together in a bowl or on a board. The mixture will be sticky. Roll a 1-tablespoon bit into a ball in the palms of your hands, then flatten it into a cake ¼ inch thick. Bake 10 to 15 minutes in hot oven to observe how it holds together; it should spread slightly, puff lightly, and brown. If it spreads out more than you wish, or is too fragile, knead in ¼ cup more flour and make another test.

lightly buttered baking sheets
1 egg beaten with ½ teaspoon water in a small bowl

a pastry brush
½ cup grated Swiss cheese
a cooling rack

When you are satisfied, form the rest of the dough into cakes and place on baking sheets. Paint the tops with beaten egg and top each with a pinch of grated cheese. Bake for 10 to 15 minutes until the galettes have puffed and browned lightly. Cool them on a rack.

Copyright © 1961 by Alfred A. Knopf, Inc. Reprinted from Mastering the Art of French Cooking *by Simone Beck, Louisette Bertholle and Julia Child, by permission of Alfred A. Knopf, Inc.*

CHEESE STRAWS

Equal quantities of grated cheese, butter, and flour. Mix butter and flour together in a bowl with a little Cayenne and salt. Add the cheese. When well mixed, roll it out thin and cut into strips, which place on a tin and bake in a moderate oven till pale brown.

From Cheeses of the World *by André L. Simon, published by Faber and Faber, London.*

CHEESE CUSHIONS

These puffy little morsels are an ideal acompaniment to salads or simple luncheon or supper dishes. Makes 62 squares.

⅔ cup shredded sharp American Cheddar cheese
½ cup butter or margarine

2 cups flour
½ teaspoon salt
⅛ teaspoon red pepper

Blend the cheese and butter or margarine thoroughly. Work in the flour sifted with the salt and red pepper. Do not add water; the mixture should be crumbly. Place in waxed paper and chill several hours. Roll to ½-inch thickness, folding the crumbs over and over until the mixture is firm. Cut into ¾-inch squares. Place on a cookie sheet, leaving space between the squares. Bake in a moderate oven, 375° F., 20 minutes.

From The Cheese Cookbook *by Marye Dahnke. Used by permission of Hill and Wang, Inc.*

PARMESAN SALAD CRISPS

½ cup butter
½ cup grated Parmesan cheese

1 cup flour
½ teaspoon baking powder
½ teaspoon salt

Cream butter until soft. Add Parmesan cheese. Mix until well blended. Add flour which has been sifted with baking powder and salt. Roll out thin on lightly floured board. Cut into rounds about 1 inch in diameter. Place on baking sheet. Bake in hot oven for 8 to 10 minutes, or until slightly brown. Cool, and put crisps together with the following filling:

Filling

2 tablespoons butter
¼ cup grated Parmesan cheese

2 tablespoons cream

Cream butter until soft. Beat in Parmesan cheese and cream. Mix until well blended. Makes 8 to 10 servings.

From The Art of Cheese Cookery *by Nika Standen. Copyright 1949 by Nika Standen and Florence Arfmann. Reprinted by permission of Doubleday & Company, Inc.*

CHEESE PIECRUST

Sift 2½ cups of flour with ½ teaspoon salt. Cut in, using a pastry blender or two knives, 1½ cups of grated American cheese, ⅔ cup of shortening, working and cutting till mixture resembles coarse meal, then add enough ice-cold water (about ⅓ cup) to make particles hold together. Pat and chill thoroughly before rolling out ⅛ inch in thickness. Line an ungreased pie plate in the usual way, pour in the filling; adjust the top crust in the usual way; make a few slits on top for the escape of steam; brush with ice-cold water, milk or beaten egg yolk, and bake according to directions, i.e., 10 minutes in a very hot oven (450° F.) to set the pastry; then at 350° F., for about 25 minutes.

Reprinted from The Gold Cook Book *by Louis P. deGouy with permission of Chilton Books, Philadelphia & New York. Copyright 1947, 1948 by the author.*

CHEESE BISCUIT

Sift one cup of flour with one fourth teaspoon of salt, cut in one third of a cup of butter. Add one cup of grated cheese. Work lightly into a stiff paste. Roll out one half inch thick and cut with very small cutter and prick tops with fork. Bake in a moderate oven about twelve minutes, but do not brown. These burn very easily.

(*Old Williamsburg Recipe. Prov'd Blair Kitchen, 1938.*)

From The Williamsburg Art of Cookery *by Mrs. Helen Bullock. Reprinted by permission of Colonial Williamsburg, Incorporated, publishers.*

CHEESE BREAD

1¼ cups milk	1 tablespoon lukewarm water
1 tablespoon sugar	2¾ cups flour
1 teaspoon salt	1½ cups shredded American
½ tablespoon butter or margarine	Cheddar
½ cake compressed yeast, or	melted butter or margarine
½ package dry granular yeast	

Scald the milk; add the sugar. salt, and ½ tablespoon of butter or margarine. Cool to lukewarm. Crumble the yeast into the water, let soften a few minutes, and add to the milk mixture. Add 2 cups flour and mix well. Add the cheese, and the remaining flour, and mix again. Knead on a floured board for 10 minutes. Place the dough in a greased bowl, brush with melted butter or margarine, cover, and let rise in a warm place until double in bulk. Knead, shape into a loaf, place in a greased 4- x 8-inch loaf pan, and brush with melted butter or margarine. Cover with a fresh towel and let rise until double in bulk. Bake in a moderately hot oven, 375° F., 50 minutes.

From The Cheese Cookbook *by Mary Dahnke. Used by permission of Hill and Wang, Inc.*

Hors d'Oeuvres

VOISIN CHEESE

½ pound Roquefort—buy cheese
high in flavor and low in salt

½ pound unsalted butter
Cayenne pepper to taste

Mash Roquefort to smooth consistency.
Cream butter.
Add to cheese.
Beat together until smooth and creamy.
Add the Cayenne and mix well.

PETITS POTS DE CRÈME AU FROMAGE

Preheat oven to 350°.

2 cups grated imported Swiss
cheese (½ pound)
6 eggs
3 cups heavy cream

¼ teaspoon Cayenne
¼ teaspoon salt
¼ teaspoons grated nutmeg

Serves 6–8.

Grate imported Swiss cheese until you have 2 cups. Beat 6 whole eggs with fork or egg whisk, adding gradually 3 cups heavy cream. Season to taste with about ¼ teaspoon each of salt, Cayenne, and nutmeg. Add 1 cup grated cheese, stir well, and pour into 8 little custard cups, being sure that part of the cheese goes into each. Place the cups in a shallow pan of hot water and bake until set, about 30 minutes. Just before serving, sprinkle the rest of the cheese over each dish.

CHEESE CROQUETTES

(a mixture with many uses)

This mixture is worth knowing about because it has so many uses and keeps so well. Shaped into pieces the size of a sea scallop, dipped in crumbs and deep-fried, it makes a wonderful hot hors d'oeuvre, in which case the following recipe makes enough for at least 14 people. Or it may be shaped into the larger, traditional croquette size and served as a luncheon dish. It is the perfect filling for little hot cheese turnovers (using the recipe for Cream Cheese Crust on page 276). And with diced ham added, it becomes the filling for the Schnitzel St. Moritz (page 290). It is also very good to slice and put on sautéed chicken breasts, with or without ham, and brown quickly under the broiler. It may be made beforehand and, if wrapped well in waxed paper, will keep in the refrigerator for a few days or in the freezer for at least two weeks. We suggest making it in a quantity not less than that given below. What you do not use immediately should be wrapped and frozen in two or three separate lumps for later use.

5 level tablespoons butter
⅜ cup flour
1 cup milk
3 egg yolks
¾ cup grated Swiss or Gruyère
½ cup grated Parmesan

1 cup of a bland, buttery cheese in small cubes or slivers (American Munster, mild Port-Salut, Bel Paese or any of the bland Scandinavian cheeses)
salt and pepper

Melt butter over a moderately low flame, blending in flour, then add the milk and stir until smooth and thick. Add whole egg yolks and stir in well, then add grated Swiss and Parmesan cheeses. When the cheeses melt and mixture is hot but not boiling, remove immediately from fire and gently mix in the cheese cubes, stirring until they melt. Add a pinch of salt and pepper. Spread in a large baking dish or pan and let cool, then put in refrigerator for about half an hour to chill. Cut, shape and use as you wish.

V.M.

Soups

CREAM OF ONION SOUP WITH CHEESE

1

4 medium-sized Spanish onions or 6 small white	1 cup sharp cheese, grated or cut into small pieces
2 tablespoons butter	pinch pepper, white or black
2 tablespoons flour	1/8 teaspoon salt
4 cups milk	

Scald milk while peeling and dicing the onions fine.

Melt the butter in the soup kettle and toss the onions in it until they are browned. Dust with flour and blend. Pour on the warm milk, a little at a time, stirring constantly, until the mixture is smooth. Add cheese and stir until it has melted. Serve with pilot crackers.

2

5 medium-sized white onions	4 cups milk
3 tablespoons butter	salt and pepper
3 tablespoons flour	4 tablespoons grated Parmesan

Peel onions and slice thin. Sauté in butter in top part of double boiler until lightly browned. Add flour and salt gradually, then the milk, stirring until smooth. Cook over the boiling water for 15 minutes more. It should be creamy and slightly thick when served. Sprinkle 1 tablespoonful of cheese over each cup.

From Onions Without Tears, copyright 1950 by Jean Bothwell. Reprinted by permission of Hastings House, Publishers, Inc.

DROVER'S INN CHEDDAR-CHEESE SOUP

½ cup chopped raw carrots
½ cup chopped raw celery
½ cup chopped raw onion
½ cup chopped raw green pepper
3 cups (lightly packed) of grated
   sharp Cheddar cheese
5 tablespoons butter

4 tablespoons flour
4 cups chicken broth
2 cups milk
salt, pepper
1 tablespoon chopped parsley
2 tablespoons dry sherry

Serves 6–8.

For years I had encountered cheese soup here and there without a thrill; then one day we had it at Drover's Inn. It was snowing hard, and we were frozen. I don't remember asking for the recipe, but I fortunately ran across it the other day scribbled on a scrap of paper. I tried it promptly, following the directions carefully, except when it was time to strain out the vegetables. These I decided to leave in. Please try the recipe and see how superb it is, the perfect soup for a very cold night.

Prepare ½ cup each very finely chopped raw carrot, celery, onion, and green pepper. Grate or shred enough sharp Cheddar cheese to make 3 lightly packed cups. Melt 5 tablespoons butter over a low flame in top of 3-quart enamel double boiler. Add the chopped vegetables and cook slowly, without browning, stirring constantly, about 5 minutes. Sprinkle over vegetables 4 level tablespoons flour and stir well for a minute, then add gradually 4 cups hot clear chicken broth. Continue cooking over low flame, stirring constantly, until it comes to a boil and has thickened slightly; then cook at least 5 minutes longer. Add 3 cups grated Cheddar cheese and stir constantly, still over low flame, until the cheese has just melted, then add gradually 2 cups cold milk. Place over boiling water and continue cooking until scalding hot, stirring constantly, about 10 minutes. Season to taste with a little salt and plenty of coarsely ground black pepper; pour into a warmed tureen, sprinkle with chopped parsley, and serve at once.

NOTE: Two tablespoons of good dry sherry may be added. Also, if you wish to be more elegant, the vegetables may be strained out of it at the moment of serving. This soup may be made ahead of time, even the day before, but heat it carefully over boiling water on low flame, stirring constantly, until scalding, but not boiling.

STRACCIATELLA ALLA ROMANA

A favorite Roman soup, Stracciatella, combines eggs and cheese and is easy to make. For six portions, beat together three eggs, three tablespoons of fine flour, and three tablespoons of grated Parmesan. Add one ladle of cooled soup to the mixture, little by little. Bring a pot of broth to a boil and add the mixture, a bit at a time, stirring continuously with a fork. Boil gently a few minutes, and continue to stir until the "shreds" are cooked.

Pasta, Crepes and Rice Dishes

FETTUCCINE ALL'ALFREDO

1 *pound of fettuccine or broad egg noodles (green noodles may also be used)*	8 *ounces sweet butter* 1½ *cups of the best Parmesan, freshly grated*

This is one of the best dishes on earth, and one of the simplest.

Cook egg noodles in a large pot of briskly boiling, slightly salted water until they are tender but still firm. Pour into a colander at once to drain.

Have ready a large, deep serving dish (warmed) into which you have placed half the butter, in small bits. Now put half the hot fettuccine into the dish. Add half the remaining butter and half the grated cheese. Add the rest of the fettuccine and the rest of the butter and cheese. Toss quickly until the butter and cheese are well blended throughout. The whole trick is to get it mixed evenly while the noodles are still hot, so the butter and cheese melt to an intensely delicious cream. Serve at once.

As served at Alfredo alla Scrofa, Rome.

Variation

1 *pound of fettuccine* 6 *ounces sweet butter*	½ *cup heavy sweet cream* 1½ *cups grated Parmesan*

The addition of cream makes it even easier to blend the other ingredients.

Cook the noodles and drain them as before, then put them into a large chafing dish over a low flame. Mix in butter and cheese, while slowly adding the cream, until all is well blended. Serve at once.

V.M.

LASAGNE IMBOTTITE

Sauce

1 large can plum tomatoes
½ can tomato paste
½ cup hot water

4 tablespoons olive oil
2 cloves garlic
1 stalk celery, diced
salt and pepper to taste

Stuffing

1½ pounds ricotta
¾ pound sausage
1½ pounds broad noodles

1½ cups cubed mozzarella
1½ cups grated Parmesan
salt and pepper to taste

Blend tomato paste with hot water. Brown garlic in hot olive oil about 3 minutes; mash slightly and then remove. Add celery, blended tomato paste and plum tomatoes; boil over high flame for 3 minutes; lower flame; cover; simmer for 1 hour. Add pepper and salt.

Broil sausage under high flame about 15 minutes or until brown on both sides; cut into small pieces.

Cook noodles in rapidly boiling salted water about 15 minutes or until tender, but not too soft. Drain.

Pour ½ cup sauce into bottom of baking pan; over this place layer of noodles, then layer of grated Parmesan, a layer of sauce, a layer of mozzarella, sausage, and a tablespoon of ricotta here and there. Repeat this process in layers until all ingredients are used. Top layer should be sauce and grated cheese. Bake in moderate oven for 15 minutes or until firm. When done, the Lasagne Imbottite is cut into serving portions. Place on individual plates; top with more sauce and grated cheese.

Serve very hot. Serves 8 to 10.

From The Art of Italian Cooking by Maria Lo Pinto and Milo Miloradovich. Copyright 1948 by Doubleday & Company, Inc. Reprinted by permission of the publisher.

MANICOTTI WITH RICOTTA

Boil prepared manicotti (packaged or frozen) according to instructions until they are tender but not too soft, and fill as follows:

Filling
(for 8 manicotti)

2 *cups ricotta*	3 *well-beaten eggs*
salt and pepper	5 *tablespoons grated Parmesan*
1 *tablespoon parsley, chopped*	*dash of nutmeg*

Mix all ingredients well and spread this filling into each tube of cooked manicotti. Arrange the stuffed manicotti side by side in a well-buttered baking dish and cover with the sauces below.

Sauces

1 *cup Béchamel sauce (see page 280)*   1 *cup tomato sauce, made as follows:*

Take 2 cupfuls of drained, stewed tomatoes and cook them without any fat or liquid, uncovered, over a good brisk fire until they are cooked down to a thick pulp. Use a small saucepan, stir from time to time. Then take off the fire and stir in a good piece of butter or a spoonful of olive oil, which will turn the pulp into a smooth puree.

First spoon the Béchamel sauce over the manicotti, spreading evenly over each roll. Then spoon a covering of tomato sauce over the Béchamel, dot with small pieces of butter, sprinkle generously with Parmesan over all, and put under a medium broiler flame until bubbling and lightly browned around the edges. Serve with additional grated Parmesan if desired.

V.M.

CREPES FREYA
Filling
(for 1 crepe—multiply by number of crepes you will be making)

3 tablespoons heavy cream
1 thin slice boiled ham
2 tablespoons grated Gruyère
or Swiss

½ teaspoon grated Parmesan
1 teaspoon chopped toasted
almonds, unsalted

Spread 1 tablespoon cream over the crepe, add the slice of ham, sprinkle with 1 tablespoon of the Gruyère, sprinkle again with 1 teaspoon of the almonds and moisten with another tablespoon of cream. Roll and place in an au gratin or other shallow baking dish. Add the remaining tablespoon of cream, the rest of the grated Gruyère and top with the grated Parmesan. Place in hot oven to bake for 5 or 6 minutes, then brown under the broiler for 3 or 4 minutes more.

Crepes

2 whole eggs
½ cup flour
1⅛ cups milk
1½ tablespoons melted butter

1 teaspoon sugar, scant
1 teaspoon salt, scant
a little extra butter for cooking

Beat all the ingredients (except the extra cooking butter) into a smooth batter, and make each crepe separately, as follows:

Quickly spoon about 3 tablespoons of batter into a large, hot, buttered pan over a medium flame. (Pan should have 10- or 12-inch diameter so crepes can spread out thin.) Let cook without stirring for about a minute, or just until underside of crepe sets and becomes golden. Then turn it and let the other side cook for a minute, or until golden. At once slide out of the pan into a warmed dish. Stack crepes one on top of the other as they are done.

Crepes may be made an hour or two in advance, in which case they should be kept covered at room temperature until they are used.

V.M.

RISOTTO ALLA MILANESE

For 4–6 people.

1½ cups rice	3 cups (or more) good chicken
marrow bones (or marrow)—	or beef stock
enough to make 3–4	a pinch of saffron
tablespoons when melted	2 tablespoons butter
1 medium onion	4 tablespoons grated Parmesan

Get marrow bones (in short lengths) from the butcher, or a few ounces of marrow if possible. Put the bones (or the marrow, cut up) into an open saucepan over a moderate fire until the marrow melts. Discard the bones and any unmelted fibers.

Chop the onion and sauté it gently in the marrow until transparent and golden, but not browned. Add the rice, stirring until well coated with the marrow, and hot. Bring stock to the boiling in a separate saucepan, and keep hot.

Lower the flame under the rice, and add a cupful of the hot stock, stirring from time to time until it is absorbed. Stir in the saffron, which has been diluted in a bit of stock or water, then add another half cup of hot stock. Keep adding more hot stock, a half cup at a time, as it is absorbed, stirring frequently over the same low fire. Different rices may absorb a little more, or less, stock. Toward the end of the cooking, add the stock in small quantities, so that the finished risotto will not be too liquid.

When the rice is soft, remove from fire and add the butter (in small bits) and the grated Parmesan. Stir well to melt and blend them evenly throughout, and serve at once.

From Il Nuovo Cucchaio D'Argento (The Silver Spoon), *edited by* V. R. Lodomez *and* F. Matricardi. *Editoriale Domus, Milan, 1950, 1963.*

CROQUE MONSIEUR

Cut the crusts off thin slices of bread and spread each slice with a mixture of grated Swiss cheese and some thick cream, well mixed to make a paste. Place a thin slice of ham between each of 2 slices of bread and dip these sandwiches in egg, then fry in butter. Serve with a beautiful cream sauce made of thick cream, butter, very little flour and some of the grated Swiss cheese.

From Clementine in the Kitchen, *copyright © 1963 by Samuel Chamberlain. Reprinted by permission of Hastings House, Publishers, Inc.*

CROQUE VIVIENNE

For each sandwich:

1 slice sour rye bread	lemon juice
1 thin slice Switzerland Swiss	butter
or Gruyère	salt and pepper
1 veal cutlet pounded thin	

For best flavor, get a Jewish sour rye with seeds; if packaged rye must be used, get a brand that has as much body and flavor as possible.

Butter a slice of bread lightly and lay over it a layer of thin Swiss or Gruyère, trimmed to fit the bread. Take a slice of thin veal cutlet (cut from leg of veal and pounded), season on both sides with salt and pepper and moisten liberally with lemon juice. Dust lightly with flour. Put a good lump of butter in frying pan over a medium-high flame and when it is hot but not smoking throw in veal cutlet and brown it quickly on the underside. Then turn it over and place bread and cheese —cheese side down—over the veal. Lower flame a little and cook another minute or two till the second side of the veal is golden brown. Put another lump of butter in the pan. When it melts, turn the whole sandwich over, using spatula, and cook till the bread turns golden brown and crisp. By this time the cheese will be melted. Serve at once.

V.M.

MATZO KUGEL

3 eggs	1½ tablespoons granulated sugar
⅓ cup milk	⅔ cup heavy sour cream
1½ squares matzo	salt and pepper
4 tablespoons butter	
4 ounces American Munster cheese, sliced thin (and preferably at room temperature)	

This makes a wonderful dish for Sunday breakfast.

Beat up eggs with milk and a little salt and break matzo into this mixture, crushing it in the hand till it is about the size of corn flakes (some of it will be in crumbs). Let soak in the milk-and-egg mixture for about 15 minutes.

Using a large skillet, 10 or preferably 12 inches in diameter, melt 2 tablespoons butter, and when pan is hot but before butter has browned, pour in mixture so that it forms a large pancake. Cook over medium flame, until bottom side has set and begins to turn golden. Cover top with slices of Munster. Continue cooking over low flame until cheese begins to melt and turn translucent. Fold the pancake in half so it forms a semicircle and cook for a minute or two more, making sure that the bottom does not get too brown. Turn the semicircle over and cook the other side till lightly golden brown.

Remove instantly to warm platter, spread with rest of butter and sugar and add large dollops of the sour cream. Serve at once.

Serves 2.

V.M.

Welsh Rabbit

THE SIMPLEST WELSH RABBIT

INGREDIENTS—3 *slices cheese, bread, mustard.*

HOW TO USE THEM—Make 3 rounds of toast, lay a slice of cheese on each with a little mustard over, and bake till the cheese is done.

From Beeton's Cookery, Containing Useful Instructions and Economical Recipes for the Practical Housekeeper. *Ward, Lock & Co. Ltd., London.*

WELSH RABBIT WITH BEER

To make a good Welsh rabbit I prefer a Cheshire cheese with a good crumb. The extremely smooth cheeses which many provision merchants sell as Cheddar are much less suitable.

Let the cheese be finely grated. Then let it be put into a saucepan with 1 tablespoonful of beer to 2 ounces of cheese. A little pepper and some made mustard [dry English mustard made into a paste with a little water] should be stirred into the cheese and beer over the fire or stove. The stirring must never cease until the cheese becomes quite smooth and begins to thicken in the pan. A yolk of an egg, worked in at the last moment, is a great improvement. The cheese ought to be spread on strips of buttered toast, toasted at the last minute.

The beer does not taste like itself after being cooked in this way. I may say, however, for those who object to beer on conscientious grounds, that milk can be used instead, although the Welsh rabbit will not be so satisfactory.

From Home Cookery in War-Time *by Ernest Oldmeadow. Grant Richards, Ltd., London, 1945.*

WELSH RABBIT WITHOUT BEER

8 *ounces Cheddar*   *dash Worcester sauce*
2 *ounces butter*   *paprika, pepper*
1 *teaspoon mustard*   4 *tablespoons milk*

Grate the cheese and place in a bowl with mustard, pepper and sauce. Warm the milk and the butter. Add to the cheese mixture until it forms a smooth consistency. Spread on toast and grill until golden brown.

From The English Country Cheese Council.

Soufflés

THE EASIEST CHEESE SOUFFLÉ

The merit of this soufflé is that the eggs don't have to be separated, that it takes about 25 minutes instead of the usual 40 to cook, and that it rises perfectly.

2 eggs
⅔ cup heavy cream
¾ cup Cheddar, grated

¾ cup Parmesan, grated
pepper
⅓ teaspoon salt

Add eggs to cream and beat slightly, then add cheeses, a little pepper and ⅓ teaspoon salt, and beat again for a moment. Pour into a 1-quart baking dish (or pour into slightly smaller baking dish until it is ⅔ full) and bake in a hot oven (preheated to 450° F.) for about 25 minutes or until golden brown. If desired, ¾ cup Swiss cheese may be substituted for the Cheddar.
Serves 2.

V.M.

CHEDDAR SOUFFLÉ

4 to 6 servings

¼ cup butter (4 tablespoons)
¼ cup flour
1½ cups milk
salt

Worcestershire sauce
Cayenne pepper
½ pound Cheddar, finely grated
4 eggs, separated

Preheat oven to moderate (375° F.).

In a saucepan melt the butter over low heat and add the flour; stir with a wire whisk until blended. Meanwhile, bring the milk to a boil and add all at once to the butter-flour mixture, stirring vigorously with the whisk. Season to taste with salt, Worcestershire and Cayenne pepper.

Turn off the heat and let the mixture cool 2 to 3 minutes. Add the cheese and stir until melted. Beat in the egg yolks one at a time and cool.

Beat the egg whites until they stand in peaks, but do not overbeat. Cut and fold the egg whites into the mixture. Turn into a 2-quart casserole (greased or ungreased, as desired) and bake 30 to 45 minutes.

From The New York Times Cook Book *by Craig Claiborne. Copyright © 1961 by Craig Claiborne. Reprinted by permission of Harper & Row, Publishers.*

CHEESE SOUFFLÉ

1 cup milk	1 teaspoon English dry mustard
small bay leaf	½ teaspoon French mustard
1 shallot, sliced	¼ cup Camembert cheese,
small clove garlic	strained
small piece celery	¼ cup freshly grated Gruyère
1 teaspoon salt	cheese
6 mixed peppercorns	¼ cup grated Parmesan cheese
3 tablespoons butter	5 egg yolks
3 tablespoons flour	few bread crumbs
⅛ teaspoon (scant) Cayenne	7 egg whites
pepper	a little paprika

Put milk, bay leaf, shallot, garlic, celery, salt and peppercorns in a pan. Stir over slow fire till mixture comes to a boil. Cover, allow to steep for 5 minutes. Melt butter in small heavy pan. Stir in flour off fire. Add Cayenne pepper, mustards, and strain on milk. Stir over fire till it comes to a boil. Add Camembert and Gruyère cheeses and ½ the Parmesan cheese. Mix well. Beat egg yolks until light and fluffy, and mix into sauce. Butter an 8″ soufflé dish and dust with a few breadcrumbs and a little Parmesan cheese. Put egg whites into metal bowl and beat by hand with wire whisk until very stiff. Add cheese sauce. Fold gently but not too thoroughly so that a little of the egg white still shows. Fill soufflé dish, leaving ¼" rim at top. Sprinkle top with rest of Parmesan cheese and breadcrumbs. Stand in shallow pan of water. Bake in preheated 375° F. oven for 45 or 50 minutes or until just firm to the touch. Do not open door until soufflé has been in oven for at least 25 minutes. Remove and sprinkle with a little paprika and serve at once. Serves 4.

By Dione Lucas, in House and Garden's Cook Book. Copyright © 1956, 1957, 1958 by The Condé Nast Publications, Inc. Reprinted by permission of Simon and Schuster, Publishers.

CHEESE SOUFFLÉ

For 4 persons.

5 *tablespoons butter*	*salt, pepper, nutmeg*
¼ *cup flour*	½ *cup grated Swiss cheese*
1 *cup scalded milk*	½ *cup grated Parmesan cheese*
4 *egg yolks*	4 *egg whites*

Melt 5 tablespoons of butter in the top of a double boiler over a direct medium flame. Stir in flour and blend well. Then slowly stir in the scalded milk, and continue cooking and stirring until the mixture is thick and smooth. Remove from fire. Stir in 4 egg yolks, previously well beaten, and salt, pepper and nutmeg to taste. Put the top of the double boiler over hot water, and stir in the grated Swiss cheese and the grated Parmesan until well blended. Remove from fire and cool slightly. Beat 4 egg whites until stiff but still moist and fold them gently into the mixture, using a wooden spoon. Butter a soufflé dish or casserole and lightly flour it (dust with flour and shake out the excess). Pour in the soufflé batter (it should come ¾ of the way up) and bake in a moderate oven, 325° F., until puffed up and delicately browned, about 35–40 minutes. Serve at once.

To make a decorative design on top of the soufflé, cut very, very thin slices of cheese into diamond shapes and arrange them in a circle around the top just before the soufflé is put into the oven. Serve with mustard sauce in a separate dish.

As made at Jack & Charlie's "21," New York.

Fondue

SWISS FONDUE

1 pound Switzerland Swiss
cheese, shredded or finely
cut
1 teaspoon cornstarch
1 clove fresh garlic
2 cups white wine (Neuchâtel
or any light dry wine of
the Rhine, Riesling or
Chablis types)

salt, pepper; nutmeg or paprika
to taste
2 loaves French or Italian
bread with a hard crust
cut into bite-size pieces,
each of which must have
at least 1 side of crust
3 tablespoons kirsch

Rub an earthenware or cast-iron casserole with garlic. Pour in the
wine and set over very slow heat. When the wine is heated to the
point at which air bubbles rise to the surface (it must not boil), stir
constantly with a fork, adding the cheese by the handful, pausing until
each handful has completely dissolved before adding another.

Dissolve cornstarch in kirsch. Add to cheese mixture. Stir again for
about 2 or 3 minutes or until the mixture starts to bubble lightly. Then
add a little salt and pepper and a dash of nutmeg or paprika to taste.

Remove the fondue casserole from the heat and set it on the table
over a heating element.

Spear a piece of bread with a fork, going through the soft part first
and securing the points in the crust. Any type fork can be used, but
the most suitable has a heat-insulated handle and sharp prongs. Dunk
the bread in the fondue with a stirring motion. This helps maintain the
proper consistency of the fondue.

Keep the fondue bubbling lightly by regulating the heat, or by turning it off or on. If the fondue becomes too thick, stir in a little preheated (never cold) wine. Toward the end, a brown crust of melted
cheese will form at the bottom of the casserole. At this point, turn off

the heat to keep the casserole from cracking. The crust can be lifted out with a fork and is considered a delicacy.

Makes 4 servings.

From The Switzerland Cheese Association.

FONDUTA

Fondue, Piedmont Style

¾ pound Fontina, diced
milk to cover cheese
1 tablespoon butter
6 egg yolks

¼ teaspoon white pepper
1 white truffle, sliced paper thin
1 tablespoon butter

Place diced cheese in dish and cover with milk. Let stand for at least 6 hours, overnight if possible. Place butter and egg yolks in upper part of double boiler, add cheese and milk and place over boiling water. Beat with a rotary beater. At first the cheese will melt and then will become a little harder. When it becomes harder, remove from over boiling water, add pepper, truffle and butter and mix well. Serve on toast or with rice or polenta. Serves 4.

From The Talisman Italian Cook Book by Ada Boni. Copyright 1950 by Crown Publishers. Reprinted by permission of the publisher.

CAERPHILLY FONDUE

2 tablespoons butter
2 tablespoons flour
½ teaspoon salt
1½ cups milk

2 cups Caerphilly cheese
pepper, black and red, freshly
  ground
fingers of toast

Melt butter in top of double boiler. Add flour, salt and pepper. Stir until flour and butter are smooth. Add milk, stirring constantly until sauce is smooth. Add shredded Caerphilly cheese. Stir continuously in one direction only until cheese is melted. Serve immediately on fingers of toast.

From The English Country Cheese Council.

Bread and Cheese Puddings

MRS. BEETON'S CHEESE PUDDING

INGREDIENTS—*Dry pieces of cheese, some bread or the crusts, an egg, a spoonful of butter, a little milk, pepper.*

HOW TO USE THEM—Grate the cheese to the thin rind, and rub the bread into crumbs through a sieve or on a grater, making equal quantities of cheese and bread, about a pie dish full in all; add the egg, beaten, the butter, some pepper, salt, if needed, and a little milk to make a soft paste, then bake in a greased pie dish for ¾ hour.

From Beeton's Cookery, Containing Useful Instructions and Economical Recipes for the Practical Housekeeper. *Ward, Lock & Co. Ltd., London.*

ERMA'S CHEESE BREAD PUDDING

Preheat oven to 325°.

16 slices white bread	salt, pepper
butter	8 eggs
4 cups grated sharp Cheddar	7 cups milk

Serves 6–8.

Butter 2 baking dishes or pans, 11" by 7" by 1½". Cut crusts from 16 slices white bread, butter one side of each slice, then cut into four pieces. Arrange 16 bread squares, buttered side up, on the bottom of each dish and sprinkle with 2 cups grated cheese, a bit of salt, and a generous shower of pepper. Cover, making another layer, with remaining bread squares, and 2 cups grated cheese; add salt and pepper.

Beat 8 eggs slightly and stir in the milk; pour over bread-cheese combination. Let it rest 10 minutes so that milk soaks into the bread.

Bake 40 minutes, or until puffy and nicely browned. Makes a delicious supper, lunch, or dinner dish.

BREAD AND ONION CUSTARD WITH CHEESE

1 cup sharp cheese cut in small
    slices
2 eggs
2 cups milk

1 Spanish onion
1 tablespoon butter
½ small loaf white bread

Peel and mince the onion and sauté in the butter until clear. Remove crusts from the bread and cut in 1-inch cubes.

Butter a baking dish and place in it alternate layers of bread, cheese slices and onion, seasoning with salt and paprika.

Combine the beaten eggs with the milk, pour over the whole and bake about ½ hour or until the custard is set.

Cheese Pies and Tarts

QUICHE LORRAINE

Makes 6 to 8 servings.

1½ cups pastry flour	4 eggs
½ teaspoon salt	2 cups thick or thin cream
¼ pound salt butter	1 pinch nutmeg
4 tablespoons ice water (about)	1 pinch sugar
1 cup grated Swiss cheese	¾ teaspoon salt
1½ dozen strips bacon (about)	1 big pinch Cayenne
	black pepper

First make a paste in the following manner. Sift pastry flour with salt. Work into it with fingertips the bar of salt butter. Moisten with just enough ice water to make it hold together.

Make a smooth ball of it, wrap in waxed paper, and place in refrigerator for ½ hour or so, before rolling it out thin on a lightly floured board. Line a large 10-inch Pyrex pie pan with it, trim the edges, roll them under and crimp prettily. Prick the surface with a fork and place in refrigerator, while you prepare the following ingredients. (But first set your oven at 450° F. and light it.)

Fry or grill about 1½ dozen bacon strips until crisp, but don't overcook. Break or cut into small pieces.

Break eggs into a bowl and add to them thick or thin cream, nutmeg, sugar, salt, Cayenne, and plenty of freshly ground black pepper. Beat with rotary beater just long enough to mix thoroughly. Now rub a little soft butter over the surface of the pastry and sprinkle the bacon over the bottom, sprinkle the cheese over the bacon, and pour the egg mixture over all.

Place in preheated hot oven and bake 10–15 minutes, then reduce the temperature to 325° F. and continue cooking until an inserted knife comes out clean, showing the custard has set (about 25–30 minutes).

If not a light golden brown on top, place under a hot grill for a second before serving piping hot. Cut in pie-shaped pieces.

From The Best I Ever Ate *by June Platt and Sophie Kerr. Copyright 1953 by June Platt and Sophie Kerr Underwood. Reprinted by permission of Holt, Rinehart and Winston, Publishers.*

CHEESE PIE
(with Cream Cheese Crust)

Serves 6.

For crust

1 package cream cheese
  (3 ounces)
3 ounces soft butter

pastry flour

For filling

a few drops of milk
½ pound Swiss cheese, grated
  or shredded
1 tablespoon flour

1 cup cream or milk
3 well-beaten eggs
pepper, salt

Cream Cheese Crust

Line a 9-inch glass pie plate with crust to be made as follows:

First: Blend 1 package cream cheese and 3 ounces soft butter until thoroughly combined.

Second: Add enough sifted pastry flour to permit the dough to be handled. Knead thoroughly by hand. Place in refrigerator overnight.

Third: If you leave the dough in the refrigerator overnight, you will have no trouble rolling it out. If you cannot spare the time, you may find it somewhat difficult to handle, in which case pat the dough by hand into the pie plate you are going to use.

Filling

First: Brush the dough with milk and fill it with ½ pound finely grated or shredded Swiss cheese.

Second: Combine 1 tablespoon flour with 1 cup cream or milk. Add 3 well-beaten eggs and season the mixture with pepper and salt. Pour this over the grated cheese in the pie shell.

Third: Bake the pie 15 minutes in a 400° oven. Reduce the heat to 300° and bake an additional 30 minutes, or until a knife inserted in the center of the pie comes out quite clean. Serve hot or cold.

NOTE: This makes an excellent dish for luncheon served with a green salad.

IMPORTANT: Follow the baking directions carefully and do not overbake.

SIMPLE CHEESE TARTLETS

Preheat oven to 400°.

Same recipe as for pie crust and filling for cheese pie (page 276), plus 1 tablespoon grated cheese for each tartlet.

First: Line tartlet forms or the back of muffin tins with 1 recipe pie crust (page 276). Cover each tartlet before baking with 1 tablespoon shredded Swiss cheese. Bake in a 400° oven until light gold.

Reduce oven to 350°.

Second: Fill each tartlet ⅔ full of the custard mixture described under Cheese Pie (also on page 276), and bake the tartlets in a 350° oven until a knife inserted in the center of a tartlet comes out quite clean. Serve hot or warmed over.

NOTE: Excellent for afternoon tea. The amount of Swiss cheese is not given as it depends entirely on how many tartlets are required. Each tartlet calls for 1 tablespoon grated Swiss cheese.

CREAM OF LEEK PIE

pastry to line 8-inch tin (see
   recipe page 276)
1 large bunch leeks
3 egg yolks
¼ pint heavy cream

4 tablespoons grated Parmesan
4 tablespoons milk
butter
salt and pepper

Line an 8-inch tin with pastry.

Use white parts of leeks and the first inch or so of the pale green parts near the white; cut into pieces about 1 inch long. Wash well, salt lightly and melt in butter, removing from pan as soon as they turn soft, but while they are still firm.

Beat together 3 egg yolks, the cream, 4 tablespoons grated Parmesan and the milk, salt and pepper to taste, and pour this mixture over leeks. Dot with pieces of butter and dust with a little more Parmesan. Bake in medium-hot oven for 30 to 40 minutes.

V.M.

Sauces

MORNAY SAUCE

To each cup of cream sauce or hot Béchamel sauce add ¾ scant cup of dry white wine and let this reduce to ⅓ its volume over a bright flame, stirring frequently. Then stir in 2 tablespoons of your favorite grated cheese or equal parts of two different kinds. When ready to use, blend in 1 tablespoon of sweet butter and taste for seasoning.

NOTES: When using Mornay Sauce to top a dish to be made au gratin, it is usually, in the French cuisine, considered improved if a tablespoon or two of whipped cream is folded into each half cup of Mornay Sauce before spreading over top of fish or other main ingredient. The top then takes on an even golden brown glaze.

Home Style Mornay Sauce

Simply add ⅓ cup of grated cheese to each cup of cream sauce and stir until the cheese is melted. It is merely a cheese sauce.

This sauce cannot be boiled when it is made, lest it curdle, so, if for any reason it has to stand, keep it over hot, never boiling, water. This applies to any sauce containing eggs.

BÉCHAMEL SAUCE

Béchamel Sauce, a simple combination of butter, flour and milk, is a foundation sauce which everyone should know how to make. An onion cooked in it gives added flavor, and other seasonings such as mustard are often added. For a richer sauce, it can be combined with eggs, cream, cheese and so on. Béchamel Sauce, or any of its variations, is served on vegetables, fish, hard-cooked eggs, poultry and other cooked foods.

⅓ cup butter	1 teaspoon salt
½ medium onion, minced	few grains white pepper
⅓ cup flour	2 sprigs parsley
3 cups hot milk	a little nutmeg

Melt butter in a saucepan, add onion and cook until onion becomes very light brown. Add flour, cook a few minutes longer, add milk and seasoning, stirring vigorously. Cook gently 25 to 30 minutes, stirring constantly until sauce is thick and smooth and then occasionally for the remaining time. Strain. If sauce is not to be used immediately, stir occasionally as it cools to prevent a crust forming on top.

WHITE SAUCE

For a good, all-purpose white sauce, use above recipe, leaving out the onion and parsley; a few gratings of nutmeg are optional.

From French Cooking for Americans *by Louis Diat. Copyright 1946 by Louis Diat. Published by J. B. Lippincott Company.*

Sea Food

COQUILLES ST. JACQUES À LA MORNAY
Scallops with Cheese

6 large scallops
juice ½ lemon
salt and pepper
3 tablespoons butter
1 bay leaf

1½ tablespoons flour
¾ cup milk
2 tablespoons cream
4 tablespoons grated cheese
handful freshly chopped parsley

Wash the scallops well in lemon juice and water. Put in a pan and pour over a little water, seasoning, 1 tablespoon butter and the bay leaf. Bring slowly to a boil and simmer for 5 minutes. Remove the coral of the scallops; cut the white part in slices.

Melt 2 tablespoons butter and stir in the flour and seasoning. Pour on the milk and bring to a boil. Reduce the liquor in which the scallops were cooked to 1 tablespoon and add the cream and 3 tablespoons cheese. Simmer for 3 to 4 minutes.

Mix into the sliced scallops and fill the shells. Sprinkle tops well with grated cheese and brown quickly under the grill. Place on top the coral of the scallops, sprinkle with freshly chopped parsley and serve.

From The Cordon Bleu Cook Book *by Dione Lucas. Copyright 1947 by Dione Lucas. Reprinted by permission of Little, Brown and Co.*

MIXED SEAFOOD AU GRATIN

NOTE: This casserole can be assembled beforehand; in that case combine all ingredients except for topping of cheese and breadcrumbs (which should be added just before baking). Cover with plastic wrap (which should lie directly on the sauce so it will not form a skin) and refrigerate. If possible, bring to room temperature before baking.

½ pound shrimp
½ pound scallops
½ pound crabment, lump or
   Alaskan King, preferably
   fresh or frozen (if canned,
   use Japanese Alaskan King)
¾ pound halibut
¾ pound fresh salmon

3 cups white sauce (see
   recipe page 280) mixed
   with 3 tablespoons
   medium-dry sherry
1½ cups Parmesan, grated
⅓ cup grated Cheddar
1 tablespoon fine breadcrumbs

In lightly salted water gently parboil raw shrimps, scallops, halibut, and salmon, each separately, then remove all bones and waste and break fish into scallop-size lumps. None of the seafood should be fully cooked because it will be cooked further. Pick over the crabmeat to remove any shells or membranes but do not cook.

Make white sauce. Mix all seafood together gently in a large bowl with 2½ cups of the white sauce and put about half of this mixture into a large, well-buttered casserole. Sprinkle with half the Parmesan. Add the rest of the mixture to the casserole and spread the remaining white sauce on top. Sprinkle with remaining Parmesan and with the Cheddar and then with the breadcrumbs. Dot with butter. Place in oven preheated to 350° F. and bake for 35–45 minutes. Top should be golden brown and bubbling.

V.M.

MIXED SEAFOOD COQUILLE

2 cups white sauce (page 280)
chives
parsley
½ cup shrimp, half-cooked
2 ounces butter
a few mushrooms
2 shallots or 1 small onion

3 tablespoons dry white wine
½ cup scallops, raw
½ cup crabmeat (fresh, frozen or canned)
½ cup lobster meat, cooked
pinch of dry mustard
salt and pepper
grated Parmesan

Make white sauce. Chop chives and parsley and set aside.

Half-cook the shrimp by dropping them, in their shells, into boiling water for 1½ minutes. Drain; shell and devein them.

Heat 2 ounces butter in frying pan over a moderate flame. When hot, add a few mushrooms cut into pieces and sauté mushrooms until golden brown. Add chopped shallots or onion and the white wine. Add the raw scallops, the half-cooked shrimp, the crabmeat and cooked lobster meat, cover pan and cook for about 2 minutes over medium flame. Add the white sauce and cook uncovered for 5 minutes more. Remove from fire and add dry mustard, salt and pepper to taste, and a scant handful of chopped chives and parsley mixed. Stir all together.

Spoon the mixture into individual buttered coquille shells (or small ramekins or a large baking dish) and cover generously with the Parmesan. Broil under medium flame only as long as needed to brown.

V.M.

Vegetables

CHEESE AND ONIONS

1

Boil the onions in milk with a little salt, and when they are done drain them but do not dry. Then chop them up, stir in some grated cheeses, warm them up in the pan again and eat them as they are.

2

Boil some onions, chop them roughly and put them into a fireproof dish with a very little of the water in which they were boiled. Season them and cover them with a 50-50 mixture of breadcrumbs and grated cheese, and bake in the oven until the top is nicely browned.

3

Boil the onions in milk till they are tender, then cut them up and pass through a wire sieve. Mix up this pulp with pepper and salt and some milk mixed with a yolk of egg. Butter a fireproof dish, spread the onion puree in it, sprinkle well with grated cheese and a little melted butter and brown in oven. Breadcrumbs can be added to the cheese covering if desired.

From Good Cheese Dishes *by Ambrose Heath, published by Faber and Faber, London, 1943.*

POIREAUX AU GRATIN

Blanch 8 leeks with all green cut away for 20 minutes in salted water, drain and wrap each leek in a thin slice of cooked ham. Prepare a Mornay sauce of

3 tablespoons butter	3 cups milk
2 tablespoons flour	⅔ cup grated cheese

Put leeks in a buttered baking dish, pour the sauce over them, dot the surface with butter and bake for 15 minutes or until nicely browned on top.

From Contemporary French Cooking *by Waverly Root and Richard de Rochemont. Copyright © 1962 by Waverly Root and Richard de Rochemont. Reprinted by permission of Random House, Inc.*

SPINACI FIORENTINA

Serves 3.

⅓ stick butter (1⅓ ounces)	4 ounces mozzarella
1 medium onion	½ cup Parmesan, freshly
2 pounds fresh spinach or	grated
1 package frozen spinach,	salt and pepper
whole or chopped	

Melt the butter in an open pan, add the onion and sauté till golden over low flame so that butter does not brown. Set aside.

Cook spinach, fresh or frozen, very briefly in a little boiling salted water. When just done, drain it well and chop coarsely (unless you are using frozen spinach that is chopped already). Leave whatever additional juice is released in the chopping. Add the spinach to the sautéed onion in its pan, mix well, and put over a moderate flame to reheat. Meanwhile, slice the mozzarella very thin. As soon as the spinach is piping hot, take off the fire, pepper to taste, and add the mozzarella and the grated Parmesan, mixing lightly so that it melts through. Serve at once in individual bowls, with additional Parmesan on the table.

V.M.

VEGETABLES PARMESAN

(For asparagus, broccoli, cauliflower, Brussels sprouts, leeks, young green cabbage, escarole, endive, etc.)

Cook vegetable rapidly in very little boiling salted water until just done, but still firm. Drain and place in a buttered shallow baking dish. Dot liberally with sweet butter, sprinkle with Parmesan and put into a hot oven (preheated to 400° F.) for 3 or 4 minutes, or until cheese is melted. It need not be brown.

V.M.

SCALLOPED POTATOES

3 or 4 medium potatoes, sliced thin	5 slices Swiss cheese, cut in strips
4 medium onions, sliced thin	½ cup Parmesan, grated
3 or 4 tablespoons butter	1½ cups milk
	salt and pepper

Butter well a 1-quart heatproof dish and arrange in it a layer of potatoes, lightly salted and peppered, a layer of onions, dots of butter, a layer of Swiss cheese strips, and a light sprinkling of Parmesan. Repeat layers in this order until casserole is almost filled. Add cold milk, making sure that it runs through to the bottom of the dish and around the sides, and coming to the level of the mixture. Add the rest of the Swiss cheese strips and a good sprinkling of Parmesan, and bake in a preheated 350° F. oven until potatoes are soft (about 50 minutes). Reduce temperature if necessary (and compensate by allowing a little longer cooking time) so the potatoes do not get darker than a rich golden brown.

Serves 4.

V.M.

Poultry and Meat Dishes

POULET ESTRAGON

breasts of 3 medium-size
    chickens, boned
¾ cup of milk
salt and pepper
1½ cups grated Parmesan

8 ounces sweet butter
3 level tablespoons shallots
    or onions, chopped very fine
¾ pint heavy sweet cream
2 large pinches of tarragon
3 ounces dry sherry

Skin the chicken breasts, dip them in milk, sprinkle with salt and pepper, and dredge on both sides in the grated Parmesan. Place in frying pan with 4 ounces of the butter and cook over a low flame, uncovered, until chicken is golden (6 to 8 minutes on each side should be enough because chicken will have a few minutes' further cooking later). Remove chicken from pan.

Use the same pan, and place in it the remaining 4 ounces of butter, and the shallots or onions. Scrape to deglaze any crumbs and crusty bits that may adhere to the pan, and blend them with the butter and onions. Cook for five minutes over a fairly high flame.

Lower the flame, add sweet cream, sherry and tarragon and let it heat over a very low flame, stirring till it thickens. Then return chicken breasts to pan for about 2 minutes, turning them so that they become well coated with the sauce.

Place the chicken breasts on a hot platter, pour the sauce over them and serve.

Serves 6.

V.M.

CHICKEN OR TURKEY DIVAN

Put in a shallow oblong baking dish
    4 stalks cooked broccoli or 8 stalks cooked asparagus
Sprinkle with
    1 tablespoon melted butter
    1 tablespoon grated Parmesan or Romano cheese
    2 tablespoons sherry
Lay over the vegetable
    4 thick slices cooked turkey or chicken breast
Sprinkle with
    1 tablespoon grated Parmesan or Romano cheese
    2 tablespoons sherry
Beat together
    1 cup Béchamel Sauce (see page 280)
    2 egg yolks
Season to taste with
    salt and pepper
Fold in
    1 tablespoon whipped cream
Pour over the chicken or turkey.
Sprinkle with
    1 tablespoon grated Romano or Parmesan cheese
    2 tablespoons sherry
Bake at 350° F. until delicately brown (about 12 minutes).
Serves 3 or 4.

From The All New Fanny Farmer Boston School Cookbook. *Copyright* © *1959 by Dexter and Wilma Lord Perkins. Reprinted by permission of Little, Brown and Co.*

CHICKEN BREASTS ALLA VALDOSTANA

4 large chicken breasts, skinned
and boned
a little flour
salt and pepper
4 tablespoons butter

2 white truffles or ½ pound
mushrooms
⅓ cup dry white wine
2 tablespoons Madeira
¼ pound Fontina or mozzarella,
cut into 4 slices

Dust chicken breasts with flour, season with a little salt and pepper and brown in hot butter for 6 to 8 minutes on each side in a large open pan. Remove chicken breasts and put them into a shallow baking dish, and keep them warm. Over each breast sprinkle a few slivers of white truffles or a more generous quantity of slivered mushrooms which have been previously sautéed in some butter until soft. Do not wash the pan you have cooked the chicken breasts in, but turn up the flame under it. Add the dry wine and the Madeira, and scrape well to loosen and deglaze any crusty bits or caramel that may have adhered to the pan. Then lower heat and simmer for about 5 minutes or less until the liquid has reduced by half. Pour this sauce over the chicken breasts in the baking dish and then cover each with a slice of Fontina or mozzarella and put under a hot broiler just long enough to melt the cheese.

V.M.

VEAL CUTLETS IN SHERRY

Serves 6.

2 pounds very thin veal cutlets
salt, pepper, paprika
1½ cups freshly grated Parmesan
¼ cup olive oil
1 mashed clove garlic

1 cup very dry sherry
2 cups freshly cooked and
buttered peas
additional grated Parmesan

First: Have the butcher pound the veal cutlets very, very thin with the flat side of his cleaver. Cut them into individual portions, add salt, pepper and paprika. Then scatter each portion with an equal share of grated Parmesan. Pound the cheese gently into both sides of the meat with a wooden meat-pounder.

Second: Heat olive oil and garlic in a large skillet. Quickly fry the cutlets on both sides until appetizingly brown. Cover with dry sherry, rapidly bringing to a boil.

Third: Remove to a hot platter, drain the sauce over them, and cover with freshly cooked and buttered peas. Sprinkle the peas with added grated Parmesan cheese.

NOTE: Be certain that the cutlets remain juicy!

SCHNITZEL ST. MORITZ

a Wiener Schnitzel
stuffed with a fondue of ham and cheese

4 slices leg of veal	salt, pepper, flour
cheese croquette mixture (see page 254)	1 large whole egg, beaten
	fine dry breadcrumbs
3 thin slices of boiled ham, slivered	corn or olive oil, or butter, for frying

Ask the butcher for cutlets from the leg of veal, sliced thick enough for him to cut pockets in for stuffing. After the pockets are cut, have the cutlets flattened.

With your fingers, stuff enough cheese-croquette mixture and slivered ham to fill each cutlet till it is smoothly rounded but not bulging. (Mixture will go in more easily if it is chilled and cut into small dice.) Press veal cutlets closed, securing with a toothpick; then salt and pepper them, and dust with a little flour. Dip into beaten egg and then into the fine breadcrumbs. (Try to do this beforehand so the breaded cutlets can be chilled in the refrigerator for half an hour or longer. Chilling makes the breading adhere better in the cooking.)

Put enough oil or butter into your largest skillet to come about ¼ inch deep. Put over a brisk fire, and when fat is very hot, fry the cutlets in it for about 2 minutes on each side, or until brown. Remove and drain both sides on paper towels, and serve at once. Serves 4.

V.M.

STUFFED PILLOWS

12 *small slices veal cutlets, cut very thin*	½ *cup butter.* .
	½ *cup Marsala or sherry wine*
12 *small slices prosciutto or cooked ham, thinly sliced*	1 *teaspoon butter*
	⅛ *teaspoon salt*
¾ *pound mozzarella cheese, thinly sliced*	⅛ *teaspoon pepper*

Flatten out veal cutlets with a mallet or ask butcher to do it. Place 1 slice of prosciutto or ham and a thin slice of mozzarella cheese on each cutlet, and fold together like an envelope, using toothpicks to hold together. Melt butter in frying pan. Brown pillows well on one side, then turn gently, and brown on other side. They should be cooked in a short time.

Remove meat from the pan, pour the Marsala or sherry into it, scraping bottom and sides of pan well. Add 1 teaspoon butter, salt and pepper and pour sauce over pillows on serving dish. Serves 4.

From The Talisman Italian Cook Book by Ada Boni. Copyright 1950 by Crown Publishers. Reprinted by permission of the publisher.

A GRATIN OF HAM AND LETTUCE

8 *thin slices boiled ham*	1 *tablespoon butter*
Crisp green leaves of iceberg lettuce, shredded	1½ *cup Béchamel Sauce (see page 280)*
8 *tablespoons grated Swiss or Gruyère*	

For each ham slice: moisten a small handful of shredded lettuce with ½ tablespoon of Béchamel and mix in ½ tablespoon of grated cheese. Spread this mixture over ham slices and roll them. Place in a well-buttered shallow baking dish with folded side down, to keep them from unrolling. Cover well with the Béchamel Sauce and sprinkle with the rest of the grated cheese. Place in hot oven for about 5 minutes and then brown gently for 2 or 3 minutes more under the broiler flame.

Serves 4.

V.M.

CERVELLE À L'ITALIENNE
(as served at Au Caveau Montpensier, Paris)

2 calf's brains	⅓ cup rich veal stock
½ cup chopped mushrooms	6 tablespoons butter
2 shallots, chopped	2 tablespoons olive oil
5 ounces ham, chopped	1 teaspoon wine vinegar
4 tablespoons grated Gruyère	salt, pepper

Soak the brains in cold water for ½ hour. Remove the membrane and poach the brains in salted water with a teaspoon of wine vinegar. As soon as the water boils remove from the fire and leave the brains until cool. Drain and reserve.

Sauté the shallots in a frying pan in 2 tablespoons butter until they become soft (they should not color). Add the mushrooms and stir the mixture gently until there is little liquid left in the pan. Add the veal stock and cook for 7 or 8 minutes. Add the ham and after 1 minute remove. Keep hot.

Slice each brain in two and sauté very gently in the oil and the rest of the butter for 4 or 5 minutes. Drain and arrange on a hot serving dish. Pour over the sauce and sprinkle with the grated cheese. Brown quickly under the grill and serve at once.

Serves 4.

Salads and Dressings

ROQUEFORT SALAD DRESSING

1 cup Roquefort
garlic
1 tablespoon Worcestershire
  sauce

1 tablespoon lemon juice
⅔ cup salad oil
2 tablespoons vinegar

Mash cheese with a little of the salad oil. Add bit of finely minced garlic. Add Worcestershire sauce, lemon juice, vinegar and balance of oil. Shake well until creamy. Serve on lettuce, cucumbers or endive.

From The Roquefort Association.

SALAD DRESSING À L'ANCIENNE

You will need

cream cheese
dry mustard
chervil
estragon

olive oil
lemon juice
salt
pepper

Mix ½ cup cream cheese with ½ teaspoon dry mustard, 1 teaspoon chopped estragon. Beat in drop by drop, 4 tablespoons olive oil, 1 tablespoon lemon juice, ½ teaspoon salt, and ¼ teaspoon ground pepper.

From Aromas and Flavors by Alice B. Toklas. Copyright © 1958 by Alice B. Toklas. Reprinted by permission of Harper & Row, Publishers.

SALADE AVEYRONNAISE
Roquefort and Lettuce Salad

2 ounces Roquefort
½ pint sweet cream
1 teaspoon vinegar or lemon
    juice
1 head lettuce

chopped chervil
chopped tarragon
salt and pepper

Crush Roquefort cheese. Blend with cream and vinegar until it looks smooth and pasty. Add salt, pepper, chervil and tarragon, mixing well for even distribution.

Slice the lettuce over a salad bowl. Pour the cheese sauce over the leaves, tossing them gently until they are thoroughly coated with mixture.

Serve with pumpernickel bread.

[NOTE: If you cannot get fresh chervil and tarragon, a little dried tarragon, soaked first in the cream, may be used, or fresh chives and parsley, or other herbs of your choice.]

From François L. Schwarz.

CAESAR SALAD

2 cups croutons
olive oil
2 heads romaine
¼ teaspoon dry mustard
¼ teaspoon black pepper
½ teaspoon salt

6 to 8 anchovy fillets
4 ounces Parmesan or blue cheese
2 medium lemons, juice
2 eggs

Rub a wooden bowl with garlic. Add the chilled romaine, torn into bite-size pieces; season with mustard, pepper, salt. Add the grated or crumbled cheese, the anchovies, 6 tablespoons olive oil and the lemon juice. Boil 2 eggs for 1 minute—no more—and break them over the greens. Toss contents thoroughly but carefully. Add croutons, tossing just enough to mix. Must be served at once.

From The New Settlement Cook Book, *copyright 1954 by the Settlement Cook Book Company. Reprinted by permission of Simon and Schuster, Inc.*

Desserts

COEUR À LA CRÈME

For 6 persons:

2 cups cottage cheese   2 cups heavy cream
2 cups cream cheese

Force the cheese through a fine sieve and beat it well with a rotary beater. Whip the cream stiff and stir it into the cheese. Line a heart-shaped basket mold with cheesecloth and turn the cheese mixture into it. Put the mold on a plate and let it stand overnight in the refrigerator. To serve, unmold the heart on a chilled serving dish and pour some light cream over it. Surround the heart with chilled strawberries sweetened to taste.

CHEESE PASTRY AND PEARS

[For this recipe, which was written in wartime, it is suggested that butter be used instead of the margarine and that the pear be fresh-cooked—and not cooked too much—instead of tinned.]

An unusual combination which, if you like the mixture of cheese and apple, you will like as well. Make some cheese pastry [see page 248], roll it out an eighth of an inch thick and cut it into four-inch-sided squares. Put half a well-drained cooked or tinned pear on each pastry half and fill the hollow where the core was with a teaspoon of brown sugar and half a teaspoon of margarine. Fold over the other half to make a triangle, press the edges together with a fork, and prick a few holes in the top. Bake in a hot oven for about a quarter of an hour.

BLINTZES

Makes about 14 thin pancakes (average serving 3 to 4 per person)

Pancakes

6 eggs, beaten   4 tablespoons flour
⅛ teaspoon salt   2 tablespoons water

Beat eggs and salt. Mix flour and water in small bowl and gradually add to it about a cupful of the beaten egg. Then add this mixture to the rest of the beaten egg. (This is to prevent lumping.)

Cover work surface near your stove with wax paper on which pancakes can be tossed as cooked.

The secret of making thin, tender blintzes is to watch the heat of the pan carefully. Use a 6-inch iron skillet. Heat this gradually until a bit of butter dropped in it will sizzle but not spatter or smoke. Try to keep pan at this same heat.

Grease pan lightly but completely with butter. Hold handle of pan with your left hand as you pour enough batter to make a thin layer that will just cover the pan. Turn your left hand back and forth as you are pouring so that the pan will be covered quickly and evenly.

If your pan is correctly heated, the thin pancakes should start bubbling almost immediately. Give the pancake just a few seconds until "set" and then invert pan over wax paper so that pancake will drop out.

NOTE: Pancake is now lying raw side down, cooked side up.

Continue making rest of pancakes, greasing pan with butter as needed.

Filling

1½ pounds farmer cheese   pinch salt
    (dry cottage cheese)   dash of pepper
½ of a beaten egg

Blend filling.

Then place heaping tablespoonful in center of cooked side of each pancake. Roll pancakes and place, side by side, in greased, open baking pan.

Twenty to 30 minutes before serving, place baking pan in pre-heated 350° F. oven. Bake until pancakes are golden brown.

Serve on very hot plates and pass garnishings. These can include sour cream, cinnamon, apple sauce; or apricot, blueberry or straw-berry jam.

From Mrs. Arthur Murray.

CHEESECAKE UNDER THE COVERS

Line a 9-inch spring-form pan with a good
> *Graham cracker crust (add a tablespoon of cinnamon to it, and ½ cup of very finely chopped walnuts).*

Pat it thinly into the pan, and chill it well while mixing
> *4 eggs, beaten until lemon-colored and thick*
> *½ cup sugar*
> *1 teaspoon vanilla*
> *2 large, or 4 small, packages cream cheese*

Beat the cheese into the eggs and sugar until it is creamy and thick, and pour it into the pie shell. Bake for 20 minutes at 375 degrees, or until "set."

Cool it 10 minutes, while you are mixing
> *1 pint sour cream*
> *4 tablespoons sugar*

Spoon this gently over the cheesecake or it will fall. Return it to the oven, which you have increased to 400 degrees, for 8 to 10 more minutes. Remove from oven, cool, cover, and place in the refrigerator for at least 6 hours, or until firmly cold and well set.

Reprinted with permission of The Macmillan Company from The Eating-in-Bed Cookbook *by Barbara Ninde Byfield. Copyright © 1962 by Barbara Byfield.*

LINDY'S CHEESE CAKE

Filling

2½ pounds cream cheese
1¾ cups sugar
3 tablespoons flour
1½ teaspoons grated orange rind
1½ teaspoons grated lemon rind

pinch of vanilla bean (inside pulp) or ¼ teaspoon vanilla extract
5 eggs
2 egg yolks
¼ cup heavy cream

Combine cheese, sugar, flour, grated orange and lemon rind and vanilla. Add sugar gradually, then remainder of ingredients in order given. Beat in electric mixer at second speed.

Add eggs and egg yolks, one at a time, stirring lightly after each addition.

Stir in cream.

Cookie Crust

1 cup sifted all-purpose flour
¼ cup sugar
1 teaspoon grated lemon rind

¼ teaspoon vanilla
1 egg yolk
¼ cup butter, melted

Combine flour, sugar, lemon rind and vanilla. Make a well in center and add egg yolk and butter. Work together quickly with hands until well blended.

Wrap in waxed paper and chill thoroughly in refrigerator about 1 hour.

Roll out ⅛ inch thick and place over oiled bottom of a 9-inch spring-form cake pan. Trim off the dough by running a rolling pin over sharp edge.

Bake in hot oven (400° F.) 20 minutes or until a light gold. Cool.

To Assemble and Bake the Cake

Butter sides of cake form and place over base. Roll remaining dough ⅛ inch thick and cut to fit the sides of the oiled band.

Fill form with cheese mixture.

Bake in very hot oven (550° F.) 12 to 15 minutes. Reduce temperature to slow (200° F.) and continue baking 1 hour. Cool before cutting.

Makes one 9-inch cake.

From Lindy's Restaurant, New York City.

Index

Index of Recipes is on page 315

Index of Recipes